KU-411-166

Making Sense of Modern Times

Making Sense of Modern Times

PETER L. BERGER AND THE VISION OF INTERPRETIVE SOCIOLOGY

EDITED BY

James Davison Hunter
Stephen C. Ainlay

ROUTLEDGE & KEGAN PAUL
London and New York

First published in 1986
by Routledge & Kegan Paul plc
11 New Fetter Lane, London EC4P 4EE

Published in the USA by
Routledge & Kegan Paul Inc.
in association with Methuen Inc.
29 West 35th Street, New York, NY 10001

Set in Imprint by Inforum Ltd, Portsmouth
and printed in Great Britain
by T J Press (Padstow) Ltd
Padstow, Cornwall

Library of Congress Cataloging in Publication Data
Main entry under title:
Making sense of modern times.
'The bibliography of Peter L. Berger': p.
Bibliography: p.
Includes index.
1. Berger, Peter L. 2. Sociologists—United States—Addresses, essays, lectures. 3. Sociology—United States—Addresses, essays, lectures. I. Hunter, James Davison, 1955– II. Ainlay, Stephen C., 1951– . III. Title: Interpretive sociology.
HM22.U6B456 1986 301'.092'4 85-25611

British Library CIP Data available

ISBN 0–7102–0826–X (c)
ISBN 0–7102–0745–X (p)

Contents

Contributors

NICHOLAS ABERCROMBIE is Senior Lecturer in Sociology, University of Lancaster

STEPHEN C. AINLAY is Assistant Professor of Sociology, Holy Cross College

PETER L. BERGER is University Professor of Sociology, Boston University

S. D. GAEDE is Professor of Sociology, Gordon College

PHILLIP E. HAMMOND is Professor of Religious Studies and Sociology, University of California, Santa Barbara

JAMES DAVISON HUNTER is Assistant Professor of Sociology, University of Virginia

JAY MECHLING is Associate Professor of American Studies, University of California, Davis

JAMES P. O'LEARY is Associate Professor of Political Science, Catholic University

DONALD L. REDFOOT is Post-Doctoral Research Associate in Sociology, Duke University

ROBERT WUTHNOW is Professor of Sociology, Princeton University

ANTON C. ZIJDERVELD is Professor of Sociology, Erasmus Tilburg University

Preface

In this volume, we have employed several editorial conventions. The first is that all editions of Berger's work, published outside of the United States, have been referred to by their U.S. titles. For example, *The Social Reality of Religion* (Britain) is consistently referred to as *The Sacred Canopy* (U.S.). The second is that coauthored works cited in the text are listed only in Berger's name. This is in no way intended to minimize the significant contributions by his coauthors, but only to make the frequent references to these works less stylistically burdensome to the reader. Full author citation can be found in the bibliography.

The editors, along with individual contributors to the volume, would like to acknowledge and thank the generous support of several organizations. Hunter received support from the Subcommittee on Research Grants of the University of Virginia. Ainlay was aided by grants from the Committee on Professional Standards as well as the Committee on Research and Publications at Holy Cross College. Redfoot wrote his contribution to the volume with support of a grant from the National Institute of Mental Health (#5T23 MH14660). Hammond was the recipient of funding from the Lilly Endowment.

In addition, the editors and contributors would like to acknowledge a number of individuals with whom discussions provided valuable insights and encouragement. Among these would be Paul Kingston, Charles Cappell, Rogers Johnson, Victoria Swigert, David Hummon, Stanley DeViney and Kurt Bach. We also gratefully acknowledge the assistance of the editorial staff at Routledge & Kegan Paul, in particular Peter Hopkins and Terry Quigley.

Introduction

The problem of modern social theory

There is an unhappy irony about modern social theory. Virtually all academic disciplines can claim to have made notable if not extraordinary advances in this century in the elaboration of theoretical perspective or in their critical application to various empirical problems. This is unfortunately not the case with sociology and, most distressingly, its handling of social theory. Indeed, one can hardly say that social theory thrives when its most prominent characteristic is the extent to which it has turned in on itself. There is currently more social theory written about social theory than about the social world itself. What is even more strange is the fact that the most recent developments in this area of intellectual discourse take it one step further: theory about theory about theory or an interpretation of an interpretation of a social theory. This is not to say that there is no validity in this kind of work. On the contrary, intellectual history, social philosophy and even empirical research have been well-served by the many useful and clarifying insights into theoretical logic and conceptualization made in some of these efforts. The problem from our perspective is that virtually all of the intellectual work falling under the heading, 'social theory' is taken up in precisely this kind of conceptualization to the second, third and even fourth degree of abstraction. (How *does* Alexander interpret Gouldner's interpretation of Parson's interpretation of Weber? And what did Marx's historical materialism really, really, really mean?) Introverted in substance and often inaccessible in style, the 'queen of the sciences' has become languid if not inert in intellectual vision.

There are, of course, a few significant exceptions to this tendency, exceptions representing most theoretical traditions. One of these is Peter Berger. Berger is one of the most prolific sociologists of the twentieth century. He has authored, coauthored, or edited over twenty books and 100 articles, many of these with translations in German, French, Spanish, and Italian. While there are a number of sociologists as prolific as Berger, few are as widely read. According to figures provided by Doubleday (one of two presses which, by and large, handle Berger's work), his books have sold in excess of a million and a half copies. Few also are as widely cited. Since 1980, for example, Berger has averaged roughly 300 listings per year in the *Social Science Citation Index*.

This merely, and perhaps unnecessarily, documents the national and international stature most sociologists readily accord him. But what distinguishes his work? Why is he prominent? Columnist Russell Baker once said that 'the young cult of sociology, needing a language, invented one. There are many dead languages, but the sociologists' is the only language that was dead at birth.' On the whole Baker may be correct, but one glaring exception he missed is the writing of Peter Berger. There is a stylistic sassiness and wit that marks his work that few if any have equaled. Whether or not one agrees with his sociology, one cannot help but be impressed with the elegance of his analyses and the eloquence of his prose. Whatever else one may say, one must agree that he knows how to write with clarity and punch.

Another trademark is his aloofness from the gamesmanship of professional sociology. He is committed to the intellectual discipline of sociology, but almost contemptuous of the profession of sociology. This is rather boldly illustrated by a comment he made in 1983 in a discussion of the moral vitality of the American population:

> If one is concerned for the future of America, one might willingly exchange the entire membership of the American Sociological Association . . . for the people who cross the Rio Grande in any given year (1983e:136).

Needless to say, such comments and others like this have not ingratiated him to the many sociologists who do take the profession seriously. His scorn for the mainstream sociological journals was evident in even his earliest works (1963c:11), and the paucity of his writing appearing in the disciplines 'top two' (he has only one full-length article in the *American Journal of Sociology* and one in the *American Sociological Review*) betrays the mutual suspicion that has characterized his relationship with mainstream American sociology. This is no doubt partly due to the fact that he has been exceptional in an era of sociology known more for the sharpening of methodological tools than refinement of theory. Beyond this, he has shown little interest in personal intellectual debate in public settings and only marginal interest (in his writing) in the often ritualistic act of self-consciously defining his territory through elaborate bibliographic comparisons, contrasts, cross-referencings, and the like. He would likely consider both exercises tedious and pedantic. He merely pursues his intellectual agenda whether people like it or not.

What most characterizes his work, however, is a return to the classical vision of sociology – a vision implicit in the works of Weber, Durkheim, Marx, Pareto, and the like. This is not to suggest that he elevates the 'classics' to a place of dogmatic authority on all relevant sociological issues (because there is little more to add); nor does it mean that he holds a nostalgia for a largely forgotten wisdom (to be pored over, dissected and restated). Classical sociology, particularly though not exclusively the Weberian variant, is simply a model of the practice and calling of sociology generally.

Indeed it can be reasonably argued that the classics did establish certain precedents. The first of these would have been the commitment to the scientific stature of the study of society. While this commitment reached certain excesses in the positivistic quest for social axioms, it was more typically expressed as a passion to see the world as it was, without first making political or ethical judgements about it. Though they varied widely in their degree of success, objectivity uncolored by *overt* political bias was still the goal. This was true to a certain extent even for one as politically committed as Marx. Yet, however objectively the reality of the social world was approached, its meaning was never self-evident but always subject to interpretation. A second precedent, then, was that classical sociology was *interpretive*. As employed here the word would include its ordinary usage – a theoretical concern with interpreting the subjective meanings and motives of social actors – but it also goes beyond it. The meaning is more generic, referring to the act of explaining the nature, the causal relations, and the historical significance of different institutional configurations and their meaning for and impact on various types of individuals and groups as they live out the routines of everyday life. In other words classical sociology was concerned not only with the question, 'What is?' but with the questions, 'Why?' and, 'So what?' Based upon their reading of historical, archival, and even statistical evidence, all of the early protagonists of sociology offered compelling interpretations of the past and of their present world. A third precedent concerns the level and scope of sociological analysis. By and large, classical sociology was comprehensive in its vision. As such the early statements contained a prominent historical component, a strong comparative component, and many of them even a self-conscious philosophical/methodological component. While many were sensitive to fine empirical detail, the classical statements were, none the less, unprovincial in their intellectual view. Their concerns were global even if not always macro-sociological. A sociology that strove to be objective, interpretive, and comprehensive was also a sociology that had the daring to take on the most consequential issues of time – chief among these was the problem of modernity. The fourth major precedent of classical sociology, then, was substantive in nature – it was the desire to make sense of the modern world. Methods and theoretical strategies differed, to be sure, but the understanding of a rapidly changing world and its consequences for individual existence was central to all of the lasting contributions of the period.

By setting these precedents the classics simultaneously established a vision and something of an agenda for succeeding generations of sociologists. That vision and that agenda, though, have progressively lost ground in recent decades. Against these currents stands Berger's own career. Virtually every aspect of his professional life has developed as an attempt to recover the interpretive vision of classical sociology. In his work in social theory and the sociology of knowledge (beginning with *Invitation to Sociology* (1963c), continuing through his premier work (with Thomas Luckmann), *The Social Construction of Reality* (1966e) and extending to his essay on the method and vocation of sociology (with Hansfried Kellner), *Sociology Reinterpreted* (1981d), Berger has developed a theoretical perspective and analytical model, novel for its synthesis of different theoretical strains in classical and contemporary theory. It is a perspective that comprehensively encompasses the complex relationship between the individual and society, the relationship between the micro- and macro-social worlds, the social genesis, maintenance, and distribution of knowledge, among other things. His work in religion (beginning with *The Noise of Solemn Assemblies* (1961a) and *The Precarious Vision* (1961c) and continuing in *The Sacred Canopy* (1967c) and numerous articles) carries the recognition (that the classical figures shared) that the fate of the individual in modern society is largely a religious problem. His work on modernization and social change in *The Homeless Mind* (with Brigitte Berger and Hansfried Kellner; 1973b), *Pyramids of Sacrifice* (1974f), *Facing up to Modernity* (1977b), and *The Capitalist Revolution* (1986) specifically and comparatively pursues the historical singularities of the modern world order and its political and social-psychological consequences. The effort to make sense of modern times in a sociologically responsible fashion has also taken him outside of the formal boundaries of sociology to inform his theological concerns in *The Rumor of Angels* (1969b), *Against the World; For the World* (1976a), *The Heretical Imperative* (1979a), and *The Other Side of God* (1981c) as well as his political concerns in *To Empower People* (with Richard Neuhaus, 1977e) and *The War Over the Family* (with Brigitte Berger; 1983e). It even extends to the more subjective statements he has made in his two novels, *The Enclaves* (1965b) and *Protocol of a Damnation* (1975d).

Berger in perspective

At one level, this book is simply an attempt to take stock of Peter Berger's formidable contributions to sociology. In this sense it knowingly commits the same 'sin' mentioned earlier. It is a work of social theory on a body of social theory – theiry to the third degree of abstraction from the social world. The contributors in Part I struggle with a number of Berger's theoretical contributions. Nicholas Abercrombie begins by examining his reformulation of the sociology of knowledge. Shifting his attention to the subjective reality of everyday life, Berger enters a dialogue with traditional sociologies of knowledge – particularly those of Marx and Mannheim.

Abercrombie explores this dialogue and considers ways in which Berger goes beyond these figures as well as comparing his work with the likes of Foucault, Gramsci and Garfinkel. Stephen Ainlay then pursues the phenomenological influence on Berger's work. He examines the notable influence of Alfred Schutz as well as Berger's popularization of a variety of phenomenological concepts and presuppositions while pointing to areas of analysis that Berger seems to avoid.

In Part II the emphasis shifts to Berger's notable contributions to the study of modernization. Anton Zijderveld elucidates the relationship of technology and bureaucracy to modern consciousness – familiar themes in Berger's work. He furthermore discusses Berger's handling of such issues in relationship to classical figures like Marx, Weber, Pareto, and Gehlen. James Hunter explores the 'malaise' that is argued to be a cost of modernity. He contextualizes Berger's own brand of social criticism by discussing a half century of writing on the modern world – Mumford, Fromm, Marcuse, Adorno, Horkheimer, Ellul, Geiger, Reisman, Packard, Slater, Bell, and Lasch to name just a few. Hunter goes on to explore the interplay between political ideology and social criticism generally (and Berger's particularly) and the significance of this interplay for the task of understanding modern life.

In light of this discussion we include an excursus on the problem of freedom. Donald Redfoot approaches this as a theme common to the work of both Berger and Max Weber – examining the ways in which both have viewed the rationality of the modern world as a threat to human freedom.

Part III turns to the substantive area of religion. Berger's contributions here are perhaps best known among sociologists and theologians alike. Robert Wuthnow begins the section with a discussion of religion as 'sacred canopy.' He explores Berger's contributions to our understanding of the ways in which religion helps people face the problem of meaningfully ordering their lives. He attempts to lend empirical specificity to a variety of key Bergerian insights. Beyond this, however, he points up several analytical difficulties inherent in Berger's conceptualization. Phillip Hammond then examines Berger's interpretation of the impact of modernization on religion and belief. He suggests various ways in which Berger gives a social-psychological twist to the classical treatment of secularization and pluralism and the problems this creates.

At this point, we again interject the argument with an excursus – this time on Berger and the problem of truth. Stan Gaede uses this forum to consider the ways in which sociological assumptions inform his theology and, conversely, the degree to which his theological (and, more broadly, metaphysical) assumptions inform his sociology.

The authors in Part IV focus on Berger's contribution to our understanding of the method and vocation of interpretive sociology. James O'Leary reviews Berger's own value-free approach to sociology. He demonstrates the ways in which this approach takes empirical form in Berger's discussion of institutions, bureaucracies, and mediating structures as well as considering the more general implications for the relationship of science to politics. Jay Mechling advocates a 'Jamesian' interpretation of Berger. Mechling makes a case for the pragmatist influence on Berger's work and suggests that this may well aid in regenerating and redirecting interpretive sociology.

Finally, the volume ends with an essay by Peter Berger. Berger weighs the foregoing analysis of his work and takes his own inventory of the contribution that he has made to the sociological enterprise. Additionally, he reflects on the past and the future promise of interpretive sociology.

As we mentioned, this book is in part theory to the third degree of abstraction – theory about theory. While the volume begins there, it does not stay there. It attempts to go beyond. It can be framed this way.

It was argued earlier that Berger's career can be seen as one attempt to recover the vision of interpretive sociology, a vision established by the classical figures of the discipline. Not surprisingly, Berger has been self-conscious about this, as is clearly seen in his writing (particularly *Sociology Reinterpreted*). The present volume, then, is not only an effort to take stock of Berger's contributions to sociology, it is also (and perhaps foremost) an effort to assess how successful he is at this larger intellectual challenge. Thus, at one level, we are asking the *expository* question: what does he say? At a second level, we are asking an *evaluative* question: does his work merely rest upon the achievements of the classics by restating them for our time, or does he go beyond them, making genuinely new contributions and pointing to new directions for theory and empirical research (in the way the classical figures did?) At the third level we are asking an *interpretive* question: is social theory still alive or is it in an advanced stage of an ineluctable decline? Does Berger's contribution mark the exhaustion of social theory or the possibility that it can move in creative directions, possibly even to a paradigm shift, in the Kuhnian sense of the term?

The contributors to this volume differ somewhat in their final assessment of Berger. Some are more critical than others. What we all hold in common, however, is a recognition that he has made significant contributions – contributions that require careful and critical appraisal, both for their specific substance and for what they may tell us about the enterprise of contemporary social theory.

PART I

Social theory

CHAPTER 1

Knowledge, order, and human autonomy

Nicholas Abercrombie

Peter Berger's *The Social Construction of Reality* (1966e), coauthored with Thomas Luckmann, was one of the most influential sociological books of the 1960s. At that time, British sociological tastes (particularly those of students) were being influenced by American studies of deviant behavior which were, in turn, formed by Mead's symbolic interactionism. It was not only that these – largely ethnographic – studies were lively, intriguing, and promising as pieces of empirical research. They also aroused interest in a theory, or philosophy, of social research, radically opposed to the then prevailing orthodoxies. Most orthodox British sociological theory was organized around 'structural' conceptions which gave primacy to social determinations rather than individual agency. In turn, these conceptions derived either from the structural-functionalism of British anthropology or from a particular reading of classical sociological theory, particularly that of Marx, Weber, and Durkheim. Thus a typical debate of the period was that between consensus and conflict schools. Parsons was taken as a representative of the first, emphasizing the coherence of societies through commonly held values, while various Marxist positions exemplified the second in arguing that societies were in fact riven with conflict. Whatever the disagreements, this debate like others was pitched at the level of social structure and tended to ignore the level of individual agency. Of course, various commentators tried to rescue the hidden individual dimension by, for example, emphasizing Parsons's action theory or rediscovering Marx's early writings. None the less, the prevailing tone was structural.

In this intellectual context, *The Social Construction of Reality* promised an alternative theoretical framework, restoring human agency, and implying the political possibility of individuals acting against powerful social structures such as bureaucracies. It became influential in generating interest in a whole range of newer perspectives from phenomenology to Weber's theory of action.

Berger's main target was the classical sociology of knowledge which he believed to be determinist, thereby denying the role of the individual in actively creating bodies of knowledge. It is true that some definitions of the sociology of knowledge may have a structural-determinist flavour. Macquet, for example, argues that all work in the subject attempts to answer three questions: 'What are the social or cultural factors which influence knowledge? What are the cognitive mental productions influenced? What's the degree and kind of conditioning between the two?' (Macquet, 1951: 255–6).

For most sociologists, Mannheim probably serves as the chief representative of the classical sociology of knowledge. Mannheim is certainly not an economic determinist in the sense that Marx (misleadingly) is often claimed to be. On the contrary, he explicitly rejects Marxist connections of this kind. However, there certainly is some sense in suggesting that he stresses the primacy of social structures in the social construction of reality. Briefly, his work develops in three stages. The first phase is marked by an orientation towards a form of idealist 'pure culture' analysis, in which the concern is with the explanation of one set of ideas in terms of another set of ideas, or spiritual entity. From this, Mannheim moves to an interest in hermeneutics and the interpretation of meaning. The third and most important stage includes Mannheim's sociology of knowledge proper. He insists over and over again that knowledge is social. Despite appearances to the contrary, thinking is a collective rather than individual act: 'knowing is fundamentally collective knowing' (Mannheim, 1960: 28). Each individual thinks in a way determined by his membership in a social group. 'We belong to a group not only because we are born into it . . . but primarily because we see the world and certain things in the world the way it does' (Mannheim, 1960: 19). As social groups differ, so will members of those groups differ in the way that they perceive the world. This correlation between membership of a social group and ways of thought is reinforced for Mannheim by the importance of struggle and competition in social life. As groups struggle with one another, so they 'think' against one another. Thought is an instrument of action and is formulated and used in accordance with the interests of social groups in their conflicts with one another. Mannheim insists that many social groups will have their own systems of thought. It is not that one social class, for example, will dominate. He mentions social classes, generations, status groups, sects, occupational groups and intellectuals as having their own particular systems of knowledge. Despite this structural pluralism, however, it is clear that he does not give an explicit role to individual agency. The position of individuals as bearers of knowledge can be more or less read off from their structural circumstances.

Any suggestion that a sociological theory, like that of Mannheim, is too structurally determinist can be interpreted in either a weak or a strong fashion. As far as the former is concerned, some structuralist Marxists (Althusser, for example) would concede that even their determinist account requires a theory of the subject. They argue that human beings are best conceived simply as 'bearers' of social relations but there must be some account of *how* subjects come to bear social relations. However, such a view still implies a certain passivity on the part of human agents. A stronger account would, therefore, stress the active, creative part played by human beings in constructing their world and their knowledge of it. In *The Social Construction of Knowledge* and other writings, Berger favours this strong view.

The knowledge of the everyday world

Although I have so far introduced Berger's concerns in *The Social Construction of Reality* in terms of a debate with theories of structural determinism, this is not the explicit point of departure of the book itself. It starts, rather, from an analysis of a different but related fault of the classical sociology of knowledge. Berger argues that the sociology of knowledge has been overly concerned with the study of the theoretical or the opinions, beliefs, and theories of intellectuals, and with the implications for the truth and falsity of the beliefs concerned. Thus Mannheim's substantive illustrations were drawn, for example, from science or mathematics or the writings of conservative intellectuals. In providing a sociological explanation of these forms of thought Mannheim became worried that he might be undermining their claims to truth. If people think things as a result of being placed in particular social circumstances (as members of social classes, for example), then it might seem as if they were not using the processes of logical thought and evidence which are supposed to be independent of circumstances. Mannheim proposed several solutions to this actually self-imposed problem. The point that Berger makes is that Mannheim, in concentrating on theoretical thought and the implications of the sociology of knowledge for truth, had misconceived the central task of the subject. The sociology of knowledge should, in Berger's view, analyse 'everything that passes for knowledge in society.' Within knowledge defined in this way, theoretical speculation plays only a minor role. What is of much greater importance is the *knowledge appropriate to the conduct of everyday life*. As Berger says:

> It is our contention, then, that the sociology of knowledge must concern itself with whatever passes for 'knowledge' in a society, regardless of the ultimate validity or invalidity (by whatever criteria) of such 'knowledge.' And in so far as all human 'knowledge' is developed, transmitted and maintained in social situations, the sociology of knowledge must seek to understand the processes by which this is done in such a way that a taken-for-granted 'reality' congeals for the man in the street. In other words, we contend that *the sociology of knowledge is concerned with the analysis of the social construction of reality* (1966e: 15, authors' emphasis).

Objections to a theoretical bias and neglect of the everyday world in analysis of culture are not uncommon. Foucault's concentration on 'serious speech acts,' for example, ignores the way that intellectualized discourses are (or are not) appropriated by people in everyday life. In a different way Gramsci emphasized the analytical importance of considering various levels of thought from language itself through folklore to common sense, and he contrasted the nature of 'popular thought' with the more theoretical doctrines of intellectuals.

Berger's interest in everyday life is, however, actually quite different from that of Gramsci and has radically different theoretical origins lying in phenomenology (especially in the work of Schutz). For Berger, the everyday life world is experienced as an ordered reality, as intersubjective reality and also an objective reality – that is, a reality 'out there' which appears independent of volition. It only *appears*, however, to be independent of volition, and the process by which human creativity becomes objectified plays an important role in *The Social Construction of Reality*. Indeed social life is possible only by means of such objectivations, because it is only in this way that one can become aware of the subjective motives, intentions, and feelings of others. For example, if I am given an object as a present, the object expresses the subjectivity of the donor and his or her love and affection. The present is acting as a sign, and signs are a crucial case of objectivation. Language is the most important system of signs for it can transcend the face-to-face situation; it typifies and anonymizes. Language therefore enables the construction of a common stock of knowledge and its transmission.

The knowledge of everyday life is organized in zones both spatial and temporal around my 'here-and-now,' round the centre of my social world which is myself. Spatially, the nearest zone is that which is most easily physically manipulated, while temporally, the nearest zone comprises those things that are contemporary with me. Experience of others is arranged in zones radiating outwards from myself. Nearest and most important is the face-to-face situation which gives direct and vivid knowledge. However, much of our knowledge of others is not acquired in face-to-face encounters and is characteristically typified; we select those characteristics that interest us and ignore those that may make these persons unique. Similar points can be made about our experience of others who are not our contemporaries. Since we cannot have face-to-face relationships with predecessors or successors, our knowledge of them is bound to be typified. Everyday life is dominated by the pragmatic motive; that is, to the solving of practical problems. Given the importance of this motive, recipe knowledge (that is, 'knowledge limited to pragmatic competence in routine performances') occupies a prominent place in our stock of knowledge.

Berger adopts Schutz's view of the way that interests structure the stock of knowledge via a system of relevance. Perhaps he emphasizes the social character of everyday life more than Schutz, for he stresses the way in which relevance structures can be determined by 'my general situation in society' as well as by immediate pragmatic motives. Further, the relevance structures of different individuals intersect so that an important element of knowledge of the external world is the relevance structures of others.

Having described the structure of the stock of knowledge, Berger's next problem is to show how it is constructed and maintained. He insists that the process of construction is essentially dialectical – a dialectic of subject and object, of individual and society.

The dialectical method

Berger's method appears to be very eclectic in its origins. He borrows his anthropological presuppositions and dialectical method from Marx, and his social psychology from Mead. His view of the nature of social reality as coercive and constraining depends a good deal on Durkheim, although he follows Weber in emphasizing the construction of social reality through subjective meanings. Some of these borrowings may seem to be irreconcilable. For example, Durkheim says, 'Consider social facts as things,' while Weber observes, 'The object of cognition is the subjective meaning complex of action.' Durkheim seems to argue for a position in which individuals are moulded by social structure while Weber appears to believe that analysis has to start with subjective meaning. However, for Berger these two statements are not contradictory for society does possess objective facticity yet is constructed by activity that expresses subjective meaning. Society is a dialectical process in which subjective meanings become objective facticities and objective facticities become subjective meanings. Now, it is certainly possible to argue that Berger's reading of Weber and Durkheim is rather partial. It is difficult to maintain that Weber's primary interest was in the 'subjective meaning complex of action' and that maxim means that individual consciousness has an analytical autonomy, since so much of his empirical work takes a very different direction. As Turner argues, Weber's sociological pessimism was closely tied to a deterministic perspective of social reality 'whose structure and process has a logic independent of the will and consciousness of individual agents' (Turner, 1981: 27). It should be clear, however, that Berger's dialectic does not *depend* on a particular reading of classical sociological writers even though the theoretical device is proposed as a means of overcoming a classical sociological problem.

The dialectic in the *Social Construction of Reality* has three 'moments': externalization, objectivation, and internalization. Berger gives a good account of the three moments in *The Sacred Canopy*:

> Externalization is the ongoing outpouring of human being into the world, both in the physical and the mental activity of men. Objectivation is the attainment of the products of this activity (again both physical and mental) of a reality that confronts its original producers as a facticity external to, and other than, themselves. Internalization is the reappropriation by men of this same reality, transforming it once again from structures of the objective world into structures of the subjective consciousness. It is through externalization that society is a human product. It is through objectivation that society becomes a reality sui generis. It is through internalization that man is a product of society (1967c: 4).

I have already said that the dialectical approach is seen as an alternative to a determinism in which the individual is formed by social structure and can have no part in its creation. Berger believes that there is a sense in which individuals create the social world around them. Such theories see the social world as being like the physical world; that is, as composed of thing-like elements which impose themselves on people. Although reifying determinist social theories are incorrect, the social world is in fact reified. That is, because the social world appears to people as such a massive, real, and coercive fact, they tend to invest it with thing-like qualities, as being a reality that presses down on them. The reification of everyday perception of social reality is an instance of a larger process, that of alienation, which is again very general to social life. For Berger, people are alienated when they forget that the social reality which appears to be so massive is in fact a human creation, is *their* creation.

Society as objective reality

The next move in the argument is to show how the dialectic works in the creation first of objective reality and secondly of subjective reality. Mankind occupies a unique position in the animal kingdom. Generally, each animal species has an environment which is specific to it. This is, however, not true of man, whose lack of environmental specialization derives from several factors. The fundamental point is that man's instinctual structure is relatively unspecialized compared with that of animals. In addition, the human child is at birth very much less biologically mature than most other comparable mammals. The result is that a good deal of what might otherwise be biologically determined development in man is heavily influenced by the environment, social as well as physical. Although there are biological constraints on the human condition, it is in this sense that one can say that man is a social creature in a way that animals are not.

The same biological factors which make human nature plastic and hence uniquely social, however, also make it unstable. The unformed human being cannot cope fully with its environment; it *has* to be moulded by social forces. Social order transforms a biologically given world-openness into a socially given world-closedness. These biological facts do not imply any *particular* social order, they merely imply the fundamental necessity of social order in general. Further, it is not the case that order is biologically constructed. Although it is, in a sense, biologically *required*, social order is constructed *socially*. In order to understand how social order is constructed, maintained, and transmitted, apart from these anthropological necessities, one must have a theory of institutionalization.

The process of institutionalization begins with the patterned and habitual repetition of human action. Again, this is seen as a constant of human behaviour; generally human action is repeated in much the same form. However, the crucial feature of institutions is that they involve the interlocking of the habitual actions of a variety of actors. One can illustrate the way that an institution is built up by considering the way that two actors, A and B, coming from entirely different social worlds, meet and interact. In this interaction, typifications will be produced quickly. As A watches B repetitively act in the same way, he is able to construct these actions as typical and can posit typical motives from them. A will also assume that B is doing the same thing with regard to him.

Eventually A and B will begin to play roles with respect to each other and will make each other's roles act as models for their own role-playing. As A and B interact – as a set of reciprocal typifications are evolved – a routine is developed in which actions that originally caused surprise become taken-for-granted. Any innovations in behaviour will themselves become habitualized, further expanding the background common to A and B.

Institutionalization, however, perfects itself only when it is passed on to others. When, for example, A and B have children. When just A and B are involved, their social world has a tenuous quality. As they made it so they can unmake it. This is not true of their children for they are born into a world which they did not make. To them the social world is a massive and coercive fact experienced as possessing a reality of its own. It is, in other words, an *objective* fact.

The story of A and B provides prototypical illustration of the construction and maintenance of institutions and also of two moments of the dialectic. In the first place, one sees how A and B *externalize* in creating the institution. Then one sees how these externalizations become objectivated when it becomes a question of involving others in the institution created by A and B. The institutional order of a society is not, however, a seamless web that is uniformly and successfully massive. For example, there is no *a priori* reason to suppose that different institutional processes are well integrated with one another since they will have different histories. This implies a potential for discord, not only *between* participants in different institutional processes, but also *within* one individual as he is involved in different institutions. These imperfections demand some mechanism of reconciliation. Most importantly, such a mechanism is also required by a much more general characteristic of the social world than institutional imperfection, for Berger believes that the world is endemically, fundamentally, and systematically chaotic and precarious. He can be lyrical on this subject:'The thought keeps suggesting itself. . . That, perhaps, the bright reality of everyday life is but an illusion, to be swallowed up at any moment by the howling nightmares of the other, the night-side of reality' (1966e: 116). Again, all social reality is precarious. All societies are constructions in the face of chaos' (1966e: 121). As we have already seen, however, social order is an anthropological necessity. Thus, there must be procedures which restore or maintain order in an intrinsically chaotic social world. These procedures are generically known, perhaps rather unfortunately, as legitimations (not in the sense of justifications).

Legitimations throw some kind of protective canopy over fragile social reality in such a way that people have their lives meaningfully ordered; they put everything in its right place. Four levels of legitimation can be distinguished, differentiated by the degree to which they are abstract or theoretical. First, at the lowest level of abstraction, language itself is legitimating, for legitimating explanations are built into the vocabulary. Thus the fact of naming another person a 'cousin,' legitimates the behaviour that is appropriate to cousinhood. The second level of legitimation is made up of proverbs, maxims, and folk tales. Third, there are more or less explicit theories about the rights and duties of cousinhood or about the appropriateness of various marriage partners that might be developed and promulgated by the old man of the tribe. Symbolic systems make up the fourth level of legitimation. These are theories at the highest level of abstraction that integrate all institutional processes. They provide a total and overarching system of meaning. All events can be given a meaning within a symbolic universe which can have this totally encompassing character. This is because they are symbolic; that is, they refer to realities which do not occur in everyday experience. However the importance of symbolic universes – and their total and theoretical character – means that they tend to be promulgated by experts, priests, or theologians, for example, who will also specialize in a kind of second-order activity by legitimating the symbolic universes.

It is uncertain from Berger's works which level of legitimation he believes to be the most significant. In *The Sacred Canopy*, he holds the pre-theoretical level to be the most important, perhaps because it is so pervasive. Language, after all, is everywhere. In *The Social Construction of Reality*, however, symbolic universes are given more emphasis. In any event, it is plain that legitimating agencies cover a very wide range of social phenomena. One of the most important of such agencies is religion. The legitimating role of religion is, incidentally, one of the main reasons for the intimate connection between the sociology of knowledge and the sociology of religion in Berger's work.

Religion is, historically, the most obviously successful symbolic universe. In that its symbolism is typically far removed from the realities of everyday experience, it is able to provide a peculiarly all-embracing framework of legitimation not restricted to the details of social life. It is able to provide individuals with a means of coping with 'marginal situations' (particularly death) which are otherwise deeply threatening. It can achieve the integration of the independent institutional processes so that the entire society now makes sense. In the past, 'religion' meant formal church religion but more recently there has been a decline of these public religious observances. They have been replaced by other agencies – not only a more private religious commitment but also such systems of belief as psychiatry or communism (see Berger, 1963f).

Religion is an effective agency of legitimation not only because it creates an encompassing universe of meaning but also because it makes the world seem an objective fact independent of man's volition. The other side of the coin is that the more effective it is in this latter function, the more alienating a force it becomes. Plainly, the more autonomous and coercive a religiously legitimated world is, the more man is unable to conceive of his role in creating and maintaining that world (see Berger, 1967c, Chapter 4). It is not only religion that alienates and reifies as it legitimates. *Any* legitimation agent of this generality and power, in that it provides a total and objective canopy of meaning, will do the same.

Society as subjective reality

The dialectic of externalization, objectivation, and internalization now has to be applied to subjective reality. In the individual's biography the process begins with internalization which is the apprehension of an objective event as expressing meaning, that is, as an manifestation of another's intentions. More generally, internalization is an understanding of one's fellow-men and the apprehension of the world as a meaningful reality. Berger's treatment of internalization is essentially a discussion of the traditional problem of socialization although it is presented in a fairly unconventional way. But first, a distinction has to be made between primary and secondary socialization. Primary socialization is effectively childhood socialization by which the individual becomes a full member of society. Secondary socialization is any subsequent process that inducts an individual into a new sector of social life.

Berger's discussion of primary socialization is heavily dependent on the social psychology of Mead. Every individual is born into a social structure; there is a fixed objective world there before his arrival. He encounters the 'significant others' – parents, siblings, for example – who have responsibility for his socialization and whose definitions of reality will appear to the child as objective facts over which he has no control. The child identifies with the significant others. That is, he takes on their roles and internalizes them. By being able to take on the role of others, the child is able to see himself through their eyes. Thus, the process of taking on another's role is also a process of self-identification. The world presented by the significant others is not internalized as one world among many possible. It is internalized as *the* world. Socialization then proceeds from taking on the role of the significant others to a more generalized identification. This process is founded on the realization by the child that the attitudes and roles of his significant others are in, fact, more widely shared. Instead of taking on the role of significant others only, the child is able to take on the role of the 'generalized other.' He now has an identity, not only *vis-à-vis particular* persons, but an identity in general. This is a decisive phase for 'it implies the internalization of society as such and of the objective reality established therein, and, at the same time, the subjective establishment of a coherent and continuous identity. Society, identity, and reality are subjectively crystallized in the same process of internalization' (1966e: 153).

The necessity of secondary socialization arises in any society in which there is a considerable division of labour, and hence some differentiation of institutional processes each of which requires some measure of socialization. Secondary socializations are not nearly so well entrenched as primary ones, for it is no longer a question of internalizing *the* world but of internalizing sub-worlds. Further, those involved in the transmission of institutional realities are not so much 'significant others' as functionaries with whom there is little emotional involvement.

So far, I have presented socialization as a universally effective method of induction into social reality. This is far from being the case for Berger for there are a number of imperfections that are systematic to the whole process. Thus socialization can never, in the nature of things, be complete over the life-cycle. Again, there is always the possibility of inconsistency between primary and secondary socialization and between the secondary socialization appropriate to different social sectors. Further, with any degree of social differentiation, the actual content of the socialization process will differ as between different social groups. In most societies therefore, there will be competing definitions of reality between social groups which may well be threatening to individuals. These imperfections indicate that socialization cannot ever be totally successful in the sense that there will always be a lack of fit between subjective reality and objective reality. That is, the reality that is subjectively appropriated, which results from socialization, cannot ever quite match objective reality. In Berger's view, this lack of fit can produce a division of consciousness which 'results in an internal confrontation between socialized and non-socialized components of self, reiterating within consciousness itself the external confrontation between society and the individual' (1967c: 84).

The necessary imperfection of socialization means that every viable society must develop procedures of reality-maintenance to ensure a measure of symmetry between objective and subjective reality. This is the same problem that I have already discussed in connection with legitimation. Now the emphasis is on the protection of *subjective* reality rather than *objective*, institutionally defined, reality. In a similar manner, Berger suggests that reality-maintaining procedures are also demanded, separately from the imperfections of socialization, by the innate instability of everyday life. Everyday life may seem solid and real enough, but 'it is threatened by the marginal situations of human experience . . . There is always the haunting presence of metamorphoses, those actually remembered and those only sensed as sinister possibilities' (1966e: 167. Again note the evocative language). These marginal situations represent the subjective side of the precariousness of all socially constructed worlds discussed at some length earlier in this essay. The marginal situation *par excellence* is death. Death threatens the taken-for-granted realities more than anything else and its incorporation within some meaningful structure is of paramount importance.

The most effective device which maintains a person's sense of reality against ever-present terror is the simple routine of everyday interaction with others. In effect, subjective reality is maintained in the same way as it was created and by similar personnel. Thus, it is the set of significant others – supported by a chorus of less significant others – who, in their daily interactions, are chiefly responsible for repetitively confirming the individual's identity.

If it is daily life that generally maintains reality, it is conversation that specifically sustains it. It is not that conversation is always about the meaning of life, but rather that every conversational exchange necessarily presupposes a whole world, a whole background of shared assumptions which are implicitly invoked and confirmed by every sentence spoken. An experiment conducted by Garfinkel (1967) nicely illustrates this point. He asked a married couple to write down an ordinary conversation that they had had one morning. It quickly became apparent that the conversation made sense only to the participants because they shared a set of background assumptions which effectively filled out the more telegraphic spoken words. He then asked them to write down those background assumptions that they thought made sense of their interchange. The couple found that this was almost impossible because every assumption that they recorded was in turn dependent on further assumptions. The efficacy of conversation in the maintenance of reality depends on the objectifying power of language. In the discussion of objective reality I indicated how important language was to Berger in the creation of an ordered, objective world. In conversation, the objectifications of language became part of the individual consciousness. Thus, in a very basic sense, everyone who employs language is maintaining reality.

In sum, subjective reality is maintained principally by everyday life. Berger suggests that the force of this claim can best be appreciated by considering what happens when everyday routines are disrupted. Thus, odd, random, or unexplained, behaviour on the part of others, can have shattering consequences for the individual; he may literally not know who he is. Indeed, this phenomenon is the basis of certain kinds of film. Hitchcock, for example, was a director who made a good deal of use of the consequences of the sudden disruption of everyday life – often in the case of mistaken identity. Films of this kind (*North by Northwest*, for example) derive their peculiar terror from the feeling that, if others around one start behaving in a quite different way, then one may not be the person one thought one was. Further poignancy is often added by the contrast between the collapse of the everyday world of the central character and the maintenance of the everyday world of others remote from him. Thus the hero, pursued by nameless and inexplicable terrors, may run through a street crowded with shoppers going about their normal business. Often his fears are compounded by the fact that his disrupted world is insulated from the normal world. For some reason he cannot have recourse to the normal world of shoppers who might otherwise be sympathetic, and he has to grapple with the new identity that the new, terrifying world is trying to thrust upon him.

The terror that we, as spectators, feel when confronted by such dramatic disruptions often seems quite out of proportion to any real threat. A similar kind of point is made by yet another of Garfinkel's experiments. In this he persuaded his students to go home and try to behave, say, as a lodger, instead of what they were, son, daughter, wife, or husband. Plainly the point of these experiments was to see what would happen when everyday reality was experimentally disrupted. In fact the response on the part of those whose routine was thus disturbed was extraordinarily violent, seemingly disproportionately so.

Although in conventional accounts socialization is often thought of as a rigid process, the implication of Berger's remarks is that subjective reality can be transformed even after primary and secondary socialization. In its most drastic form, this will be a total transformation of the kind that occurs in religious conversion. This is in effect a process of resocialization which will involve the destruction of previous socialization, both primary and secondary. The most important requirement for conversion processes of this kind is the existence of a legitimating apparatus not only for the new reality but also for the rejection of the old. Conversion or 'alternation' is only an extreme form of the transformation of subjective reality. In a sense, secondary socialization itself is also such a transformation. There will be a whole range of resocializations – of varying degrees of thoroughness – between secondary socialization and alternation, and in modern society such processes will be commonplace as individuals are socially and geographically mobile between different social worlds.

It will be obvious from this discussion of subjective reality that the creation and maintenance of identity is closely bound up with the creation and maintenance of subjective reality. Therefore, theoretical work in social psychology is intimately connected with the sociology of knowledge, as it is defined by Berger (1966a). A theory of identity is a theory of the appropriation of a particular reality.

Order, uncertainty and the dialectic

The argument of *The Social Construction of Reality*, while it appears to be a treatise in the sociology of knowledge, is actually much more wide-ranging than that. In its criticism of the classical sociology of knowledge, it starts from an insistence that the knowledge of the everyday world should be the most significant focus of the subject but moves to an ambitious solution for one of the most important problems in classical sociological theory, the relationship between individual and society. One of the consequences of this is to move the sociology of knowledge to the centre of the stage. In doing so the book achieves a great deal. It stimulated interest in phenomenological approaches to sociology, it contrived a theoretical framework which united diverse branches of sociology, and it brought an original solution to a classical sociological problem. I shall want to argue in the last section of this essay, however, that *The Social Construction of Reality* and Berger's other work makes its impact not because of, but in spite of, its methodological innovations.

As I have indicated in the body of this essay, at the root of much of Berger's work is the insistence that the social world is *naturally* chaotic and precarious. The very texture of Berger's language changes when he is describing the 'fundamental terrors of human existence.' It becomes more lyrical, powerful, and evocative. The basic assumption is that mankind is beset on all sides by uncertainties, instabilities, and terrors, whether biologically, environmentally, or socially induced. One is reminded of Lucky's speech in Beckett's *Waiting for Godot* (1965) in which he contrasts ordinary life which is like a game of tennis with what lies underneath, the 'great cold' and 'the abode of stones.' For Berger, human life in such a context is literally impossible. In emphasizing the *naturalness* of this, Berger makes a deliberate comparison with the physical world in saying that social life abhors disorder as nature abhors a vacuum (1971d). Human life is only possible if the precarious, threatening, and frightening world is kept at bay by a protective canopy of systems of meaning. 'To be human means to live in a world – that is, to live in a reality that is ordered and gives sense to the business of living' (Berger, 1973d: 62). Legitimations are a functional requirement; no human society can exist without them. Cracks in the canopy must necessarily begin to let the terrors in. For example, Berger's analysis of the modern world is that there is a pluralization of legitimation that is much less effective than is a single monolithic system. People are not as safe with them and modern societies have begun to show the effects in the greater precariousness of life. In a telling description, Berger argues that modern life exhibits a peculiar 'homelessness' due, in part, to the fragmentation of systems of meaning (1973d).

There are a number of difficulties in the assumption of precariousness and the consequent necessity of order and legitimating systems. The theory is functionalist as it is expressed; ordering processes exist to meet disorder. In addition a large number of agencies of legitimation are cited. For example, Berger says that 'all socially objectivated "knowledge" is legitimating' (1967c: 30). Legitimation becomes such a general category that it is almost as if social life was required to keep social life ordered. One does not have, in other words, a ready notion of what would count as the counterfactual. A related point concerns the difficulty of establishing the necessity of order. On a number of occasions Berger provides some basis for holding this belief. In *The Social Construction of Reality*, as has been seen, it is argued that human beings are less formed at birth than are animals and are less able to cope with their environment. This implies that human nature is, at birth, unstable and that the most important requirement of the process of socialization is the construction of *order*. One might have thought that socialization involves all sorts of other things, including the provision of certain sorts of skills necessary for coping with the physical environment and that this provision is fundamentally important.

If there was no process of socialization and a human being had to rely on the skills available at birth, it would simply die. Berger seems to think, however, that without socialization human existence would be merely chaos. 'Chaos' is an odd way to describe such an extreme contingency. It is none the less revealing since Berger is deriving *order* as the prime requirement of human existence from the incompleteness of the human being at birth. Not only is it eccentric to suggest that order is *fundamental* in this sense but Berger does not succeed in showing how *order* is derived from the biological facts of human infancy. At times he attempts to derive order from other postulates. For example, in *The Sacred Canopy*, Berger says, 'put differently, the most important function of society is nomization. The anthropological presupposition for this is a human craving for meaning that appears to have the force of instinct. Men are congenitally compelled to impose a meaningful order upon reality' (1967c: 22). This is not exactly an attempt to derive order from human nature, it is a suggestion that order *is* human nature. Indeed, more often than not the polar opposites chaos and order are presented as axioms not otherwise derivable. However, one ought to experiment with contrary axioms and see if there is any argument that might help in deciding between them. It could be argued, therefore, that mankind can tolerate a good deal of uncertainty, without the need of a legitimating apparatus, and, of course, it has been argued that the human condition positively benefits from a measure of risk and uncertainty. Doubtless human nature requires a certain minimum of stability, but more from this to exaggerate the amount of order demanded. Societies can tolerate a good deal of dissensus and conflict and, indeed, one of the sources of such dissensus may be the very existence of the legitimating apparatus.

One last difficulty in the assumption of order should be mentioned. This concerns an ambiguity in the conception of social stability. Sometimes Berger talks of legitimation as giving meaning and sometimes as giving order or certainty. However, these are very different notions and will not always run together. It is possible for a system of belief to give meaning but create uncertainty. To some extent this point is realized in *The Social Construction of Reality* where a distinction is made between cognitive and normative aspects of legitimating systems. Thus there is a difference between saying that 'X is your sister' and saying that people should not sleep with their sisters. None the less, Berger does not recognize that there may be a certain tension between giving meaning in the sense of explaining and giving order in the sense of moral certainty; one can give meaning without giving certainty.

The concern with order is closely related to other features of Berger's work. For example, reification, defined earlier in this essay, while it is not intrinsically bound to the human condition, is, in fact, present in most societies. It will, indeed, assist in the legitimating processes 'by bestowing ontological status on social roles and institutions' (Berger, 1965c). In general, throughout Berger's work there is an emphasis on the role of anthropological constancies and necessities in the determination of social life. Indeed, the phrase 'anthropological constancy' occurs over and over again. Sometimes this will be in association with comments about the biological nature of human beings. Thus, in *The Social Construction of Reality*, death, sleep, hunger, sloth, and forgetfulness play an important theoretical role. These issues are nicely summarized and extended in an address given by Berger, which is reprinted in the *American Sociologist* (1971d). Here he argues that sociology performs two apparently contradictory functions. On the one hand, it is subversive of established patterns of thought. On the other, it is conservative in its implications for social order. Sociology has the latter function because it shows that every human community is importantly characterized by order, continuity, and triviality. The question of order has already been dealt with at length. Continuity is important because all societies have to see their current behaviours as part of an historical stream. Triviality is crucial to social life because mankind can only tolerate a limited amount of excitement and change. 'Trivality is one of the fundamental requirements of social life' (1971d: 4).

What do the importance of social order, the prominence of anthropological constancies, sloth, forgetfulness, death, sleep, hunger, continuity, and triviality have in common? Their crucial import, in my view, is that they all represent *limitations on autonomous human activity*. Together they give an oppressive feeling of weight. Surrounded by such forces, human beings have little scope for activities other than the routine. As Berger himself says of his view of reification: 'Such a perspective, I admit, is pessimistic. It is probably "conservative" ' (Berger, 1966c: 77). In sum, one half of the dialectic of *The Social Construction of Reality*, the stress on human activity in the construction of the social world is, *in practice*, suppressed by the sheer weight of forces, not only biological, but also social. The conversation between the individual and social structure is entirely one-sided. The implication of this is that those critics who accuse Berger of neglecting social structure are entirely wrong (see Lichtman, 1970 and Wisdom, 1973). On the other hand phenomenologists who suggest that Berger does not follow Schutz far enough in incorporating the actor's view may be nearer the truth (for example, Speier, 1967).

It would be tempting to draw the conclusion from my analysis that Berger is a conservative theorist. There are conservative themes in his work: the emphasis on order, the significance of the family, the importance of religion, and the analysis of modern society as fragmented and potentially anomic. His position is, however, more complicated than that, for he has consistently stressed the importance of the analysis of creative human activity and individual autonomy. This is evident in his book *The War Over the Family* (1983e), for instance, besides the programmatic declarations. Again, one other theme in his work is the nature of sociology as *subversive* as well as *conservative* discipline (Berger, 1963c; Berger, 1971d), although even here he cannot resist saying that subversiveness gives an ecstasy of freedom which can be personally dangerous, as in the case of Weber. My point, however, is that these counter-conservative concerns remain submerged and residual and without adequate theoretical development when compared to the detailed elaboration of conservative themes. There is therefore a tension in his work both theoretical *and* spiritual, between structure and human activity, and between pessimism and the possibilities of human autonomy – a tension that, perhaps, remains unresolved in sociology as a whole.

CHAPTER 2

The encounter with phenomenology

Stephen C. Ainlay

With varying attention to disclaimers, many writers have categorized the work of Peter L. Berger as 'phenomenological' (see, for examples, Wisdom, 1973; Abercrombie, 1980; Wuthnow *et al.*, 1984). He is minimally assigned a historical role as a popularizer of that hybrid, phenomenological sociology, or sometimes even suggested as one of its key founding figures. Yet Berger, although acknowledging his intellectual debts to phenomenology, would not be likely to categorize himself in these terms. In a sense, this chapter seeks an answer to the question, 'Just how phenomenological is Peter Berger?'

The interest in this question is not a matter of sociological book-keeping. The concern of this chapter is not with attaching a label to Berger's work. Rather, by examining his dialogue with phenomenology, one can better understand the nature of his contribution to interpretive sociology. How has phenomenology influenced his vision of the method and substance of the sociological enterprise? How has his use of phenomenological concepts illuminated human experience in the modern world? Has he exhausted (did he ever intend to) its usefulness?

Certainly some phenomenological pedigree exists. Berger was a student of Alfred Schutz. To be more accurate, he took courses with Schutz while a student at the New School of Social Research and Schutz's conceptual baggage is readily apparent to even the most phenomenologically naïve reader of Berger's work. Yet – perhaps indicative of the distance Berger has always maintained from phenomenology – Carl Mayer directed his dissertation. Likewise, his earliest publications betray little evidence of his phenomenological training (consider, for example, *The Noise of Solemn Assemblies*, 1961a or *The Precarious Vision*, 1961c). By contrast, Berger's consistently informative footnotes to most of his work after *Invitation to Sociology* (1963c) as well as discussions within the texts themselves show extensive reading in the phenomenological literature. Yet Berger never really self-consciously embraces phenomenology as did others who studied with Schutz (Thomas Luckmann or Maurice Natanson to name just two). Furthermore, he has not authored nor edited any lengthy tomes that engage the traditional debates within phenomenology (contrast Berger's work with *Structures of the Life-world*, coauthored by Luckmann with Schutz – posthumously in the case of the latter – or Natanson's two-volume edited collection on *Phenomenology and the Social Sciences*). The answer to the question that this chapter poses is not, therefore, self-evident.

Phenomenological baggage in Berger's corpus

It should be made clear from the outset that Berger's work is informed by a variety of writers and theoretical traditions. Wuthnow, *et al*. (1984: 21) are correct in observing that to place him in any one theoretical camp ('phenomenological' or other) is to reduce him to a mere caricature of the complex array of theoretical influences that guide his thought. One needs to be cautious, therefore, so as not to over-interpret the phenomenological character of his writings.

Berger's (1966b) own antipathy to such over-generalizations can be anticipated in view of his response to Edward Tiryakian's (1965) attempt to identify the threads of existential phenomenology in sociology's theoretical mainstream. Tiryakian described the work of writers ranging from Vierkandt to Parsons as falling within the purview of phenomenology. Berger correctly criticized Tiryakian for mistakenly interpreting every reference to 'structure' or 'meaning' as phenomenological and suggested that he did a disservice to both sociology and phenomenology. One should accept Berger's caution and refrain from substituting phenomenological intent for mere theoretical sympathies.

By way of introductory remarks, Berger's exchange with Tiryakian is worthy of additional consideration. It provides clues about the former's place in phenomenological circles. To begin, although quite brief, this is one of the few times that Berger sets himself up as 'expert' in phenomenological matters (Tiryakian, in his 1966 response, disapprovingly refers to Berger's 'pontifical pose of expertise'). While Berger reveals a comfortable fluency with phenomenology's founder – Edmund Husserl – and makes lucid criticisms of Tiryakian's loose usage of key phenomenological concepts, this exercise proves an exception. Most of his work borrows liberally from phenomenology – especially the phenomenology of Schutz – but leaves the more esoteric intraphenomenological discussions and debate to others. This has helped make his work accessible to the larger sociological community but again raises issue as to the appropriateness of the phenomenological label.

Secondly, the Berger/Tiryakian exchange represents one of Berger's few forays into the halls of sociology's 'top journals.' It is indeed surprising that a sociologist as reputable and prolific as Berger has had (in addition to this page and a half 'correspondence') only one full-length article in *The American Journal of Sociology* and again only one in the *American Sociological Review*. I think it is fair to suggest that this speaks, in part, to the professional costs brought on by the phenomenological flavor of Berger's work. While keeping phenomenology at arm's length, Berger sufficiently links his work to that movement through the use of some key assumptions and concepts that his contributions are often viewed as on the fringe of traditional sociology. This again reveals the elusive nature of the phenomenological influence on Berger.

Having said all this, I will try to identify both the spirit and conceptual substance of phenomenology in the writings of Peter Berger. This is, after all, where the case can best be made. The Berger/Tiryakian exchange may be his most phenomenologically self-conscious exercise but he more fully develops its conceptual apparatus in other works. While his most systematic attempt to apply phenomenological insights and concepts to sociological theorizing can be found in *The Social Construction of Reality* (1966e), coauthored with Thomas Luckmann, both his earlier and later works provide insights into the origins and applications of his approach. *Invitation to Sociology* (1963c), for example, reveals phenomenological sympathies and Berger makes prophetic references to the certain popularity of the then forthcoming English version of Schutz's collected papers. Other early work (see Berger, 1965c) demonstrates his understanding of key phenomenological insights and anticipates further theoretical contributions to come. Work after *The Social Construction of Reality* turns more toward the application of his unique brand of interpretive sociology to traditional sociological problems but retains the same phenomenological flavor. *The Sacred Canopy* (1967c), for example, struggles with religious consciousness in the modern world. *The Homeless Mind* (1973b), as another example, struggles with the impact of bureaucracy on various aspects of human experience. More recently, *Sociology Reinterpreted* (1981d) reassessed sociological method in ways that some have termed phenomenological (Wuthnow, 1984: 33). Berger has even toyed with overtly phenomenological projects (see his essay 'The Problem of Multiple Realities: Alfred Schutz and Robert Musil,' 1970c, in a volume of essays dedicated to the memory of Schutz). All of these writings can help document and assess the phenomenological influence on Berger.

Existential foundations

Berger (1966e: 173) concludes the *Social Construction of Reality* with the observation that sociology must be carried on in constant conversation with both philosophy and history. Since Berger has remained faithful to this mandate, it is in some ways easier to trace the social philosophical assumptions that guide his sociological theory than it is for others (his introduction is a rare exercise in sociological reflexivity). While it would be a mistake to characterize him exclusively in terms of any one tradition, his work bears the unmistakable mark of existential phenomenology.

In saying this I accept Giddens's (1977: 136) distinction between three phases of phenomenology – the transcendental (a phenomenology in search of knowledge free from presuppositions), existential (primacy of the self in the lived-in world) and hermeneutic (stressing the linguistic character of human 'being in the world'). Berger is clearly most influenced by the second or existential phase. One measure of this is the literature that he cites to legitimate his claims about the nature of human experience. Throughout his work, Berger relies more heavily on writers in the existential phenomenological tradition – notably Alfred Schutz, Max Scheler and Jean-Paul Sartre. He makes relatively little of Husserl's transcendental writings and likewise makes only marginal use of hermeneutical authors (he shows, for example, little interest in Gadamer).

Berger accepts the existential assumption of 'world openness'. As Berger (1966e: 45) puts it, 'Man's relationship to his environment is characterized by world-openness.' Here he directly follows Schutz (1970: 135)) who insists 'my world . . . has from the outset the sense of being typically a world capable of expansion; it is a necessarily open world.' Furtheremore, Berger argues for the essential 'plasticity' of the human organism and emphasizes our relative freedom from instinctual drives. He (1966e: 47) suggests that 'while it is possible to say that man has a nature, it is more significant to say that man constructs his own nature, or more simply, that man produces himself.'

While the world represents an open horizon of possible interpretation, Berger (1967c: 19) insists that 'man . . . is compelled to impose his own order upon experience.' In fact, it is the sense-making activity of people that gives them their very humanness (Berger, 1973b: 63). Borrowing from Sartre's notion of 'totalization,' Berger argues that this ordering activity is an ongoing, always incomplete process. As he puts it,

> While man, as an acting being, is constantly engaged in structuring the world as meaningful totality (since otherwise he could not meaningfully act within it), this process is never completed. Totality, then, is never a fait accompli, but is always in the process of being constructed. Therefore, the term totalization can be applied to this meaning-building process (1965c: 201).

It is this ongoing, always incomplete, process of giving meaning to the world – both physical and social – that distinguishes Berger's view of human experience itself.

Here Berger echoes the declaration of the French phenomenologist Maurice Merleau-Ponty (1962: xix): 'We are condemned to meaning.' It is not entirely clear, however, if he accepts Merleau-Ponty's criticism of Sartre's notion of absolute freedom. For Merleau-Ponty, existence is imbued with sense, not unlimited freedom (hence the poignancy of paraphrasing Sartre). On the one hand Berger endorses Sartre – accepting the notion that, while we may try to deny it, we are free to say 'No.' Borrowing from Sartre,

Berger insists that to deny our human capacity to make (and remake) a world is to be guilty of 'bad faith' (1963c: 143; 1967c: 93). As he (1963c: 144) puts it, 'They are in bad faith when they attribute to iron necessity what they themselves are choosing to do.' On the other hand, 'freedom' in Berger's framework can only be understood as existing within the context of society and its institutions which continually confront the individual with 'coercive' and 'compelling' 'facticity'.

This is consistent with an ongoing tension that characterizes the 'Bergerian' approach. Throughout his work, Berger attempts to balance the power of society over its participants with the power of the individual to create the world. Berger continually affirms the essential humanness of the social world and he continually guards against reification. Social order itself owes to human production. Its appearance owes to human biological incompleteness. Its perpetuation and maintenance owes to human activity. Berger (1966d: 49) insists that in 'both its genesis (social order is the result of past human activity) and its existence in any instant of time (social order exists only and insofar as human activity continues to produce it) it is a human product.' He accomplishes this sort of sociological juggling act by relying on the phenomenological doctrine of intentionality.

The intentional nature of human experience

Berger (1966e: 20) observes that 'consciousness is always intentional; it always intends or is directed toward objects.' In saying this he explicitly affirms their reliance on the phenomenological doctrine of intentionality. This doctrine is so central to phenemenological thinking that Natanson (1973a: 103) has suggested that it is the very axis of phenomenology.

Intentionality was essentially the key conceptual mechanism by which phenomenology sought to overcome the apparent polarization between 'empiricism' and 'intellectualism' (this reflects Merleau-Ponty's choice of terms). 'Empiricism,' in this sense, denotes an approach to understanding human existence that stresses all things to be external to one another and related in a cause and effect way. It is a way of understanding the world which belittles the roles of consciousness in explaining human activity. 'Intellectualism,' by contrast, represents that way of thinking which believes all things to be created solely by consciousness. It does so at the expense of the object world. While empiricism seems to rob consciousness of any constituting responsibility in its encounter with a pregiven, predefined world, intellectualism assigns independence to that consciousness by denying the import of the external environment. Phenomenology sought to redress these extremes by arguing that consciousness has a ubiquitous referrant quality – referrant to the object world.

Developing the original concept that was introduced by Brentano, it was Husserl who cemented intentionality into phenomenological terminology. Engaging the polarity imposed by empiricism and intellectualism, he insisted that both positions sever the essential link between subject and objective environment and as such are untenable descriptions of human experience. Human experience has a dialectical character. It cannot be reduced to one-sided causality. Rather, 'epistemology implies ontology; knowledge implies being' (Giddens, 1976: 25). Husserl (1970b: 544) puts it quite succinctly by stating 'in perception something is perceived, in imagination something is imagined, in expression something is expressed, in love something is loved, in hate something is hated, in desire something is desired, and so on.' For Husserl (1970a), human experience could not be described in terms of perceptual sensations alone as is done by the empiricists, but rather only in terms of things perceived ('cogitatum') and of consciousness directed toward something ('cogito'). Intentionality proposes a dialectical reformulation of consciousness in relation to the world. As such it aims at preserving both objective and subjective efficacy.

It can be argued that Husserl eventually abandoned this position – searching instead for the constituting, transcendental subject. Nevertheless, the referrant quality of consciousness inherent in the doctrine of intentionality becomes a permanent part of the phenomenological stance. Most pertinent to our understanding of the place of intentionality in Berger's work, it takes a prominent position in the work of Alfred Schutz.

Reviewing Husserl, Schutz (1971: 107) observes that, 'There is no such thing as thought, fear, fantasy, remembrance as such; every thought is thought of, every fear is fear of, every remembrance is remembrance of the object that is thought, feared or remembered.' The intentionality of consciousness is again affirmed and subjective, free cognitions of the world are held in check by an objective environment. 'Each act of perceiving and its intentional objects are indubitable elements of my stream of thought' (Schutz: 107). As Schutz extends his analysis beyond a sort of perceptual phenomenology to a phenomenology of the social world (defined narrowly by Schutz as a phenomenology of interpersonal relationships) this guiding insight continues to inform his approach. Schutz presumes the existence of an objective social reality, that is, a reality that 'precedes any possible analysis of mine,' and which presents the individual with a 'horizon' of possible interpretations. Imposing environment and acting subject *in relation to* one another are stressed.

Some writers have ignored the full complexity of the intentional dialectic. Consequently, they have concluded that phenomenologically inspired sociologies are necessarily overly subjectivistic and introspective. To some degree, this was true of Schutz. In his zeal to demonstrate the open possibilities of human action he (similar to Husserl before him) often seemed to lose touch with the objective environment to which consciousness refers. Whether his is an error of commission or omission is subject to argument. Similarly, some sociologists who rely heavily on Schutz have been preoccupied with/reduced to a sort of 'methodological individualism' (see Ainlay, 1983). This need not, however, be the case. It is, for example, to Berger's credit that he successfully avoids this problem. He appreciates the essential unity of subjective and objective realities as characteristic of the whole of human experience ranging from people's experience of their bodies to their relationship with institutions. In his agenda, Berger resembles Merleau-Ponty more than Schutz (as Merleau-Ponty was concerned with extending his intentional analysis from issues pertaining to simple reflex behavior to the complexities of class consciousness and industrial capitalism) although he relies on the conceptual framework of the latter much more so than the former.

In explaining people's elementary relationships to their bodies, for example, Berger attempts to preserve the ambiguity that the dialectics of intentionality necessarily impose. He insists:

> On the one hand, man *is* a body, in the same way that this may be said of every other animal organism. On the other hand, man *has* a body. That is, man experiences himself as an entity that is not identical with his body, but that, on the contrary, has that body at its disposal. In other words, man's experience of himself always hovers in a balance between being and having a body, a balance that must be redressed again and again (emphasis in the original, 1966e: 48).

For Berger, then, the relationship between self and body is an 'eccentric' one. While constrained by the objective limitations of the organism, people are, nevertheless, granted the intentional capacity to interpret their experience of that organism – it is, for better or for worse, at their disposal. The organism neither exhausts people's experience of themselves nor can they transcend the parameters that the body sets for them.

Berger extends this intentional relationship of the self and body to include a second dialectic between self and social world when he articulates a theory of identity. For him identity is exhausted neither by people's socially produced sense of self nor by some sort of biological substratum. Nor can it be conceived of as some sort of ethereal reality. For Berger, identity is bound to an ongoing dialectical process of considerably more complexity.

> There is an ongoing dialectic, which comes into being with the very first phases of socialization and continues to unfold throughout the individual's existence in society, between each human animal and its socio-historical situation. Externally, it is a dialectic between the individual animal and the social world. Internally, it is a dialectic between the individual's biological substratum and his socially produced identity (1966e: 165).

Berger never fully develops the internal dialectic (a point to which we will return later). Nevertheless, his appreciation for the intentional unity of experience (between subjective consciousness and objective experience, biological and social) is again affirmed. Organism and society, mediated by individual consciousness, limit each other and yet all are necessary for us realize ourselves in the world.

Berger's descriptions of our experiences with society's institutions continually reveal his rejection of one-sided causality. Perhaps most notably in his treatment of religion, he speaks to the same intellectualist/empiricist (substituting the words 'idealist' and 'materialist') tension that informed the original phenomenological agenda. He insists on the dialectical relationship of religious ideas and social structure.

> Only a dialectical understanding of these relationships avoids the distortions of the one-sidedly 'idealist' or 'materialist' interpretations. Such a dialectical understanding will insist upon the rootage of all consciousness, religious or other, in the world of everyday praxis, but it will be very careful not to conceive of this rootage in terms of mechanistic causality (1967c: 128).

For readers familiar with Maurice Merleau-Ponty's (1973) essay on 'The Crisis of Understanding,' Berger's discussion here bears an uncanny resemblance with Merleau-Ponty's treatment of the intentional unity of religious consciousness and social structure. This sympathy of Berger and Merleau-Ponty have been pointed out by others. Laurie Spurling (1977: 86), for example, insists that Berger's treatment of institutions (religious and other) is fully consistent and complementary to Merleau-Ponty's phenomenological approach. Berger goes far beyond Merleau-Ponty (religion for the latter is more an aside) but the similarities in their handling of this relationship betray common theoretical assumptions.

Berger perhaps most extends our insight into the intentional nature of human experience in his discussion of the dialectic by which society and social actor are created and maintained. Summarizing this dialectic in the beginning moments of *The Sacred Canopy* (but dealing with it more systematically in *The Social Construction of Reality*), he insists:

> Society is a dialectic phenomenon in that it is a human product, and nothing but a human product, that yet continuously acts back upon its producer. Society is a product of man. It has no other being except that which is bestowed upon it by human activity and consciousness. There can be no social reality apart from man. Yet it may also be stated that

> man is a product of society. Every individual biography is an episode within the history of society, which both precedes and survives it. Society was there before the individual was born and will be there after he has died. What is more, it is within society, and as a result of social processes, that the individual becomes a person, that he attains and holds onto an identity, and that he carries out the various projects that constitute his life. Man cannot exist apart from society (1967c: 3).

In arguing this, Berger rejects both idealist and materialist views of people's relationship to the social world in which they live. This point is obviously central to arguments put forth in *The Social Construction of Reality* but cannot be explained away as a Luckmannian theme as Berger returns to it time and time again in his subsequent works – such that it becomes an earmark of the Bergerian thesis (see, for example, Berger, 1966a; Berger, 1967c; Berger, 1973b). True to his word ('What interests us here is the common intentional character of all consciousness,' Berger, 1966e: 20), Berger has used this dialectical process to illuminate many different social phenomenona: religion (1967c), marriage (1964c), bureaucracy 1973b) to name just three.

There are three ongoing 'moments' to this dialectical process: externalization, objectivation, and internalization. Externalization is the continual outpouring of both mental and physical activity that characterizes human being. For Berger, it is an anthropological necessity born out of human incompleteness at birth (contrary to other animals which are born 'finished'). 'Deprived of a man-world, he [man] constructs a human world' (1967c: 6). As such, externalization is at the core of people's world-building activity. That is, the human world is one 'that must be fashioned by man's own activity' (1967c: 5). In Berger's conceptual scheme, creating a world is a collective enterprise and speaks to the essential sociality of humans.

While people are continually creating their world through their activities – they invent tools, language and even institutions – 'all human activity is subject to habitualization' (Berger, 1966e: 50). The habitualization of activity does not mean that people lose their ability to create a world. On the contrary, 'the background of habitualized activity opens up a foreground of deliberation and innovation' (Berger, 1966e: 51). Nevertheless, activities begin to take on an object-like character and as such begin to constrain those who produced them in the first place. Activity, once objectivated, takes on a coercive character. On a more sociological note, Berger insists that habitualization of activity at the societal level gives way to institutionalization. All of this is central to the process of objectivation by which people's externalized activities take on an object-like quality, confronting actors with a sort of external facticity.

It is through internalization of the objectivated world that people can be thought of as products of society. Internalization is 'the reabsorption into consciousness of the objectivated world in such a way that the structures of this world come to determine the subjective structures of consciousness itself' (1967c: 15). Accomplished primarily through socialization, internalization enables society to solve the problem of passing habitualized solutions to human problems on to succeeding generations. Although consistent with the principle of intentionality, here Berger extends his analysis well beyond the scope of most phenomenologists and accordingly has to rely heavily on complementary theoretical models – notably the social psychology of George Herbert Mead.

Typical of Berger, these three moments are born out of both phenomenological and non-phenomenological (although sympathetic) literature. Berger's treatment of externalization is clearly indebted to Hegel, yet the influence of Schutz is also apparent (see the latter's discussion of the 'postulate of subjective interpretation,' 1971: 11), as is that of Sartre (relying on his ideas of 'totalization.' See Berger, 1965c). Yet its biological foundation is indebted to Gehlen (see footnote attesting to the same in Berger, 1966e: 180). Similarly, for the concept of objectivation, Berger gives a phenomenological twist to Hegel and Marx (he is most self-conscious of this in Berger, 1965c). Most obviously, while his treatment of internalization relies heavily on Schutzian discussions of the shared nature of everyday life, Berger gives it a pronounced Meadean emphasis.

It is reasonable to ask, then, whether or not the Bergerian dialectic truly has phenomenological origins (a question that seems even more reasonable since Berger (1966e: 15) suggests that his dialectical perspective is derived from Marx). Typical of his entire sociological corpus, Berger's dialectical method appears eclectic in its origins (Abercrombie, 1980: 148). Indeed, Berger's treatment of these three moments demonstrates that the dialectics of Berger's sociology are not simply the dialectics of phenomenological intentionality. The dialectics of Hegel, Marx, and even Mead (especially between the 'I' and the 'me') influence his work. Nevertheless, I would argue that his readings of these other writers are filtered by phenomenological assumptions (rather than the other way around).

The life-world as paramount reality

It is the mark of Berger's sociology of knowledge that he has concerned himself not so much with the knowledge of ideologues or intellectuals but more so with knowledge that is 'pretheoretical' and possessed by the 'man on the street,' in 'everyday life.' (For reviews of his contribution in this regard, see Abercrombie, 1980 as well as his contribution to this volume; Wisdom, 1973). Not only is this focus consistent with (and inspired by) Schutz, but his reliance on Schutz's conceptual scheme for its exposition is apparent.

Berger's approach to everyday life mirrors the phenomenologist's interest in the 'natural attitude.' He insists that 'the reality of everyday life is taken for granted *as* reality. It does not require additional verification over and beyond its simple presence. It is simply *there* as self-evident and compelling facticity' (Berger, 1966e: 23). Here again, Berger demonstrates his embrace of Schutz by accepting the latter's inversion of the phenomenological 'epoche'. Whereas Husserl intended the epoche to refer to the phenomenologist's suspension of *belief* in the world as he/she knows it, Schutz used the expression to refer to the suspension of *doubt* that characterizes our everyday experience. For Berger, like Schutz, the taken-for-granted character of everyday life figures prominently into his argument. Rather than getting beneath life's taken-for-grantedness, they are both concerned with its detailed explication.

Taken together, the whole of people's unquestioned, subjective experience of their biological and social worlds can be termed their 'life-world' (or 'Lebenswelt' in Husserl's terms). Berger (1966e) observes that the reality of everyday life – the life-world – is organized around a variety of concerns, most of which reflect traditional areas of phenomenological discourse. Among such organizing concerns are the 'here' and the 'now' (1966e: 22). People organize their experience in terms of relative closeness and remoteness to where they are located spatially (the 'here' provided by the individual's body) and temporally (the 'now' provided by the individual's present). Correspondingly, we are more concerned about what is closest to us in space and time. While Berger spends little time developing this theme in any of his work, he pays homage to the phenomenological insight that the subjective ordering of time and space are fundamental foundations to knowledge in everyday life. Pursuing another Schutzian theme, Berger furthermore insists that the world of everyday life is dominated by the 'pragmatic motive.' This is to say, 'my attention to this world is mainly determined by what I am doing, have done or plan to do in it' (1966e: 22).

People assume that the world of everyday life is an intersubjective world. For the so-called 'man on the street,' the solipsistic question of the existence of others simply doesn't occur. People 'know' that they share the world with others and – except in a dream state – they are necessary to its constitution and maintenance. In fact, it is its collective nature (it 'has been established collectively and is kept going by collective consent', Berger, 1973b: 63) that allows it to be taken for granted, without question, until further notice. Berger elaborates on Schutz, not only discussing face to face interaction and the central role of language in the process of world maintenance, but also outlining the importance of institutions – especially as they pertain to the problem of legitimation (see Berger, 1966e; Berger, 1967c).

At the level of subjective experience, a person's involvement in everyday life is facilitated (and, in fact, enabled) by the 'typifications' that he/she carries. Typifications, or, as Berger also likes to call them, 'recipes'. Rather than having to be continually negotiated, the world is more often experienced as typical. A person carries with her/him types which offer a comparative basis by which sense can be made of the world as it is confronted. People know what the 'typical' house is, such that whether or not they are interested in buying a colonial, salt-box or ranch they know them all to be houses. Most typifications emerge through the process of socialization but some result from repeated exposure to variations of some type. Thus, through typifications that emerge from one's own experience and through those that are passed on by predecessors and contemporaries, a person routinely make sense of the world around her/him. People not only come to know what the typical house looks like but, in a similar fashion, they come to know how the typical encounter with a bureaucrat should go.

The sum total of all that a person knows about the world and how to act in it, is contained within her/his 'stock of knowledge'. People's stock of knowledge emerges from a combination of typifications passed on to them by others ('biographical situation') and the sedimentation (see Berger, 1966e: 63; Schutz, 1971: 76–7) of their own personal experience. For Schutz, and for Berger after him, this understanding of the typificatory process preserves the objective reality of an external social world acting on the individual while also preserving the individual's ability to modify pregiven typifications or innovate new ones.

The reality of everyday life is our 'paramount reality' (Berger, 1966e: 24). This implies that there are 'multiple realities' but, compared to the paramount reality of everyday life, all others are 'finite provinces of meaning.' In observing this, Berger is again resonant with the Schutzian corpus (see Schutz's extensive discussions, 1971: 229f; 340f). People enter a finite province of meaning whenever by definition, they turn their attention away from the reality of everyday life. Berger uses the illustration of the theater, insisting that between the time that the curtain rises and falls, the patron is transported to a sort of other world. But the same can be said for the artist, the physicist or anyone else who for artistic or professional reasons leaves the world of mundane interpersonal experience behind. According to Berger, each of these finite provinces of meaning requires a sort of 'secondary epoche' (1970c: 224); that is, one can successfully exist in each finite province of meaning as long as one suspends doubts about it as well. Although he is less reflexive about it, this approach informs Berger's understanding of the sociologist's problem of studying a world of which he/she is also a part (1963c). Clearly a central part of his scholarly publications, Berger has also developed his interest in multiple realities in his writings outside the domain of traditional sociological discourse; that is, in his novels (Mechling, 1984).

It is also in this context that Berger makes one of his greatest contributions to a new language, if not new understanding of modernity and its impact on consciousness. Modernization itself has brought about a 'pluralization of life-worlds' (Berger 1973b: 63ff). Not only do we carry out our lives in relationship to a variety of institutions but our attachment to multiple institutions impacts the structure of consciousness itself. Berger insists that 'modern life is typically segmented to a very high degree, and it is important to understand that this segmentation (or, as we prefer to call it, pluralization) is not only manifest on the level of observable social conduct but also has important manifestations on the level of consciousness' (Berger, 1973b: 64–5). Most notably, modernization has resulted in the fundamental pluralization of 'private' and 'public' spheres. Thus, in typical Bergerian fashion, classic sociological debate is given a phenomenological face-lift.

Extending the intentional dialectic

The preceding review of the phenomenological assumptions and concepts that appear throughout the corpus of Berger's work would seem to provide some answer to the question that was initially posed. It is certainly safe to conclude that to fail to account for the phenomenological influence on Berger's work is to miss a major intellectual force behind his analysis of the modern world. Yet to say this is different than to conclude that he is a phenomenologist.

Part of the problem in assessing the work of anyone as phenomenological is that there are so many variations within the movement itself that coming up with a set of criteria by which to judge them proves difficult. As Merleau-Ponty (1962) observed, there are nearly as many phenomenologies as there are phenomenologists. This has led some to conclude that it may even be inappropriate to refer to phenomenology as a 'school' or 'movement' at all (Spiegelberg, 1971). One's attempts to identify a coherent phenomenological tradition will be continually frustrated if Husserl (especially his later writings) is used as a standard. Even Heidegger (who Husserl thought would be his philosophical heir, see Spiegelberg's discussion, 1971: 154) failed by Husserl's assessment. Attempting to issue phenomenological licenses certainly seems a questionable undertaking at best.

To the extent that he uses phenomenological baggage to accomplish his sociological aims, Berger is distinctly Schutzian. This is not to say that he relies exclusively on Schutz (the influence of Sartre and Merleau-Ponty – see his acknowledgement of the latter's impact, 1964c, for examples – is noteworthy). Berger's dependency on Schutz in itself makes his phenomenological loyalties suspect. In view of the fact that he deviates from the transcendental vision of the later Husserl, Schutz himself is suspect as a phenomenologist. Berger shares even less in common with Husserl's phenomenological idealism.

Beyond this, as Wuthnow *et al.* (1984: 21) observe, 'Berger demonstrates a genuine eclecticism and a propensity for synthesis of the finest kind.' Berger, by his own assessment, blends Schutzian phenomenology with Weberian interpretive sociology and Meadean social psychology (1966e; 1964c). It is, therefore, probably a mistake to pigeon-hole him at all. His dedication to 'eclecticism' and 'synthesis' propels him far beyond the original phenomenological agenda articulated by Husserl and past the substantive interests of Husserl's 'students.'

As has already been noted, it is typical of Berger's approach that traditional sociological debates are enlivened by the introduction of phenomenological assumptions and conceptual tools. He has accomplished this in such an appealing way that it is easy to ignore the complexity (and even the origins) of his analysis. Some will undoubtedly argue that he has further complicated an already impenetrable sociological jargon (Berger's own criticism of 'sociologese', 1963c: 14, is brought to mind). For others, Berger's facile handling of phenomenological insights allows them to rethink anew issues that were seemingly lost to American sociology.

It is instructive that Berger's approach is marked by a consistent refusal to argue about these phenomenologically based concepts and assumptions 'qua phenomenologist.' Berger picks and chooses from phenomenology's conceptual cornucopia without regard to intra-movement debates nor does he ever intend to really refine phenomenological analysis. He is better thought of as a sort of sociological pirateer rather than loyalist to phenomenology.

Furthermore, Berger never really expresses any interest in utilizing a true phenomenological method to accomplish his sociological aims. As Spiegelberg (1971: 655) observes, phenomenology may be best identified by its method for it is one of the few aspects of the movement about which most adherents agree. He goes on (1971: 659ff) to list seven positive steps of that method: 1) investigating particular phenomena; 2) investigating general essences; 3) apprehending essential relationships among essences; 4) watching modes of appearing; 5) watching the constitution of phenomena in consciousness; 6) suspending belief in the existence of the phenomena; 7) interpreting the meaning of the phenomena. Berger in no way identifies himself with nor ties himself to these methodological directives. This may be his clearest point of departure from phenomenology. Schutz (1971: 116) cautioned that 'it must be clearly stated that the relation of phenomenology to the social sciences cannot be demonstrated by analysing concrete problems of sociology or economics, such as social adjustment or theory of international trade, with phenomenological methods.' Similarly, Merleau-Ponty attempted to contrast phenomenology with 'scientific' explanation by suggesting that 'it [phenomenology] tries to give a direct description of our experience as it is, without taking account of its psychological origin and the causal explanations which the scientist, the historian or the sociologist may be able to provide' (1962: vii). Even more to the point, Merleau-Ponty suggests, 'phenomenology stops where the mundane sciences begin.' Berger is in accord with both these opinions.

Berger undoubtedly accepts that sociologists have an obligation to make sure that their social scientific typifications ('constructs of a second degree') jive or fit with the typificatory scheme of people in everyday life. In this he is consistent with the spirit of Schutz's directives on the role of the social scientist. As Schutz (1971: 27) observes, 'The scientific observer of human interrelation patterns, the social scientist, has to develop specific methods for the building of his constructs in order to assure their applicability for the interpretation of the subjective meaning the observed acts have for the actors.' Yet Berger never questions the sociologist's ability to generate second-degree constructs. He would not handcuff sociologists to the same degree as other writers who have clearly asserted their phenomenological allegiance. Consider, for example, the methodological argument of Michael Phillipson (1972). Moving from Schutz's (1971: 44) 'postulate of adequacy', Phillipson (1972: 17) insists 'The meanings given to human action by members (of the situation under investigation) are the ultimate data with which the social sciences must concern themselves. As they are the well-springs of action, social science cannot meaningfully go beyond them in its explanation.' Berger's view of the sociologist, in contrast, retains some explanatory prowess. This is apparent, for example, in his discussion of the place of statistics in sociological reasoning. Berger (1963c: 11) observes that 'statistical data by themselves do not make sociology. They become sociology only when they are sociologically interpreted, put within a theoretical frame of reference that is sociology.' Or again, 'The interpretation, however, must be broader than the data themselves.' Perhaps most conclusively, Berger declares in *Sociology Reinterpreted* (1981d: 39) that 'The sociologist cannot simply adopt the typifications as they are, but she or he must *take cognizance* of them' (emphasis in the original).

Accepting Berger's methodological standards, he is certainly not a phenomenologist *per se*. But then, much of his contribution to interpretive sociology would be lost had he been. Rigorous description should be central to any sociology that owes even the slightest debt to phenomenology. In order to understand human experience and people's activities in-the-world, it first becomes necessary to describe their typifications of everyday life and the meanings they hold in all consistencies and variations. Much of Berger's appeal lies in the success he has realized in describing the experiences of people in the modern world. But true to the sociological mandate, Berger also examines the ways in which these typifications and meanings are built up for people and by people as well as the means by which they become their social 'reality.' Borrowing from the phenomenological literature, this could be called the 'constitutive' phase of Berger's work. Furthermore, while he demonstrates a marked sensitivity to Schutz's concerns with biography and personal socialization, Berger goes beyond these to accommodate a variety of external factors: most notably, economic and technological organization and their relation to structures of consciousness.

One might usefully distinguish here between social phenomenology and phenomenological sociology (a distinction that is largely overlooked). What should ultimately distinguish a phenomenological sociology from a social phenomenology is the former's ability to persist in going beyond common-sense explanations of experience. Consistent with the grammatical intent of adjectives, phenomenological sociology need only be qualified by phenomenology's assumptions and conceptual tools. It need not persist in all of its philosophical goals – transcendental or otherwise. In fact, Spurling (1977: 91),has noted that if phenomenologists want to speak of society, it will be necessary for them to leave aside questions raised by the phenomenological reduction and take the social world for granted. In these conditional terms, then, it would be accurate to term Berger a phenomenological sociologist. I would note again, however, that the variety of writers calling themselves phenomenological has been so great that a qualifier of this sort is almost useless. Indeed, the phenomenology that Berger ignores greatly outweighs that which he integrates into his theorizing.

Nevertheless, I might go so far as to suggest that the greatest contribution of Berger's theoretical eclecticism has been his unfolding of the ubiquitous character of people's intentional relationship with the world – an insight that, as alleged, is greatly indebted to phenomonology. By refusing to dismiss either individual consciousness or social structure as appropriate objects of inquiry – focusing rather on their inseparable unity – Berger considerably expands the horizon of sociological interest. This emphasis brought the sociology of knowledge from the periphery to center stage. More than this, however, Berger provides a theoretical vehicle for incorporating an understanding of people's biological, psychological, and social experience without capitulating to the causal oversimplifications that both determinism or idealism impose.

It is in his treatment of intentionality that Berger most clearly supersedes Schutz. While Schutz remains locked to the standpoint of the ego (for a similar but more extensive treatment see Giddens, 1976: 31ff), Berger truly attempts to preserve the referrant quality of consciousness. He demonstrates that individual projects, relevances, and typifications are bound to the social environment in which a person finds her/himself.

At the same time, it is in further revealing the intentional unity of experience that one can go beyond Berger. In accord with Abercrombie's (1980: 164) criticism, Berger does not fully explain the individual's ability to 'act back upon' the socially imposed, external constraints on her/his behaviour. As early as *Invitation to Sociology*, Berger sensed the import and the enormity of this task. Discussing the role of human freedom, he observed, 'We contend that here is an important area of dialogue between philosophy and the social sciences that still contains vast tracts of virgin territory' (1963c: 141). It is perhaps because of its vastness or because others (Berger points to the work of Schutz and Natanson) had set it as their task, or because he himself is sociologically wary of its implications, that Berger never really answers the question of human autonomy in the face of external constraints. He gets close to it in his discussion of 'bad faith.' At one point he observes, 'Bad faith is that form of false consciousness in which the dialectic between the socialized self and the self in its totality is lost to consciousness' (1967c: 93). But then such false consciousness seems inescapable in the natural attitude, given the 'coercive facticity' of society itself.

Although the model is squarely in place, Berger also fails to fully develop the role of the body as both limiting and enabling human expression in the world. Berger does speak of the biological incompleteness of humans at birth which gives rise to the need for externalization as well as the eccentric relationship that exists between self and body but he only hints at its fundamental role in day-to-day experience.

Berger's relative inattention to the role of the body may be due, in part, to phenomenology from which he draws his inspiration. Schutz allows for the active role of the body in the intentional dialectics of human experience. Following Husserl, Schutz acknowledges the central role of the body in the recognition of the 'Other' (1971: 124), the use of language (1971: 296) and the establishment of projects that are 'within reach' (1971: 306). But a concern with the body remains a relative aside for Schutz as compared with the French phenomenologists – perhaps best represented in the work of Merleau-Ponty, Sartre and Marcel. Their respective explorations into the relationship of the body both with self and interaction with others could greatly aid the complete disclosure of the internal dialectic of which Berger speaks. One cannot expect Berger to be all things to all people, but the need to integrate a greater appreciation of the body into sociology – especially interpretive sociology – is glaringly apparent. Developing an adequate sociology of the body is certainly among the chief mandates for a phenomenologically inspired interpretive sociology.

Berger's heavy reliance on the phenomenology of Schutz allows him to avoid a number of other debates which preoccupy other phenomenologists. Most notable in this regard is the dialogue with Marxism. For Sartre and Merleau-Ponty, the struggle with Marx (and the Communist party) continually lurks in the background (if not looming in the foreground) of their writings. Merleau-Ponty (1962: 443), for example, concludes his *Phenomenology of Perception* with a critique of vulgar Marxism and a brief exposition on the nature of class consciousness – using intentionality to argue against both reflex theory in our understanding of the body as well as vulgar Marxism. Various contemporary sociologists, who also trace their intellectual roots to the French, have turned to traditional Marxist issues with greater enthusiasm (Piccone, 1971; O'Neill, 1972 – note that O'Neill self-consciously attempts to integrate Berger and Merleau-Ponty). Berger has confronted Marx and Marxism, to be sure (for a recent example see 1981d: 140ff), but more as a theoretical aside than major substantive focus.

To be fair, however, it is inappropriate to affix blame to Berger for a failure that has characterized most of American sociology. What concerns us here is that this would have been impossible had he paid greater attention to French phenomenology. To the degree that sociology in the U.S. has conversed with phenomenology, Schutz is viewed as the pertinent link and Schutz's writings are entirely devoid of a conversation with Marx. We carry high expectations for Berger. We expect him to transcend disciplinary provincialism. We expect him to say (and to pursue) that 'sociology must return to the "big questions" ' (1981d: 9) posed by the classical period of sociology. In accord with Zeitlin (1968), the 'big questions' of the classical period were born out of a struggle with the ghost of Marx and one cannot help but wish that Berger had struggled more self-consciously with this same spirit.

Finally, Berger can, to some degree, also be criticized for a sort of 'equivocal negativism' (see Paul Filmer, *et al.*, 1972: 205). That is, he seems to criticize traditional sociology, either explicitly or implicitly, yet never really tells us how we might go about studying the social world. Even the student who first came to sociology via Berger's 'invitations' must have sensed his methodological ambivalance. When Berger (1963c: 11) says, 'The sensible person reads the sociological journals mainly for the book reviews and the obituaries' or when he talks of sociology's 'methodological inferiority', we sense that he intends something more than the 'N' is too small. Yet he (1963c: 13) also insists, 'If the sociologist remains faithful to his calling, his statements must be arrived at through observation of certain rules of evidence that allow others to check on or to repeat or to develop his findings further,' and we imagine him survey in hand. His most recent thoughts on method (Berger, 1981d) fail really to reduce the ambiguity. We do not mean to complain (as others have done) that Berger is not empirical – on the contrary, he is empirical in the best sense of the word. We must, on the other hand, lament that he has not developed a clearer statement of method. How do we go about studying the social world? Do some methods do too much damage to the reality of those we seek to understand? Are some methods better than others in preserving the integrity of the actor's own story? For many, phenomenological insight carries with it a methodological agenda (Psathas, 1973), and one must wonder how Berger resolves these tensions.

Conclusion

In the final analysis, I think one must agree with Giddens (1976: 33) that it is not really useful to pose a question as whether there 'can be' or 'cannot be' a phenomenological sociology in an unequivocal way. The terms 'phenomenology' and 'sociology' are in some way contradictory in both intent and method. Pointing out the grammatical intent of using phenomenology as a mere qualifier may ease some of this tension. Yet Berger is least useful for resolving such debates. He shows little interest in engaging in such debates and he certainly never intended to carry on philosophy but simply to demonstrate the utility of a sociological conversation with philosophical insights.

Berger's incorporation of phenomenological insights into the tradition of interpretive sociology has been an attempt at carrying on the dialogue with philosophy that he advocates. His success results from that conversation. The criticisms that weighed against him here rest in his failure to carry the conversation far enough. But then, Berger cannot be faulted for failing to map the whole of human intentionality. In fact, it is more appropriate to applaud the extent to which he expanded the role of the intentional dialectic. He has provided a model that can integrate the intentional relationship of the self to body and self to society alike. The challenge that remains for interpretive sociology is the pursuit of this dialectic into all the various domains of human experience, revealing the fundamental complexity and ambiguity that the intentional nature of consciousness necessarily implies.

PART II

Modernization

CHAPTER 3

The challenges of modernity

Anton C. Zijderveld

Berger's corpus has often perplexed those schooled in America's mainstream, functionalist, and positivist sociology – a style of sociological reasoning that has often displayed a chilling disregard for the classical European tradition of the discipline. For such people, his work is very often judged as superficial. Yet to conclude this is to fail to appreciate the profundity of Berger's cognitive and stylistic virtuosity.

Right from the beginning of his writings in the 1950s, Berger had the rare gift to formulate his thoughts and ideas on even the most difficult problems and issues with uncompromising clarity. His concepts are always lucid, and seemingly easy to understand, and if he has to use sociological jargon, he will always meticulously clarify its meaning. This cognitive and stylistic lucidity of Berger has often been mistaken for superficiality and that is a grave misunderstanding. What Nietzsche (1955) once wrote about the ancient Greeks applies to Berger. They were, he said, always profound at the surface. Berger differs in this respect from most contemporary French and German philosophers and social scientists, who all too often confuse (on purpose, I am afraid) profundity with conceptual murkiness and stylistic heaviness. If one takes the considerable trouble to read them closely, one frequently discovers that their thoughts and ideas are rather shallow and conventional.

Furthermore, Berger's sociology is not only characterized by its debunking, rational analysis of the prereflexive, world-taken-for-granted. It also possesses an intrinsic relationship with humor and laughter (which fits with his sociology of knowledge as well as his own construction of reality, Zijderveld, 1963). In a sense, Berger's sociology has always been a *fröhliche Wissenschaft*, a gay science in which there is a titillating mountain air. But unlike Nietzsche's philosophy, Berger's sociology is not, in the end, run down by the forces of tragedy. Maybe in his sociology comedy wins over tragedy, because it is ultimately based on Christian faith and hope.

It is precisely on this point that I have come to differ with Berger. Very much like Max Weber, one can argue that in truly modern life the collapse of the traditional, religious canopy of meaning is final and irreversible – that it is a fate to be borne, if possible, with one's head up high and with a sense of honor and dignity. After this collapse, general world-views and comprehensive ethical systems have not just become impossible and implausible, but very suspicious. This too is, of course, a world view, but a very minimal one. In it, tragedy always lurks behind comedy, and the most hazardous and frightening aspect of modernization is not so much, as Berger claims, its endemic homelessness – that is, its alienation and anomie – but the gradual decline of the sense of honor.

It is from this Weberean awareness of tragedy and of fate that I shall discuss Berger's theory of modernization as the historical process of expanding homelessness, and of concomitant streams of demodernization and counter-modernization. The latter try, mostly in vain, to curb alienation and anomie. Berger is in basic sympathy with them, but we shall see that he views most of them as either insufficient or dangerous. With great lucidity, the ideologies of demodernization and counter-modernization are dissected by him. Yet I shall argue that his own answer to the problem – an inductive type of religion and theology – proves to be far from convincing.

Modernization: the classical heritage

Berger's thoughts and theories are firmly rooted in the classical tradition of sociological theory. Basic concepts that at regular intervals show up in his general sociology and sociology of religion (for example, anomie, alienation, bureaucracy, class structure, theodicy, etc.), derive from the writings of Durkheim and Marx, and above all from Max Weber's *oeuvre*. There is, of course, no need to elaborate this point in further detail here, but I want to emphasize Berger's creative and very free use of these classical concepts and theories. Unlike many theorists these days, Berger is not at all interested in painstaking exegeses of the words of the 'masters of sociological thought.' He has read them all once – not just Weber, Durkheim and Marx, but also de Tocqueville, Pareto, Simmel, Mannheim, Lukacs, Gehlen, Plessner, etc. – and applies their theorems eclectically to his very own conceptualizations and theories. Being trained phenomenologically by Alfred Schutz, he demonstrated from his first publications on that he was not going to be just another theoretical synthesizer, who lives intellectually from the thoughts and theories of others. On the contrary, he has constructed his own theoretical universe, but he has done so in a continuous debate with classical theorists.

The process by which the world (first in Europe, then in the U.S.A., later in Japan, and nowadays in the Third World) began to depart and deviate from the traditional, essentially religious and magical world, first drew the attention of Alexis de Tocqueville. De Tocqueville envisaged modernization primarily as a gradual but very influential and deeply penetrating process of democratization, in which not only political but also social-cultural and economic structures, and consciousness itself as well, began to change and alter. Having been born into the aristocracy, de Tocqueville viewed this process with anxiety, yet rather fatalistically, he realized at the same time that it could not be stopped or reversed. He also warned not to make too much of such symptomatic eruptions as the revolutions of 1789 and 1848, since the process of democratization and its social and cultural levelling took place on a much deeper level of structure and consciousness, and would in fact continue far beyond the age in which he lived. He was right. Democratization continued to keep Western societies in change and turmoil up to the present day. Some decades later, Durkheim focused on the expanding differentiation and specialization of structures and functions due to increasing demographic density and increased division of labour. He believed that this structural differentiation was particularly salient in his own lifetime. Whatever progress this modernization might bring about, Durkheim believed, its structural and, therefore, unintended consequence was the threat of normlessness and pluralization of values – a psychological, institutional chaos which he termed *anomie*. Marx, as is well-known, linked modernization to the rise of capitalism, and thus to historically concrete phenomena. To him modernization was primarily the spectacular expansion of exploitative structures which would cause above all structurally rooted *alienation*. The contours of a classical theory of modernization found a further, very essential elaboration in the writings of Max Weber, who placed prime emphasis on the ever-expanding rationalization of the world primarily through the capitalist mode of production but also through legal bureaucracy, science, and technology.

In all these theories an evolutionist type of analysis was apparent. They focused on various processes which could easily be detected (although, as it were, *in nuce*), in still premodern societies: democratic tendencies were present in the European Middle Ages, structural and functional differentiation and specialization do occur in almost any human group of a certain size, exploitation and alienation began at the very moment people started to divide the necessary labor amongst each other, and rational tendencies could be found easily in all the major world religions. The point is that these processes which have been called modernization, accelerated and expanded widely and deeply within the Western world. Together they indeed constituted a Great Transformation. In order to highlight this structural transformation, various typologies have been proposed. It has been called a transition from *Gemeinshaft* to *Gesellschaft*, from society ruled by status to one governed by contract, from a mechanical to an organic solidarity, from a traditional folk society to a functional, urban culture, and so on.

Incidentally, not all the classics of sociological theory contributed to this theory of modernization. Pareto, for one, scorned the evolutionist thrust of such theories. In his cynical eyes this history presented but one vast reservoir of usually rather senseless rationalization of non-rational actions. In his own terminology, non-rational residues rule the world and rationalizing derivations try *a posteriori* to make sense of it all. Since these residues do not change very much, history is but one chain of similar events. We think things are new and different all the time, because we believe in the rationalizing derivations which give us the illusion of change. Derivations, Pareto (1935: 751) said, are like rubber bands which can be stretched to any length required. In Pareto we find an early form of structuralism and thus a rejection of historicism and voluntarism in sociology.

Georg Simmel always emphasized the fact that in the process

of modernization cultural values, norms and meanings tend to become general and abstract. In his monumental *Philosophie des Geldes* money is taken as a prime example of such abstraction, and the argument in this book presents a very impressive sociological theory of modernization and modernity, although the title of the book – 'philosophy of money' – suggests otherwise. In his well-known essay on the web of group affiliations, Simmel also argues that cultural abstraction increases, when in a fully modernized society the individual is forced to play different roles in several, partially overlapping groups. As a result, a distance grows between the individual as a person on the one hand, and the functional requirements of these roles on the other hand, causing a kind of double consciousness, namely an awareness of an I-here and Society-there. This distance between person and roles, incidentally, enabled the emergence of psychology and sociology as separate disciplines, but it also led to a growing sense of abstraction and alienation. I have tried to elaborate on this theme elsewhere (Zijderveld, 1970).

Following Weber's well-known typology of rationality (*Wertrationalität-Zweckrationalität*), Karl Mannheim distinguished between substantial and functional rationality. Our rationality is functional, Mannheim argued, if we are able to search prudently for means and methods which can successfully realize certain goals and objectives. The prime focus in this type of rationality is on the techniques, the methods, the means, rather than on the goals, the aims, the objectives of human action. Substantial rationality, on the other hand, is the ability to understand reality in all its complexity, to draw, as it were, meaningful coordinates through reality, to connect seemingly autonomous phenomena. To the substantially rational person reality is not a senseless and meaningless chaos of facts, things, persons, and events. On the contrary, in substantial rationality reality appears as a meaningful *Gestalt*, above all as an understandable reality. As a result, we may add, the cognitive mode of functional rationality is causal explanation, whereas *Verstehen* constitutes the cognitive mode of substantial rationality, and since neither means and ends, nor functional and substantial rationality can be separated, it does not make much sense to separate both modes of cognition within the social sciences.

With the help of this set of concepts, Mannheim defined modernization as a process in which substantial rationality became ever more superseded (though not destroyed) by functional rationality. The more our world began to modernize, the more we became functionally rational, and the more we began to lag behind in substantial rationality. With the help of modern science and technology we can explain a lot, but we have become rather weak when it comes to a meaningful understanding of reality. This is a very important addition to Weber's theory of rationalization. This gradual supersedure of substantial rationality by functional rationality may lead eventually to a decline of rationality. How? Because functional rationality depends upon substantial rationality for a clear determination of the aims and goals which are to be realized functionally. In such a situation, means, methods, and techniques have the tendency to become goals-in-themselves which, of course, is functionally as well as substantially irrational. The pedantic bureaucrat, not able to think about anything else but the regulations of his organization; the legal specialist in the spell of the procedures; the social scientist enchanted by methods and research techniques – they are but seemingly rational. This line of argument has been further elaborated in so-called Critical Theory, in particular by Herbert Marcuse. Berger, however, has worked it out in a distinctly different direction.

Following some main tenets of Talcott Parsons's theory of social evolution, we could summarize all this in a simple definition: modernization is a process of social-structural differentiation and a concomitant cultural generalization of values, norms and meanings (1977). That is, when under the impact of industrialization, institutional and organizational structures multiply, the cultural canopy of meaning will not only pluralize but also grow general and abstract, not in the least because it will have to cover a wide range of realities. In fact, pluralization and generalization may cause the collapse of this canopy. Incidentally, we see here how Alfred Schutz's theory of multiple realities (1971: 207–59), which played such a dominant role in Berger's sociology of knowledge, can be tied conceptually to the classical theory of modernization. This is precisely what Berger has done in his own theory of modernization to which we shall turn presently.

However, one essential component should still be added to this classical theory of modernization. It has been forcefully formulated by the German philosopher and sociologist Arnold Gehlen (1904–76) whose theory of institutions had a decisive influence on Berger's sociology of knowledge (1957; see also Schelsky, 1965: 250–75). According to Gehlen, modernization was above all a process in which the traditional institutions which in Durkheim's terminology can be briefly and adequately defined as collective patterns of thinking, feeling, and acting, have lost their hold over individuals. In a sense, Gehlen argued, institutions function as substitutes for the lack of well-developed and interconnected instincts. Institutionalized behavior is seemingly instinctive, the difference being, of course, that institutions are historical and thus changeable, whereas instincts remain biologically fixed and thus unalterable. When institutions begin to lose their grip on human beings, the latter will be thrown back on their own subjectivity which causes the emergence of a very influential and rather dangerous subjectivism. Motives for action are no longer sought and found in the formerly taken-for-granted institutions of tradition but now searched for in the unpredictable abodes of the individual psyche, where they are constantly subjected to scrutiny and reflection. An anti-institutional mood thus pervades all of modernity, and there is a continuous discussion and permanent reflection about values, norms, motives, and meanings, and a prime emphasis on emotional experiences. Helmuth Schelsky coined the concept of *Dauerreflexion* (permanent reflection) for this state of modern consciousness. It is often heralded as the great liberation from the confines of tradition, but Gehlen warned that it will but cause mental confusion and behavioral insecurity. Anti-institutional and anti-traditional subjectivism may well lead to the very opposite of what modern man hopes to accomplish, namely, the final break-through of human freedom, creativity and authenticity. It will, Gehlen has argued, lead to *Handlungsverlust*, that is, to the decline of the capacity to act. If human beings retreat to subjectivism, they will gradually lose the capacity to transform nature into culture, to construct socially their own human reality. That is, they will become incapable of realizing any kind of freedom, creativity, and authenticity. Freedom, Gehlen once said in a rather Hegelean train of thought, can only be realized and experienced *through* alienation of the collective, objective, and traditional institutions (1963: 232–46).

The classical theory of modernization and its contemporary elaborations have always been mesmerized by the ills of modernity: anomie, alienation, abstraction, subjectivism, rationalism turning into its opposite, etc. Most of these themes recur in Berger's theory of modernization, yet his very own sociological perspective – the humanistic approach and the sociology of knowledge – and his relativizing sense of humor prevented him from any kind of gloomy, cultural pessimism. Although he is deeply concerned about the collapse of the traditional canopy of meaning, he neither withdraws into existential despair, nor does he retreat, as we shall see presently, to a naive, religious optimism. William James once remarked about the mood of Schopenhauer and Nietzsche: 'The sallies of the two German authors remind one, half the time, of the sick shriekings of two dying rats. They lack the purgatorial note which religious sadness gives forth' (James, 1958: 47). There is no sick shrieking in Berger's prolific writing, but behind its clarity, its razor-blade sharpness, and its humor, one can detect a certain religious sadness.

From sacred canopy to homelessness

When the world was not yet industralized and urbanized, not yet dominated by the sciences, technology and bureaucracy, not yet in the firm grip of macro-economic, either capitalist, or socialist structures, culture – that is, meanings, norms, values, symbols – could still be experienced as an integrated whole. To be sure, there were fierce conflicts in terms of power and interests, there were severe social divisions and religious dissents, but despite such factions and strifes people did share some basic views about reality and super-reality. Fierce sectarian wars did take place under the sacred canopy, but it was precisely because of this canopy – the belief in it, the outspoken ideas about it – that such conflicts could erupt at all. Only in a fully modernized society that the idea of a *jihad* strikes people as utterly strange and incredible. Thus, the sacred canopy of premodern societies did not at all ensure harmony and peace, but it did provide people with a cognitive and existential taken-for-grantedness which has been lost in modernity.

To Berger, modernization was above all a pervasive pluralization of values, norms, meanings, and symbols which lead to segmentation of culture and to a plurality of life-worlds. Basic in this pluralization was the dichotomy of the private and public spheres of life, while also within these spheres themselves pluralizations have occurred. As a result, Berger argues, the modern world has become 'an ever-changing kaleidoscope' (1973b). This kaleidoscopic plurality has far-reaching consequences for the modern individual, since it forces him to make choices, decisions, and plans all the time. As a result, reality remains open and unfinished, and is subjected to a serious decline of taken-for-grantedness. The modern individual has to search for reality constantly, and in continuous deliberations and reflections future actions have to be planned. In the process, his sense of identity will change drastically. Whereas identity – that is, everything answering to the question 'Who am I?' – remained firmly rooted in a traditional, objective, institutional order prior to modernization, identity in the modern plurality of vastly different life-worlds is doomed to be subjective, highly individuated and thus malleable and unstable.

Since the traditional canopy was essentially religious, the impact of modernization was most dramatic in the sphere of religion. Therefore, most classical social theorists who have focused their analytical attention on modernization, placed religion in the center of their scientific attention. (Law, incidentally, was the other sector on which these theorists focused their attention, since here too modernization could be observed most clearly.) Also in this respect does Berger stand in the line of classical social theorists, apart from the fact that he also has a personal and normative interest in religion and theology. In any case, modernization as the pluralization of life-worlds means to him primarily the gradual transition from an overarching canopy of basically religious meanings, norms, values, and symbols to widely discrepant cultural systems, in which the religious definition of the world has lost ever more of its plausibility. This secularization, however, is not a disappearance of religion, if such a thing were at all possible. Religious definitions of the world have rather become private and subjective on the one hand, and very general and public on the other. As to the latter, long before the notion of a 'civil religion' became popular amongst the sociologists of religion in the 1970s, Berger developed a comprehensive theory of civic creeds and ideologies with vaguely religious over- and undertones (1961a). As in his first book-size publication (1961c), he confronted a sociological analysis of religion in modern society with theological reflections.

The privatization, individuation and generalization of religion lead, according to Berger, to a serious decline of religious plausibility, and thereby to a growing sense of meaninglessness and disorientation. Berger calls it a state of homelessness – an unwittingly gnostic term which refers to an existential state of anomie and alienation which is allegedly hard to bear psychologically and causes the recurrent emergence of nostalgia for a condition in which one can feel oneself at home again, at home in society, in the universe, with oneself and with one's fellow human beings.

Loyal to the basic tenets of the sociology of knowledge, Berger ties consciousness systematically to social structure. If homelessness is typical of modern consciousness, technological production (or the world of work) and the bureaucratized state constitute the main structural realities within modern society, and function as the primary agents of modernization. (Secondary agents are, according to Berger, among others: urbanization, stratification and mobility, mass education, mass media, etc.) Typical for the world of modern work is above all the fact that it is based upon scientific and technological knowledge which are spread out over various degrees of expertise. Technological expertise is in principle not bound to any specific persons and can be exchanged among people more or less freely. Berger calls this *reproductibility* which he links conceptually to *mechanisticity*, since such expert functions usually possess a machine-like character. Naturally, in modern production quantitative *measurability* is a third character trait. Furthermore, in modern production there is a strong *componentiality*, that is, production and products are distinguishable parts which are yet linked together in mutual interdependencies, making for a production system. In this system means and ends are clearly separated which results in a high degree of *abstraction*. What Berger calls the tinkering attitude is most functional in the modern production system and may spread far beyond it: the conviction that the world, yes, life itself, can be made by human beings technologically. Berger calls it *makeability*. Finally, in the modern world of work social relations tend to be anonymous: it requires functionaries and a high degree of engineering. In fact, the functionaries themselves are subjected to *anonymization* which causes the emergence of a double consciousness, because the worker will experience himself not only as a private person with an identity in a private world, but also as the player of functional roles and a technical functionary in the production system (Dahrendorf, 1964).

Technological production in modern society is, of course, highly bureaucratized. Yet Berger distinguishes from this bureaucracy the state bureaucracy which carries its very own characteristics. It is, for instance, more variable and arbitrary than the production system which is strictly tied to production schedules and output figures. Therefore, Berger views the political bureaucracy as the second main agent of modernization, and as the very nucleus of modernity.

Whereas the knowledge of technological production is specialized and hierarchical, divided over various degrees of expertise, bureaucratic knowledge consists of a vast supply of rules, regulations, and jurisdictions which are to be applied in a similar manner within substantially rather different sectors of society. *Competence* is the crucial concept here. It is based upon formal jurisdictions, proper procedures (such as referral, redress, etc.), and the continuous coverage by rules. As in technological production, anonymity is essential in the bureaucratic system. The bureaucrat thinks and works without bias, value-free, objectively. The cognitive style here is that of *orderliness*: the bureaucrat's main objective is to place certain cases and problems in certain boxes, classifying, rather than analyzing and synthesizing them. *Organizability* and *predictability* are crucial to this system and they are founded upon a general expectation of justice. Subjects and clients are to be treated equally and objectively, according to formal rules and procedures, which entails, of course, a degree of depersonalization. Meanwhile, unlike technological production, political bureaucracy is unable to separate means and ends, but the preoccupation with rules, regulations and procedures can easily cause the typically modern displacement of goals: not rarely the bureaucratic system itself becomes the final goal. Berger speaks here of a built-in bureaucratic *utopianism*, in which the perfect organization is viewed as one without bothersome clients. Some state bureaucracies, he claims, resemble a Platonic heaven, although the pragmatic realities of political life will in most cases put severe limits on such a bureaucratic utopianism (1973b).

The limits of modernization

Ever since the famous report of the Club of Rome came out, there have been heated discussions on the limits of economic growth. Much less attention has been paid to the equally important, and closely related question, whether there are limits to the process of modernization. More than anyone else in contemporary sociology, Berger dealt with this problem which he defined as one of stoppage. 'A totally modern society would be a science-fiction nightmare,' he proclaimed at the end of *The Homeless Mind* (1973b: 229). Meanwhile, if sociological analysts have usually neglected the problem, there has never been a lack of discontent with and hostility towards modernization and modernity. From nineteenth-century Romanticism to the youth culture of the 1960s various movements of counter-modernization and actual demodernization have accompanied the steady expansion of modernity.

Berger's views on counter-modernization and demodernization deserve special attention. To start with, it is arguable that his 'objective,' sociological analysis merges strongly with his personal, normative stance in matters of policy and ethics. This merging of logically rather different levels of argument does somewhat obfuscate his analyses in the last four chapters of *The Homeless Mind*. In these chapters his arguments begin to lose their customary clarity and lucidity. (To give but one example, it is not very clear what precisely the differences are, according to Berger, between counter-modernization and demodernization, since both concepts are not clarified.) What is far more important is the fact that his own stance *vis-à-vis* modernity and the various attempts to curb its homelessness, remains ambiguous. As to the latter, he does make it perfectly clear that he is not at all happy with the various demodernizing movements of our days, such as the youth culture and the counter-culture of the 1960s. Yet after having discussed them, often ironically, he admits that 'a correct intuition is involved in all of this' (1973b: 200). The correct intuition is that a full-fledged modernity causes homelessness (for example, alienation and anomie) and that this cannot and may not be the human condition of a modernized society. Thus, in a sense Berger is in sympathy with the nostalgic search for a lost paradise, for an existentially plausible home, but is at the same time convinced that various demodernizing movements, in the Western as well as in the Third World, have not much else to offer than shabby shacks or frightening prisons, figuratively and literally. The ambiguity is not solved, then, by any clear alternative.

Marxism – or, in Berger's writing, socialism – obviously saddles him with a large problem, since it not only offers modernity (that is, science, technological production, bureaucracy), but also promises a home (that is, a semi-religious, comprehensive world-view and communal solidarity). In a sense, as Berger phrases it, Marxism promises that one can have one's cake and eat it! (1974f: 43) In the Third World, Berger argues correctly, radical socialism often merges with nationalism which presents a curious mixture of modernization and demodernization. If *The Homeless Mind* is still somewhat ambiguous and vague, when it deals with these and similar problems, in *Pyramids of Sacrifice* Berger sets out to clarify his political and ethical stance on the matter.

In this book Berger begins with an analysis of the modernizing and demodernizing ideologies in terms of (semi-) religious, mythopoetic exercises. He distinguishes typologically between two basic myths: the myth of growth which is basically capitalist, and the myth of revolution which is basically socialist. Although both myths are firmly rooted in the minds of Western intellectuals, he is primarily interested in their effects on the development of non-Western, Third World countries. Meanwhile, it should be noted, he has changed his mode of analysis in *Pyramids of Sacrifice*: 'this book is not primarily a scholarly work in the sense of "value-free science." It tries to bring together scientific analysis and ethical concern' (1974f: 7). Berger calls the result 'a hard-nosed utopianism' (1974f: 15). Thus, in the background of the ideological war between the 'capitalist' and 'socialist' models of development, he sees a much more fundamental war between two fundamental myths: the myth of growth has faith in rationalism, in the need of choice and of control, and is carried by two 'archetypes,' the entrepreneur and the engineer. The myth of revolution, on the contrary, rejects the primacy of reason and is in search of a redemptive community which is led by armed prophets. In terms of modernization, the former is obviously 'progressive,' the latter 'regressive,' if not 'archaic.' Yet in Marxism the myth of revolution is mixed with elements from the myth of growth, since it claims to offer a scientific and technological, thus rational, socialism which, due to the fundamental unity of theory and practice, will lead mankind eventually to a world without alienation and anomie, that is, to communal solidarity: 'in the end, everybody will have everything – the fruits of progress without the price of alienation; redemption *and* technocratic control; community *and* individual choice' (1974f: 43). This mythological amalgam is still strengthened, if couched in nationalism, as happens in various African countries these days.

In *Pyramids of Sacrifice* Berger sets himself the hard task to discuss critically both myths and to assess the human costs and benefits of the 'capitalist' model and the 'socialist' model of development. He presents Brazil and China as the clearest examples of these two models, if they are taken to their extremes. He refuses to opt for either one of them, that is, to romanticize either Brazil or China as normative models for development in the Third World. Moreover, his own hard-nosed utopianism is based on the conviction that policies for social change are always forged by politicians and intellectuals who have faith in the superiority of their own insights, and who are prepared to sacrifice at least one generation of human beings for their political ideals and objectives: 'Both sets of sacrifice are justified by theories. The theories are delusional and the sacrifices are indefensible. Rejection of *both* the Brazilian *and* the Chinese models is the starting point for any morally acceptable development policy' (1974f: 14).

This is, of course, not the place to summarize Berger's analysis of both myths and models in further detail. One might rather ask what, in Berger's view, the desirable theoretical and political-ethical solution might be, if both myths and policy models – the myth of growth and the myth of revolution, 'Brazil' and 'China' – are to be rejected. In two chapters Berger makes up a balance of the human costs and benefits, and he does so in terms of a 'calculus of pain' and a 'calculus of meaning.' But if it comes to hard-nosed utopian conclusions, we are somewhat left up in the air of ambiguity. The calculus of pain actually ends up by saying again that 'neither model is morally acceptable,' whereas the calculus of meaning results in a plea for a humanistic approach to development. Not even the contours of a humane development policy are being traced (1974f: 192, 216).

The welfare state: between capitalism and socialism

I would argue that an alternative to both models does exist, and that it has been realized already, although not in America. Berger's plea for a re-evaluation of America at the end of *Pyramids of Sacrifice* may certainly meet with full sympathy, but is neither analytically nor politically very strong. It seems to me that a realistic, alternative development policy has been tried out in North-Western Europe in what is now called the welfare state. One can certainly argue about the successes and failures of the European welfare state (Wilensky, 1974; George and Wilding, 1976), but its original conception was precisely to reject both capitalism and socialism.

If reduced to its bare ideological outlines, the welfare state meant to erect a fully modernized society in which a state-guaranteed social and economic security for all its citizens had to be established. This security was to consist of an equal floor of minimal provisions in health care, old-age insurance, education, housing – of all those provisions, in short, which at least materially make for a civilized living. This equal floor then had to function as a basis from which individuals and groups of citizens would be enabled to develop their talents and energies according to their own initiatives. That means, the original, rather hard-nosed utopian dream of the welfare state was to establish a society in which the bourgeois values – above all, equality, liberty and solidarity – were to be balanced mutually, and maintained equally. Maybe this dream was impossible? And indeed, much has gone wrong with it recently, as the welfare state has become too bureaucratic, too state-oriented and centralized, too egalitarian, due to which intermediary structures have lost much of their autonomy and stamina, and individual citizens much of their initiative and imagination. Yet the original conception of the welfare state contains, at least analytically, a hard-nosed utopian model of modernization and development which is neither capitalist nor socialist. And in its initial mythology – equality, liberty, and solidarity – the welfare state meant to alleviate the ills of tradition (poverty, poor health, recurrent massive unemployment, squalor and misery), as well as the ills of modernity (alienation, anomie, a pervasive sense of homelessness). Moreover, the welfare state meant to balance elements of social democracy (for example, the notion of a general floor of minimal social and economic security for all citizens) with elements of liberalism (for example, the idea that from this floor citizens should be able to rise socially according to their talents, initiatives, and energies). In a sense, the welfare state could indeed be viewed as a third model of development which intended to avoid the maldevelopments of the capitalist and those of the socialist models. Understandably, the welfare state has always been rejected fiercely by both the extreme 'right' and the extreme 'left.' As such, it could, at least theoretically, have served as an example of what Berger was looking for, namely, a hard-nosed utopianism which avoids the human costs of both the myth of growth and the myth of revolution, of the capitalist and of the socialist models of development policy, of 'Brazil' and of 'China.'

However, I may be terribly wrong here. Maybe Berger believes that the ills of modernization and modernity's many-faceted discontents cannot at all be dealt with adequately on the socio-scientific level of analysis, and that, in terms of practice and policy, development and change cannot at all be left to politics and politicians. Maybe Berger believes that these issues ought to be confronted less superficially on the level of religious commitments, of theology and ethics. He does not say so explicitly in his books, and at the end of *Pyramids of Sacrifice* he refers briefly to his own Christian commitment. Yet he does not elaborate further on that point. He proposes only to search for ethical propositions which could be accepted universally by all people of good will, being Christian, Muslim or Marxist, conservative, radical or liberal. Such propositions, he hastens to add, should not merely add up to a common divisor in which syncretistically elements of various world views are put together and neutralized. He rather looks for propositions that are based upon 'a common no': '*No* to children living in garbage; *no* to exploitation and hunger; *no* to terror and totalitarianism; and *no* to anomie and the mindless destruction of human meanings' (1974f: 259). From such concrete cases of nay-saying, Berger believes, alternative policies of development could be designed. But here we meet, of course, a colossal problem: after all these concrete no's, to which nobody would object, some hard-nosed, practical and political yes's will have to be designed. Berger, however, rests his case when it comes to this highly important point. I suggest once more that the original notion of a welfare state would have given him the opportunity to go beyond the common no's he has mentioned.

However, I have the suspicion that at this point Berger prefers to transfer the discussion from social science and politics to religious commitment, theology, and ethics. To me, such a transfer is far from satisfactory, intellectually, practically or politically. Yet it must be clear by now that a discussion of Berger's theory of modernization and demodernization may not omit his views on modernity and religion.

Modernity and religious commitment

Berger's work in the area of religion is an integral part of Berger's whole *œuvre*. It should not be seen as an alien part in it, or as amateurish exercises in the margins. Moreover, they are not at all written as religiously edifying manifestos for Christians, and are far remote from what the Germans nicely call *Erbauungsliteratur*. Much like Schleiermacher, Berger seems to address the 'cultured despisers of religion,' but he does so without any missionary zeal. In fact his motive to transcend the level of scientific (that is, empirical, objective, rational) argument and to engage in religious and theological considerations about the supernatural is a very simple and very rational one. If debunking of our world-taken-for-granted is the task *par excellence* of the sociology of knowledge, one ought to debunk also this sociological debunking! To Berger this is not just a matter of intellectual honesty but also one of moral necessity. However, it is a matter of simple logic that such a debunking of the sociological debunking cannot be performed by sociology itself, nor by any other empirical social science. One has to transcend the empirical sciences and the natural world to a metaphysical level and the supernatural. As no one else in contemporary sociology, Berger had the nerve to formulate his ideas about all this explicitly, without obfuscating the logical and methodological boundaries between sociology and theology; between value-free analysis and normative commitment.

Once again, in his religious and theological writing, modernization assumes a very crucial role. If this process entailed a pluralization of values, norms, and meaning, as he demonstrated in his sociological studies, it must have had a dramatic impact on religion which in traditional society had functioned as an overarching canopy of meaning and as an institutionalized set of legitimations and theodicies. As such, modernization entailed a radical secularization which went far beyond the empirical decline of power and influence on the part of organized religion. It was a process which not only affected social structure, but caused a profound alteration of consciousness as well. In his religious and theological writing Berger tries to cope with this intellectually and religiously.

This is, of course, not the place to give a summary of his theological analysis, criticism or proposal. This is done elsewhere in the volume. It suffices to mention here that Berger opts for an 'inductive' model of theologizing, as opposed to a 'reductive' and deductive model. That is, he starts his religious analyses with very concrete, everyday life experiences, such as anxiety, humor, and laughter, love, hope, play, etc. In them he searches for signals of transcendence (that is, for clear indications of a reality which goes beyond the immediate here-and-now and which transcends our physical senses and the limits of our clock-time). Such signals of transcendence are indeed the angels of our time; harbingers of a supernatural reality. He thus tries to open our eyes for an inductive type of religion which, if systematized theoretically, would lead to an inductive type of theology. It is, of course, quite a large order, and Berger fully realizes this. He is, however, too impatient to work out the whole program in detail, and prefers just to sketch the raw outlines of it.

I am not a qualified person to assess the merits and demerits of Berger's inductive program. In such an assessment the intellectual courage and the refreshing imagination would have to be stressed. Present-day 'cultured despisers of religion' could be inspired by him at least to reflect upon their own atheism or agnosticism, and therefore, here too, Berger debunks what has been taken for granted. But one could question whether induction is really that much different from the by now rather traditional reductions of neo-liberalism. Moreover, theologians certainly will detect in Berger's angels an uncanny resemblance with the many gods of Hellenism. Through his inductive religion, the pluralism of modern society might very well lead up to a modern form of polytheism. Moreover, speaking about Hellenism, this modern polytheism might well be very gnostic, which is not that strange, of course, since gnosticism is, due to anti-institutional subjectivism, endemic to modernity anyhow.

Paradise lost

But while I am saying all this, I realize that my own Calvinist origins are still at work here, be it residually. My critical remarks, I am sure, will cause a truly Lutheran smile on Berger's face. In the Calvinist universe there is but one, rather far away, God, and there are hardly any angels. And if, for some reason, one is no longer able to believe that this far away God revealed himself through Jesus of Nazareth, whose life, death, and alleged resurrection constituted the super-theodicy of the cosmos, one will not settle for Berger's inductive experience of transcendence. Indeed, the post-Calvinist lives in a rather barren world, if it comes to the justification of suffering and death, and to the experience of Meaning. He can then swing with the times and the tides of modernity, as many do these days who gradually burn up their physical and mental energies without contributing much to culture and society. He can also stick to what Thomas Mann called *die Forderungen des Tages* – the exigencies of the day – and try to realize one's talents and one's opportunities in a humane and humanistic manner. Such an intellectual asceticism, which was also typical of Max Weber's world view, has not much to offer in terms of redemption, but after the collapse of the sacred canopy that is probably all there is left. During the course of modernization, we have eaten from a tree of knowledge, and thereby lost a paradise of faith in redemption and salvation. The true tragedy of modernization in this respect is that no deduction, no reduction and no induction can ever put the canopy of Meaning together again.

CHAPTER 4

The modern malaise

James Davison Hunter

One of the most persistent themes among intellectuals since the Enlightenment has been the belief that modern society is in a state of crisis – at a crossroads in its evolution. It will either realize the full measure of hope that technological, economic, and political progress has long promised, or (more likely) suffer decline at the hand of unforeseen forces that progress itself unleashed. To be sure, themes of crisis, malaise, and decline have been so widely promulgated that one wonders whether this conviction is not also a conceit, for nearly every generation of intellectuals since that time has made the claim that *its* generation is the decisive one. In one sense it is irrelevant whether the various claims have any basis in reality. Merely the fact that they are made repeatedly and with such passion is significant. At the broadest level it signals an almost universal perception that modernization has not come without severe, long-lasting and perhaps calamitous costs.

But what are the costs? Sociology, from its beginning, has been among the most prolific contributors to the literature of 'social criticism' and predictably, the kinds of assessments made have varied considerably. Of course, in the nineteenth century, the principal statements came from Marx, Durkheim, Weber, and Simmel, and their respective criticisms have become so familiar that they hardly need repeating. Alienation and the total estrangement of man from his exploiters, his fellow-workers, the product of his labors and ultimately, himself; the inherent disposition toward normative breakdown and the perverse 'cult of the individual;' the ineluctable rationalization, bureaucratization, and disenchantment of modern culture combined with the reduction of the human spirit to narrow specialization; the isolation of the individual in an abstract and impersonal metropolis – the early protagonists of sociology were invective about the human consequences of modernity and, in most cases, trenchantly pessimistic about the likelihood of the human circumstances getting much better.

Clearly the classical statements merely started the tradition in the discipline. Social criticism continued through the first half of the twentieth century, and even to the present it has continued to be an obligation assumed not only by popular doomsdayers but by some of the more talented and energetic thinkers of the day as well. Some of it has been intellectually defensible; much of it has not. But, successful or not, those who engage in this exercise share a breadth of vision that is nothing short of audacious. It is an audacity that Peter Berger shares as well.

Berger's own contribution to the problem of assessing the costs of modernity, though, has been neither formalized nor systematized in a single work. His contribution is, in fact, scattered throughout two-and-a-half decades of scholarly and popular writing. A review and evaluation of this criticism, then, will be the focus of this chapter. The context, however, is critical. Whatever the substance, a fair treatment of Berger's position can only begin by framing it within the large, contemporary literature appraising the human experience in the modern world.

Pathos in the modern world: a half-century of social criticism

As will become clear, many of the themes distinguishing contemporary social criticism had already been sounded in the late nineteenth and twentieth century. Even so, the substance and style has changed in unique ways.

Early criticism: 1930–1960

In the early years of modern social criticism the 'mass society critique' predominated. Jose Ortega y Gasset's *The Revolt of the Masses* (1932) set the tone for much that was to follow. Ortega argued that the contemporary West was 'suffering from the greatest crisis that can afflict peoples, nations, and civilizations,' namely, the emergence of the masses. As the term suggested, the masses were an undifferentiated agglomeration of people who were, ironically, distinguished by their conformity, by their lack of individuality and quality, by their herd mentality. Yet to the extent that the masses existed *qua* masses in the past, they always recognized and accepted their subordinate position in the social, cultural, and political life of their societies. They rarely, if ever, asserted a right to intervene in these spheres. The crisis of modern society for Ortega was that the masses were now asserting themselves in such a way as to define social, cultural, and political reality for civilization as a whole. It was now, as never before, seeking to advance its 'plebian' aspirations to the foreground of social life.

But where did mass society come from? Most of the early arguments pointed to the advanced technological quality of modern society. Oswald Spengler, for example, complained that mankind was 'becoming the slave of the Machine.' The artificial and esoteric edifice of technology was 'permeating and poisoning' all dimensions of the natural and social world to the point that every organism was subject to mechanization. Human beings were reduced to a number 'entirely without significance' (1932: 90–104). Lewis Mumford in terms less polemical sounded similar themes in *Technics and Civilization* (1934). Here he argued that among the chief characteristics of 'our machine civilization' were the regularization of time, the contraction of space and time, the standardization of performance and product, the transfer of skill to automata, and mass-production and mass-consumption, and that these foster an impersonalness and passivity among the population. For Mumford (1938) and many other sociologists in the 1930s, the modern city became a parable for the modern age. 'Life means metropolitan life,' noted Mumford, and metropolitan life was a 'rootless world' (p.255). Such statements were not entirely groundless either. The studies of city life by the Chicago school of sociology in the 1920s and 1930s all seemed to confirm this image. Community life was disintegrating under the stress of poverty and homelessness (Anderson, 1923; Sutherland and Locke, 1936); family disorganization (Mowrer, 1927; Mowrer and Mowrer, 1928; Frazier, 1932), racial unrest (Taylor, 1922), and crime, delinquency, and gang behavior (Sutherland, 1937; Landesco, 1929; Slawson, 1926).

European social scientists shared many of these views, but there was also the deep-seated belief that American problems were not entirely European problems. As such, they sought new theoretical and empirical means for exploring the pathos of modern society. With a few notable exceptions most prominent European scholars settled on a theoretical synthesis of Marxian, Weberian, and Freudian (psychoanalytic) critiques. In this development the Europeans, particularly at the Frankfurt School, came to dominate social criticism from the early 1940s through the early 1950s.

If one can speak of the perspective of the Frankfurt School at all, one can do so only in the most general of terms. Sharp disagreement existed on several matters among many of the protagonists. Even so, upon many points there was agreement – one being that there was a pathological quality about industrial capitalist society and the life it offered ordinary people. Erich Fromm, for example, maintained that modern society was, by mental health criteria, 'sick.' Though not all accepted the baldly medical/psychoanalytic presuppositions inferred in Fromm's analysis, a similar normative quality distinguished their critique: modern society was oppressive to human experience and societal evolution; it was opposed to human freedom. Alienation, in one form or another was the modern malaise. But what was its source?

For Fromm (1941) it was the unassimilable freedom man had at his disposal. Capitalism had afforded people unprecedented freedom but at the cost of their psychic isolation and alienation. Modern man had become a stranger to his own world. But more than this, Fromm (1955) maintained that modern society inhibited the satisfaction of basic needs necessary to mental health. Instead, it created 'false needs' such as the materialistic drive to possess more and more. Herbert Marcuse (1955, 1960) viewed the loss of individual autonomy as having come from the emotional and sexual repression structured into the maintenance of modern civilization and specific forms of social domination. There was, of course, a certain amount of repression which was common to all societies (as Freud pointed out), but under capitalism, according to Marcuse, an extraordinary degree of 'surplus repression' is coercively imposed on the individual, subjecting him to the 'performance principle' and, therefore, to the power of a dominating class. An even more significant source of alienation for many early social critical theorists was science and technology. Independent of their use as instruments of class domination, they existed as an autonomous form of oppressive ideology. Theodor Adorno and Max Horkheimer (1972) and Marcuse in a later work (1964) argued that class domination was rapidly becoming less important in the historical development of Western capitalism. Replacing it in significance was the progressive and all-pervasive domination of science and technology. They threatened to make culture and human consciousness 'one-dimensional' – passive and acquiescent, incapable of creative intellectual and artistic expression outside of the demands of instrumental rationality.

One of the secondary consequences of these structural changes was the creation of a mass culture. A result of a fusion of advertising and entertainment, mass culture only deepened the alienation and the false consciousness of modern experience. Among other things, it allowed for the subjugation of real human needs through newly created 'artificial' consumer needs. It also encouraged a disposition toward mass conformity. Genuine community was not possible under these conditions. Moral, behavioral, and cognitive conformity to the standards of mass society, then, provided an artificial sense of sociality, belonging, and security. The real danger of this was that it made modern individuals unusually manipulable – predisposed, as it were, to submission to an authoritarian state or charismatic leader or both. In a word, it fostered an 'authoritarian personality' which was inherently vulnerable to the totalitarian ideal (Adorno, *et al.*, 1950; Fromm, 1941; Christie and Jahoda, 1954).

This intractable pessimism was shared by other European sociologists not a part of the Frankfurt network. Jacques Ellul (1957), for example (like Spengler, Mumford, and many critical theorists), maintained that the essential tragedy of contemporary civilization was its increasing domination by 'technique.' All domains of life (the economy, the state, public opinion, education, leisure, medicine and morality) have become subjugated to the quest for the most rational and efficient means. The result was an 'operational totalitarianism' where spontaneous creativity is destroyed; where individuality is lost in a homogenous mass; where human freedom is sacrificed for tranquilizing abstraction. Unlike the Marxists, however, Ellul did not feel these distinctions were unique to Western or even American capitalism. On the contrary, capitalism or socialism, democracy or authoritarianism, all modern forms of political economy accepted the fundamental assumptions of technical rationality.

Theodor Geiger's work (1963, 1969) fell more in line with the

American mass society critique, with several important exceptions. He was sharply critical of its romanticism and its nostalgia for either a past or a future ideal. Moreover, while he agreed that modern society was characterized by a certain 'homelessness and isolation of the individual,' cultural uniformity, 'Americanization,' excessive specialization, bureaucratization, and the decline of cultural standards, these were not uniformly distributed in society but were confined to experience in the public sphere. The private sphere of 'personal singularity and intimate association,' by contrast is satisfactory to most modern individuals. The latter, then, compensates for the mass existence and atomization of the public sphere. For Geiger, the distinguishing characteristic of contemporary life was not mass existence as such but the polarization of forms of life – the dualism of social spheres.

Still another European voice of dissent during the late 1940s and early 1950s was that of Arnold Gehlen (1956, 1957). When taken as a whole, Gehlen's perspective was one of the more philosophically sophisticated and sociologically astute. The long and short of his critique, however, was simple. Modern rationality 'deinstitutionalizes' the encompassing and stable institutions of archaic society. In more common parlance, it substantially undermines the credibility of traditional routines and patterns of social life previously experienced as objective facticity. Modern society, then, has a built-in destabilizing tendency which has consequences for all dimensions of human life. One of the more important consequences is for the social psychology of modern man. Since the assumptions of everyday life are no longer taken-for-granted, in practical terms, modern man is faced with an extraordinary number of choices. Without an objective social order to turn to, modern man 'turns inward' to his subjectivity for those answers. Deinstitutionalization and 'subjectivization' are, then, the complementary problems of modern society. Not only is the social order of modernity fluid and unstable, but the personality structure of modern man is also given to change.

From the mid-1950s to the mid-1960s, the locus of creative social criticism shifted back to the United States. Curiously, life had never been better for most Americans. Virtually all areas of the economy expanded, with the effect of improving the quality of life for nearly all sectors of the labor force. Yet in spite of this (in some ways because of it), social criticism abounded. The analysis of the modern malaise, however, became more focused and empirical. It became concerned with 'massification' within specific institutional sectors of modern society.

One prominent sector was the media of mass communications and the 'mass culture' it fostered. Enormous changes had taken place in this sphere between the 1930s and early 1960s. For example, the number of households with radios increased twenty-fold between 1925 and 1965 (from 2.7 million to 55.2 million) (Bureau of the Census, 1975: 796). The number of households with televisions grew even more dramatically from 9 per cent in 1950 to 93 per cent in 1965 (Bureau of the Census, 1984: 558). Likewise in book publishing, where the number of new books published annually remained fairly constant from 1910 to 1950, between 1950 and 1964 that number nearly tripled to over 28,000 titles annually (Bureau of the Census, 1975: 808; 1984: 236). These trends had a parallel in the motion picture industry as well. Such changes were not without cultural consequences, as many were quick to point out. Mass culture, like anything mass-produced, standardized and therefore deindividualized cultural products. It aimed, as virtually all critics agreed, at the 'average of consumer tastes.' It homogenized culture and therefore destroyed all values since value judgments imply discrimination (MacDonald, 1953: 4). Real culture became 'trivialized, eclectic and styleless' (van den Haag, 1959); real taste was 'cretinized'; the senses were 'brutalized' (Rosenberg, 1957: 9). As one commentator put it, 'Mass culture was at best a vulgarized reflection of High Culture' (MacDonald, 1953: 3). Mass culture was popular among the 'masses' partly because of the effective manipulative capabilities of the mass media, particularly through advertising. These were the 'hidden persuaders' of our society (Packard, 1957), the devices of the 'mind managers' (Schiller, 1973) providing effective conduits for the 'propaganda' of a technological civilization (Ellul, 1965).

The mass media and specifically mass advertising had another consequence, of course, and this was the stimulation of mass consumption. Between 1940 and 1965 the general index of national advertising expenditures increased nine-fold (Bureau of the Census, 1975: 857). The new billions of dollars invested into this industry combined with continued mass production, growth in the real income of working Americans in the post-war period, and the expansion of credit-buying, and the result was an unprecedented surge in mass consumption (Galbraith, 1958). Critics such as Vance Packard (1960) and Jules Henry (1963) and later, Phillip Slater (1970) complained that America was becoming a 'throw-away' culture where not only material possessions but human life itself operated upon principles of 'planned' or 'dynamic obsolescence.' The economic and human foundation of such a society was waste.

Another institutional area which suffered a peculiarly modern malaise was education. As is well-known, public education experienced tremendous growth from 1920 to 1965. For example, of the population eighteen years of age or older, 16 per cent graduated from high school in 1920, but by 1965 this had grown to 76 per cent (Bureau of the Census, 1975: 379). Much of that growth took place in the post-World War II period. But what kind of system was training the future generation? Predictably, the diagnosis was not sanguine. Critics such as Jules Henry (1963), John Holt (1964) and Herbert Kohl (1967) observed that instead of seeking to develop the learning potential of children and adolescents, schools had adopted a bureaucratic model of organization and productivity. Like any large-scale organization, schools were seeking to maximize productivity and uniformity. In pursuing this goal, students were taught passive conformity to impersonal bureaucratic norms and fear of and anxiety toward bureaucratic authority. In effect, these highly 'repressive institutions' destroyed students' natural creative intelligence. As Holt put it, schools were places were students followed 'meaningless procedures to obtain meaningless answers to meaningless questions' (1964).

Community was also believed to suffer in modern societies. As of 1930, roughly 18 per cent of the American population lived in suburban areas, but in the course of the next thirty years that figure doubled – to 36 per cent (Weller and Bouvier, 1981). Changes as significant as these invariably altered the nature of community life, especially in the American middle class and, in the minds of most social critics, the change was for the worse. Studies of suburban communities like 'Park Forest' (Whyte, 1957) near Chicago or

'Crestwood Heights' (Seeley *et al.*, 1956) in mid-Western Canada showed that these transient communities were havens of status competition and middle-class conformity. What individuality did exist was merely 'marginal differentiation.' Because of its transient quality, interpersonal bonds could not be deep (though sociability required the appearance of depth) and identities could not be grounded. The high degree of mobility also seemed to create a high degree of structural instability despite a veneer of social tranquility and happiness. As the authors of *Crestwood Heights* noted, there was a remarkable degree of disorganization and change in the values and norms of everyday life for its residents (though particularly in the realm of child-rearing and socialization). One of the distinct consequences was the expanding role of mental health experts in the community to provide moral guidance. These problems (among many others), however, were not exclusively the problems of city or suburban living. As Vidich and Bensman (1958) showed in their study of the rural village of 'Springdale,' the dynamics of mass society so prevalent in metropolitan areas were also at work in the small town – what many considered to be the last stronghold of resistance to modernity.

The net effect of the changes in all of these institutional spheres (and others too) was the fashioning of a novel personality type or social character. This was the bottom line of virtually all social criticism of the period. The pathos of modern civilization achieved its most poignant and tragic expression in the flawed character of modern man.

The concern with social character cannot be over-emphasized. Though initially popularized by Riesman (1950), it became a standard methodology of social criticism through the early 1960s. The term 'social character' could essentially be understood as the aggregation of psycho-social qualities common to members of the same culture. The special utility of the concept was that it allowed the reduction of culture to a single descriptive category – an ideal-typical character structure. Practically, it allowed for shorthand historical and cross-national comparison – comparison that would ultimately highlight the singular qualities of modern existence.

This modern social character, then, was typified in a variety of ways: the 'mass man' (Ortega, Geiger, Ellul), the 'marketer'

(Fromm), 'one-dimensional man' (Marcuse), the 'other-directed personality' (Riesman), 'alienated man' (Josephson), the 'fixer' (Mills), 'organizational man' (Whyte), 'psychological man' (Rieff), and 'protean man' (Lifton). Still others, such as Paul Goodman (1956), Vance Packard (1960), Jules Henry (1963), Phillip Slater (1970) spoke of a national or social character without naming it, yet it was clear from their descriptions what they meant. In composite, the modern social character lived in conditions that were alienated, isolated, impersonal, and dehumanizing. He was virtually powerless and because of his transience, he was morally, psychologically, and socially rootless – without a sense of self or of place. All of this yielded an experience of loneliness, anxiety, uncertainty, and confusion, but also of boredom and emptiness. His life had become one of quiet and senseless desperation. In response, modern man had become obsessed with escaping the reality of his existence. But escapism came in different forms: the 'addiction to the prefabricated experiences' of mass culture, competition for popular approval (as a substitute for deep human relations) or just the passive and fatalistic resignation to the abstract structures that determined everyday existence. The end product was a mass of individuals that were conformist by nature, hedonistic ('oral,' 'wasteful,' 'materialistic') and, needless to say, profoundly unhappy.

It would be incorrect if one were left with the image that all believed these problems were uniquely the cause of modern capitalism or even American capitalism. Some did, of course, but many of mass society's most caustic critics believed that while America and the West were unique historical cases, the socialist experiments yielded their own versions of the same malaise (McDonald, 1953; Rosenberg, 1957). This fact, however, did not lessen the scorn and derision aimed at the American example. It would also be incorrect if one were left with the impression that all social critics fundamentally opposed mass society. There were a few (mainly conservative theorists) who without compromising the severity of their assessment argued that the modern malaise (variously understood) was simply the cost of modern democracy (Hughes, 1961; Shils, 1959; Hook, 1961; White, 1971). For them it was a heavy price to pay but in the end a price unquestionably worth paying.

Current criticism: 1965 to the present

While much of the social criticism written before the mid-1960s maintained its popularity through the end of the decade and through the early 1970s, very little of the criticism being produced had the same concerns. One rarely heard new complaints about mass culture, the mass media, mass consumption, the decay of urban and suburban existence, the atomization, alienation and isolation of the individual or other institutional critiques. There were exceptions, to be sure, such as Anton Zijderveld's *The Abstract Society* (1970) or Phillip Slater's *The Pursuit of Loneliness* (1970). Also, among institutional sectors, public education continued to be sharply criticized through the early 1970s (Illich, 1971; Herndon, 1971; Bowles and Gintis, 1976). The major thrust of social criticism, however, shifted. It was foreshadowed by works like Phillip Rieff's *Freud: The Mind of the Moralist* (1961) and later *Triumph of the Therapeutic* (1966). It was also implied in Seeley's *Crestwood Heights* and other empirically-oriented studies of the late 1950s and early 1960s. But by the early 1970s, it constituted the dominant theme in social criticism of the political right, left and center. *In nuce*, the modern malaise had become the psychologization of modern life.

This argument was formulated in different ways, of course, according to the intellectual (and even political) sentiments of the social critics. Reiff, for example, in one of the more creative and literary critiques of the decade (1966) argued that the anti-ascetic principle of the therapeutic attitude dominant in the West (and particularly America) was at the very heart of the impoverishment of Western culture. Orrin Klapp (1969), observing the same phenomenon, interpreted it in terms of a 'collective search for identity.' This search had taken different sectors of the population in different directions – moral crusades, nationalistic movements, religious and secular cults and the like – but they all implied the inability of modern culture to provide a stable universe of meaning from which people root their personal identity and significance. Richard Sennett, in *The Fall of Public Man* (1974), argued that what has really taken place is a fundamental redefinition of the private sphere of inter-personal and *intra*-personal reflection about psychic disposition, emotional states, authenticity, and meaning.

What is more, the private sphere has assumed a predominant place in the social world. Intimacy (narcissism) has become the central social and cultural principle of advanced societies and, as such, it has supplanted public discourse and civic responsibility. It emerged with the promise of liberation but it has become institutionalized as a sociological tyranny. Similar themes were evident in Daniel Bell's *The Cultural Contradictions of Capitalism* (1976) and prominent in Christopher Lasch's *The Culture of Narcissism* (1978). While neither critic was Marxist, both accentuated the role of capitalism (in its later stages) in undermining traditional asceticism and, in its stead, fostering a pervasive narcissism/hedonism in the culture. Bell was more theoretically sophisticated in discussing the structural roots of this problem; Lasch, however, was more relentless in uncovering narcissism in every major cultural sphere – leisure, entertainment, sport, education, family, and socialization. The first major quantitative effort to measure and interpret the psychologization of modern culture came in 1981 with the publication of Daniel Yankelovich's *New Rules: Searching for Self-fulfillment in a World Turned Upside Down*. Though only quasi-scholarly, Yankelovich's work effectively documented a decline in traditional moral and familial asceticism and the development of a new code of moral meaning based upon the quest for self-expression and self-fulfillment. A decade and a half of social criticism was justified by the evidence Yankelovich provided.

The preceding review does not begin to reflect the subtlety and depth of these analyses. Nor does it begin to highlight differences and even incompatibilities among the various perspectives. The concern, thus far, has been exclusively thematic – isolating the major strains and shifts in cultural criticism since the 1930s. It is worth observing at this point (from a sociology of knowledge perspective) that the major themes in social and cultural criticism have generally followed shifts in the social structure. This was certainly true in the earlier decades of this period – the rapid innovation of technology through the length of the century has yielded a fairly constant flow of criticism about its psycho-social effects; the emergence of mass communications (through the development and proliferation of radio, television, and the print media) yielded sharp criticism about its effects on culture and human relations; the enormous growth in public education yielded a critique of its 'massifying' consequences; the invention of mass consumption similarly yielded hostile intellectual responses. This kind of interplay was also at work in the later criticism. The critique of subjectivism, psychologization, and narcissism has followed a tremendous growth in the 'self-awareness industry.' For example, from 1965 to 1981, the number of doctorates conferred annually in psychology more than tripled whereas the number conferred in all fields just doubled (Bureau of the Census, 1984: 387). So, too, the number of psychiatrists in the United States increased by 7,400 between 1970 and 1981 at a rate which kept pace with the general expansion of the medical profession (Bureau of the Census, 1984: 110). Finally, the number of new books published annually in the area of psychology/philosophy tripled between 1960 and 1980 (to 1,430 books) – a rate higher than that in the book publishing industry generally (Bureau of the Census, 1984: 236).

The point is that the thematic shifts of social criticism in the previous half-century are not entirely fortuitous. From a sociology of knowledge perspective, then, it is not surprising that as the novelty of certain societal changes subsided (as, for example, in mass advertising and mass consumption) or as the growth trends table off (as they did, for example, in public education by the early 1970s and mass communication in the mid-1960s) social criticism also subsided or shifted its focus. This also explains in part the rise and decline of the critique of native fascism and the authoritarian personality in Europe. Thematic changes in social criticism occurred even though there was no evidence that we suffered any less from the alleged problems of mass society or that we were in any less danger from native authoritarianism and so on.

The relevance of this discussion is not tangential but essential to a proper understanding of Berger's own contribution to the literature of social pathology. The important question now, however, is simply descriptive.

Berger's contribution: toward a social psychology of modernity

If one can interpret the principal thrust of Berger's intellectual project as an attempt to come to terms with modernity, then his attempt to assess the 'modern malaise' is certainly central to it. Yet the focus of his efforts has shifted since the start of his career.

His two earliest works, *The Noise of Solemn Assemblies* (1961a) and *The Precarious Vision* (1961c) were forthright exercises in social criticism – their focus, the 'malaise' (his own word) of established religion in contemporary America. Both books fit the genre of the late 1950s and early 1960s period in social criticism. Berger in a very real sense simply applied a version of the mass society critique to another institutional area – organized religion in this case, and specifically the Protestant version. (Thus it provided an important complement to Gibson Winter's (1961) study, *The Suburban Captivity of the Churches*.) Distinguishing Berger's work, however, was an insider's loyalty – Berger wrote as a Christian and as a sociologist. The result was not only a compelling sociological critique of the American religious establishment but a religiously 'prophetic' statement about where the church had failed in its mission and what its role in the modern world should be. In a word, Berger complained that organized religion in America merely legitimated the social, political, cultural, and psychological status quo, that it lacked the intellectual honesty and moral and theological vision to address responsibly the deep crises that faced the modern world. Organized religion was systematically engaged in acts of bad faith.

Though since that time Berger has repeatedly distanced himself from this 'youthful religiosity,' these books are still highly significant both for the stir they created in ecclesiastical circles and (for our purposes) for an understanding of Berger's intellectual biography. On the latter it should only be emphasized that his impassioned critique was stylistically and moralistically compatible with other social criticism of the period. His concerns in the area of social pathology soon changed. The 'young Berger' soon evolved to the 'mature Berger', and the focus of the latter was on constructing a social psychology of modernity. Given the fact that his intellectual biography spans the late 1950s to the present, this transition is, from the perspective of the sociology of knowledge, not unpredictable.

His starting point on this later project was an application of the sociology of knowledge to the problem of identity. In this Berger has been greatly assisted by the Meadian tradition of social psychology. In brief, identity is created out of the dialectical relation between the individual and society. Society (through significant others, reference groups, and the like) assigns identities and individuals (through an ongoing socialization) appropriate identities. An individual's biography, then, is continually involved in a bargaining between an objective identity (what society tells him he is) and a subjective identity (how he perceives himself). In sum, identity is not an ontological given but a socially constructed phenomenon.

Yet identity construction always takes place within certain social and historical coordinates. Thus the range of possible 'selves' is empirically limitless. None the less, typological distinctions can be addressed. In so far as the present problem is concerned, the most important typological contrast for Berger is between traditional and modern types.

According to Berger, identity construction in traditional societies always took place within a highly stable and cohesive social arrangement. There was always a high degree of integration in the symbols that permeated various sectors of society and thus from the perspective of the individual in this context, his life was carried out in a life-world that was unified. In more technical terms, there was always a relatively high degree of symmetry between objectively assigned and subjectively appropriated identities (1973b: 64; 1973c: 85). This is not to say that he was necessarily happy with his lot in life – in all likelihood he was not. Still, his sense of location in the world and of who he was (defined largely by family, occupation (1964d: 215) and religion (1974e: 64) was a firm and unquestioned reality. He could be certain of who he was to the extent that society was consistent in its treatment of him. In this way, most people most of the time did not entertain notions of self-doubt.

Yet the strength of character traditional society fostered has progressively been undone with the advent of modernity, according to Berger. In short, since the sociological context in which identity formation takes place is inconstant and impermanent, then identities themselves will also be an alterable if not transitory phenomenon. All of the major institutional developments associated with modernization have contributed to this: the rationalization of economic life, the growth of the state, the autonomous development of technology, the decline of the hegemony of the church, social mobility in a class society, urbanization, and modern communications. Together, these factors work to draw out an increasing number of people from the culturally 'closed worlds of face-to-face community and thrust them into situations where they had to rub elbows continuously with unpredictable, often incomprehensible strangers' (1973c: 85). But admittedly there is little new in these insights. Thus the focus of Berger's concern has been in articulating the social-psychological processes and consequences inherent in this transformation.

To be specific, the symmetry between objective and subjective identity for a larger number of people is weakening. People, less and less, inwardly identify with their objective status (particularly occupational status) in society. But why? One reason, Berger offers, is that highly specialized work in an ever-changing social and work situation tends to divorce the individual from a stable set of social relationships and events that would ordinarily provide a stable source of self-identification (1964d: 216). In addition, the primary public institutions in which the individual's work is likely to be located tend to be abstract and incomprehensible to him. Their massive size and complexity, his own anonymous work within its bureaucratic structures, and its functional rationality cannot be converted into individually meaningful categories. Another reason is found in the nature of the class structure of modern society (1964e). Divisions in the class system are vague at best with no single criterion which identifies an individual as a member of a particular stratum. This, of course, contributes to an uncertainty of status. What is more, though, social mobility in this class system leads to changes in social milieu – a disruption in the primary social relationships that had for a time provided a context for meaningful social existence.

In line with Geiger's argument, Berger maintains that the solution to these problems became the division of social experience into public and private spheres (1973c: 87). Because the individual cannot fully relate to the fragmented experiences and relationships of the public sphere, more and more individuals are constrained to turn to the private sphere (a sphere geographically and socially segregated from work) of family and intimate social relations for a meaningful and stable identity. Berger is careful to observe that this solution has worked for large numbers of people, particularly in the earlier stages of modernization. Yet as modernization has advanced this solution has proved increasingly unsatisfying because of certain inherent weaknesses. The problem is that even in the private sphere, there has been a progressive pluralization. Both the experience with the modern city and modern media of mass-communications have assaulted consciousness with a variety of discrepant approaches to reality. While all of this 'broadens the mind,' as Berger puts it, it also 'weakens the integrity and plausibility of [the individual's] home world' (1974e: 67).

In terms borrowed from Arnold Gehlen, Berger argues that the institutions of the private sphere have become 'deinstitutionalized.' Due to this pluralization traditional definitions of reality which had previously provided stable coodinates for living everyday life (in courtship, marriage, child-rearing, religious faith and practice, interpersonal exchange and the like) are increasingly fluid, fragmented, and deprived of plausibility. Religion and the family are institutionally too weak to maintain a 'cognitive hold' over the individual. In brief, the quandary facing all modern individuals is that the public sphere is overly institutionalized and the private sphere is 'under-institutionalized.' Both spheres are structurally ineffectual in providing the durable and consistent environment necessary for a meaningful world and a stable identity. Yet in Berger's view human beings 'require' reliable interpretations of reality and personal existence. Where, then, does modern man look? The quest for meaning 'turns inward' to the depths of human subjectivity. Again borrowing from Gehlen, there is a process of 'subjectivization' whereby the individual is 'thrown back upon himself' or his own subjectivity in order to 'dredge up the meaning and stability he requires to exist' (1973c: 92).

This entire process can be aptly illustrated in the historical transformation of two ethical principles: sincerity and honor. In traditional Western societies, human quality was manifested in 'sincerity' – the candor and integrity with which one performed *public* roles. Yet with modernization, sincerity has been displaced by 'authenticity' – the expression of the true, undefiled self. The contrast is essential. Sincerity 'presupposes a symmetrical relation between self and society while authenticity implies a fundamental opposition between them' (1973c: 82). In different words, 'sincerity is discovered *within* social roles; authenticity *behind and beneath* them.' Likewise in traditional Western societies, human worth was defined by a sense of honor. Honor, according to Berger, 'is a direct expression of status, a source of solidarity among social equals' but it also implies certain standards of behavior in dealing with inferiors, equals and superiors (1970b). But the concept of honor has become obsolete in modern times – replaced by the concept of dignity. The latter implies that there is humanity and human significance *behind* or *apart* from socially imposed roles or norms. In short, 'the concept of honor implies that identity is essentially, or at least importantly, linked to institutional roles. The modern concept of dignity, by contrast, implies that identity is essentially independent of institutional roles' (1970b). Dignity and authenticity could only gain the wide cultural currency they have in a situation where individual identity becomes only loosely attached to institutional settings.

The illustrations are compelling but substantively Berger goes even further. Subjectivization implies a compulsive reflectiveness about everything one does and, ultimately, who one is. The activity is a solitary one by and large and because the range of possible identities, life-plans, and life-styles is open-ended and potentially changeable, this reflectiveness is perpetuated. It is here, according to Berger, that Riesman's category of 'other direction' gains theoretical relevance. The self is vulnerable to and dependent upon the expectations of a plurality of reference groups (1964e). The problem with subjectivization is plain at this point. Who one 'really' is, how one 'should' live – these reality definitions are subjectively real *only* in so far as they are continually reaffirmed by others. Because the social structures people inhabit are pluralized and relatively unstable, the subjective world they inhabit will have a quality of unreality to it. The net effect, then, is a profound crisis of meaning and certainty for the modern individual in which self-identity is perhaps the central problem. Thus, in Berger's view, it is no accident that a large identity market, replete with 'experts' marketing various ideologies of self-discovery and human potential has emerged (1967e: 337; 1974e: 175; 1973c: 87).

In brief, 'the migratory character of his experience of society and of self has been what might be called a metaphysical loss of "home." ' 'Modern man [suffers] from a deepening condition of "homelessness" ' (1973: 82). Reflectiveness and the various manifestations of emotional life are amplified to an extraordinary degree with the effect of 'paralyzing spontaneous action.' The essential point to all of this, for Berger, is that the contemporary identity crisis (which is a central part of a general crisis of meaning) is neither accidental nor transitory but rather an intrinsic feature of modern social life (1974e: 173). It will not go away.

This is the core of Berger's argument. It is an argument, however, not without some qualification. For example, Berger notes that this identity crisis is not evenly distributed in modern society. For one, youth are particularly vulnerable – adolescence and young adulthood are the locus of this malaise 'because it is the biographical phase of transition between the "softness" of modern childhood and the (inevitable) "hardness" of the major institutions of adult life' (1974e: 179). Class also accounts for some of the variance. The middle and upper-middle classes (and especially the knowledge classes) with their privileged access to the city, higher education, mobility, and the like, are also more vulnerable than those of the lower classes. In global terms, Berger even acknowledges that America is even more vulnerable than other industralized countries because 'it is in America that the forces of modernization have gone further than anywhere else' (1973c: 90).

'Social pathology' and political ideology

To summarize is to abbreviate and to abbreviate is to sacrifice depth and richness. For one, the preceding inadequately conveys much of the analytical subtlety of his work. It also fails to articulate the philosophical presuppositions out of which his analysis proceeds. Finally, it fails to communicate the grandness of Berger's vision and the almost cosmological coherence of his perspective. Even so, it does highlight the essential contours of his argument and, having done so, several observations can be made.

First of all Berger is Weberian, perhaps to a fault. Weber, of course, held that the source of the contemporary malaise was endemic to generic structures and processes of modernity and were not solely attributable to industrial capitalism (*à la* Marx). Certainly Weber was correct as far as he went but one would also suspect that political economy would imprint the manner in which the malaise is expressed and experienced. Specifically, democratic capitalism and state socialism would amplify as well as suppress different dimensions of the modern malaise. Yet Berger remains consciously and steadfastly Weberian on this issue even with the historical advantage. In this his analysis could have been developed much further. Clearly it is an important area for research. Why he does not point to (much less develop) it is not clear. My main point is only that one can be Weberian on this issue and still acknowledge empirical differences between different kinds of modern societies.

Subtlety in his analysis also would have been enhanced with a greater analytical/empirical sensitivity. In the end Berger's perspective is too broad and too general to be totally satisfying. Age and social class clearly account for a great deal of variation in the experience of modernity's discontents. But there are many other factors (demographic and otherwise) that figure in it as well, as a sizeable body of empirically oriented studies suggest. A static model of formal hypotheses would be unnecessary (and trivial). Even so the specific linkages between the unique structures of modern society and the substance of personal identity call for greater systematization.

Perhaps the most serious criticism leveled at Berger's contribution (in light of the body of literature in this field) is a lack of originality. The abstract and alienating qualities of modern bureaucracy are freely borrowed from Weber and Simmel. His indebtedness to Gehlen for a philosophical anthropology and for a theory of institutions, deinstitutionalization, and subjectivization is patent (and acknowledged). So too the signifiance of the public/private division was foreshadowed by Geiger's work. Indeed nearly every dimension of Berger's argument had been made before. From a distance, there are few real surprises.

Yet those who stop there miss Berger's contribution. First of all the distinctiveness of his work in this area as well as other areas is found in the subtlety of his theoretical synthesis and the rigor of his theoretical logic. The elegant way in which he integrates the theoretical insights of Weber, Durkheim, Marx, Mead, Gehlen, Schutz, and others, for example, is nothing short of brilliant. Beyond this, the explicit linkages he does make between the sociology of knowledge and modernization theory, though underdeveloped in my opinion, is not only original methodologically but highly promising for empirical research. In all of these areas Berger makes a contribution.

As significant as what he says about modern existence is the way he says it. I am not referring to his prose but to his intellectual style. First, he shares none of the Luddite phobias of technology that most early social critics had nor does he share any of their elitist disdain for mass-culture. Second, he is more empirically oriented than most theorists who also write in this genre. He has a strong intuitive understanding of the modern world that is both informed and confirmed by empirical research. His theoretical propositions are also presented in ways that are generally falsifiable. Certainly there are exceptions which defy scientific examination, but he is more sensitive about this than most. Finally, there is distinctiveness in the scientific neutrality with which he approaches the subject. This is not to say that his work is not colored by implicit bias, only that his critique is not laced with an overt political agenda. This deserves further elaboration.

Taking stock of modern life has, since the classical period, been a multi-faceted undertaking. Beyond analysis there is interpretation, assessment, and even prediction: what are the social consequences of modern institutions? and what are their lasting effects? It is possible to answer these questions with a fair degree of objectivity yet it is also typically at this point that the ideological sentiments of the scholar surface. (Ordinarily, though, if the scholar has an ideological predisposition and a political agenda it does not follow analysis but is intricately woven within it.) The focus, however, is on Berger. He is obdurantly Weberian about keeping politics and science as separate vocations – even when answering questions such as these. He is also relatively successful at it. But is there an implicit sense in which his analysis of the costs of modernity is ideologically colored?

The most appropriate way of answering this question is to pose another: what is really problematic about the modern situation? As we have seen, intellectuals have disagreed over the vocabulary of malaise but upon one point there has been remarkable consensus. It is a philosophical point and consensus on it lends a similar tenor to the wide variety of analyses. It is an agreement about the monstrous quality of modern social structures. They are all pervasive and exclusively to blame for the nearly intolerable alienation, anomie, etc. of modern life. The individual in this situation is a somewhat witless and certainly hapless creature who passively endures his plight as a modern (mass) man. The implication, of course, is that in order to make modern life tolerable, the structures need to be changed. In this light it is not surprising that liberal reformist and radical critiques (which call for fundamental structural change) have dominated this literature.

Berger answers this question in a different way. Modernity is certainly not all good. (He has even described contemporary society as culturally hollow or 'decadent' (1983e: 129–136).) He also shows that the discontents of modernity can generate cultural backlash in the form of political and social protest movements (1973a; 1973b). Yet the most serious problematic about modernity's discontents is that they foster a vulnerability to totalitarianism – a political solution to the social-psychological yearning for 'home' (1973c: 89).

But Berger is not an incurable pessimist either. Modernity is not all bad. The revolution of sentimentality in the family, for example, is surely more desirable than the brutality of childhood in non-modern contexts (1974c: 179); the modern discovery of human dignity and human rights even in the face of the obsolescence of honor is hardly a development deserving denunciation (1973b: 95); anonymity may come with bureaucracy but so does a relative equality of treatment (another commendable feature of modernity); and urbanization is not only an agglomeration of modern social ills from crime to poverty and traffic congestion to pollution but it is also a symbol of hope and freedom for millions of people, particularly immigrants (1977c). The list could be extended but the point is made. For Berger, modernity is a mixture, both beneficial and problematic.

Berger's 'realism' about the modern situation suggests that the crisis of modernity is born out of a dialectic between the constraints of modern social structure and the ability of the individual to adapt to those conditions. If a crisis exists, it is not solely due to structural causes. At least in part it is also due to the individual's inability to adjust. This dialectical understanding is entirely compatible with the theoretical dialectic which informs the rest of his work. The significance of this, however, is that to place emphasis on one or the other implies different prescriptions for remedial action. When fault is found within the society, structural reform is called for; when it is found within the individual, individual reform is called for – the structures do not require change. If one were to consider his sociological writings alone, it would not be clear where he places emphasis. In places he presents a model of a strong social structure against a relatively passive individual; elsewhere of a 'confidence in the common sense of ordinary people and the resilience of human beings in all sorts of circumstances' (1983e: ix). Yet simply the fact that he operates out of a dialectic as opposed to a strict materialism is suggestive. It does not necessarily make his analytical perspective conservative but it does make it implicitly anti-radical and perhaps, given his reading of present political realities, anti-liberal as well.

The vocation of social criticism

Underlying all social criticism, though Berger's contribution in particular, are the questions, 'What does it mean to be a modern person?' and 'How do we make sense of modern life?' Such broad questions were central to the classical tradition of sociology. They have remained important to the discipline in the twentieth century, at least in certain quarters. In my opinion, they still have a legitimate if not central place in contemporary sociological discourse if the discipline is to remain of intellectual consequence.

By their very nature these questions require answers that are theoretical and interpretive. Yet if the answers are at all useful, they must also proceed with careful and constant reference to the empirical world they seek to explain and interpret. In the past century, the tendency among those writing in this genre has been to stray bit by bit away from an empiricist orientation. Berger, as I have mentioned, is not faultless on these grounds. In a discipline that is already hyper-quantitative, one should be reluctant to level this criticism. Indeed, to some this may be a source of relief – at least there is one area of sociological reasoning that has not submitted to monomaniacal empiricism. All the same the criticism is valid. Without submitting to the constraints of reliable data, the intellectual quest loses sight of its goal.

One of the perils of operating outside of these constraints is that social criticism can become an exercise in hyperbole if not social fiction. Provocative they may have been, but the reductions of culture to personality popular in the 1950s and 1960s were precisely that. Survey data of the period suggest that people were not nearly as alienated, isolated, morally vacuous or unhappy as we would be led to believe. The same could be said about the alleged loss of community promulgated by early community studies. Later research has shown that the breakdown in meaningful social relationships was not nearly as bad as we were led to believe. Some atomization did take place, naturally, but the most significant reality may have been the alternate strategies of community life assumed by people living in the modern city and suburbs. In principle any sweeping generalization will exaggerate, distort, and fictionalize empirical reality. Most of the writing in this genre has been given to precisely this sort of practice. Yet if this is so then it makes one wonder whether the modern malaise, however formulated, is not but a projection of the critic's own experience. Berger himself has maintained that intellectuals are the most vulnerable group of people to the 'discontents' of modern life (1976d). When social criticism is reduced to this kind of projection, it then becomes little more than an expression of impotence – the inability of the intellectual himself to cope with or to adapt to modern life. He himself is the hapless creature enduring the modern malaise. Surely this would account for some of the hysteria of contemporary social criticism.

The *de facto* posture of discounting careful methodology has been, in some cases, an excuse for doing careful research. Social criticism, it could be argued, has been too eager to pronounce an indictment without having seen all of the evidence. But if true, is it coincidental? Clearly the ideological interests of the critic could best be served by the appearance, as opposed to the substance, of scientific rigor. It is much easier to make ideological claims if one does not have to deal with facts that might contradict those claims. Given that radical and liberal analyses have been predominant between the 1940s and 1980s, they are the most liable to this criticism. In principle, however, intellectuals of any political orientation would be vulnerable to vulgar reductions of science to ideology without a balanced commitment to empirical rigor.

Yet not only are ideological interests served in this way but so is intellectual self-interest. Anyone who writes in this genre – anyone who attempts to answer these questions – implicitly claims a special perspective. They see what few others see; they know what few others know; and it is within their power (whether or not anyone takes them seriously) to pronounce the good and the bad about a people and their way of life. In this lies the audacity of the social critic. Yet it is very easy for one answering these questions to either be put into the position or to freely adopt the role of sage or guru. All too frequently in the 1960s and 1970s, social criticism yielded to this kind of self-aggrandizement.

While few would doubt Berger's intellectual audacity or his humanistic sensibilities, to his credit he has been fairly successful at disclaiming the prophetic mantle. As he put it in 1963, 'to think of my own writing as a "prophetic" activity [is a] thought that would be at the same time, blasphemous and asinine' (1963e). His commitment to the principles of falsification (not to mention his professional commitment to value-free sociology) has also constrained him from making explicit reductions of science to ideology. Finally, though to some extent Berger's work has been given to over-generalization, this commitment has made him far less vulnerable to the propensity to write social fiction than most others who have written in this genre. Perhaps he would have gone further toward developing an empirical sensitivity but then so could most. The least one can say is that his intellectual posture is appropriately oriented for the development of a useful social criticism.

In sum, one of Berger's achievements has been simply to take up anew the grand issue of individual existence in the modern world. In this he is not alone, of course, but Berger has been more successful than most. This is not only because of the ingenuity of his theoretical synthesis. It is also because *as a sociologist* he has maintained the priority of empirical accuracy over ideological program. To put it differently, what made classical analyses of the problem of modern life important was not the volume or pitch of their moral denunciations but the creative blending of interpretive insight with a realistic and empirically grounded understanding of their world. If Berger succeeds in illuminating the nature of contemporary existence, it is due to a similar commitment. Those who share this distinction with him in contemporary intellectual life are far fewer in number.

Excursus: The problem of freedom

Donald L. Redfoot

Peter Berger (1976c: 399) once lamented that the sociological world seemed to be divided into those who are 'intimately related to computers' and those who study 'the theories of dead Germans.' While he is neither dead nor German, this essay will fall into the latter category by relating Berger's works to those of Max Weber as they share the focal concern of the German humanistic tradition with the nature of reason and human freedom. The purpose is neither to praise nor to prematurely bury Berger. Rather, I share his concern that, if sociology is to overcome its current situation in which substantive significance is subordinate to statistical significance, it must renew the discussion of the 'big questions,' among which none is bigger than the nature of human freedom. In Berger's work, we find a rare example of a contemporary social theorist whose work addresses these vital questions.

Karl Jaspers (1963: 261) described Weber as 'the exemplar of a rational man for all who wish to be rational and free,' linking his ideas to eighteenth-century liberalism. This liberalism was originally expressed by the French Enlightenment *philosophes* who praised the individual freedom that was possible through the application of human reason. Immanuel Kant translated this concern with reason and freedom to the German world, giving it a more precise philosophical form (Levine, 1981). Kant (1949: 3ff, 63ff) argued that human action may be viewed as either an empirical problem for study or as a practical problem for action. As an empirical problem, human action is part of 'the world of sense,' subject to causal explanations like any other natural phenomenon. As a practical problem, however, human action is part of 'the world of understanding,' subject to moral laws of freedom. In the first case, the observer is interested in what 'is;' in the second case, in what 'ought to be.' Morality is the realization of freedom through the subjective reason of the autonomous will and the objective reason of the civil state (1965). Late in his life, Kant argued that history has an inherent teleology, the end of which is the perfection of reason and freedom within and among human societies (1963: 11–26). His 'universal history' is unilinear in its optimistic belief in the inevitable realization of freedom. This 'historicism' reached its most monumental proportions with Hegel (1967) who read human history as a series of dialectical moments in the realization of reason and freedom, culminating in the modern, Western state.

In post-revolutionary France, on the other hand, the focus on individual freedom soured as conservative, anti-Enlightenment thinkers dominated the intellectual debate, seeking models for social order in a 'rediscovery of medievalism' (Nisbet, 1966: 9ff). Among these conservative thinkers was Auguste Comte, whose utopian vision of positivism envisioned a new social order modelled after medieval society but based upon scientific reason. While rejecting the Enlightenment's focus on individual freedom, Comte retained its confidence in scientific reason as the basis for political action and social order.

While drawing from both the humanistic and positivistic traditions in establishing the foundations for modern sociology, Weber ultimately rejected both. He rejected the faith in history as the realization of freedom found in the German humanistic tradition with his characterization of modern rationality as an 'iron cage.' As Levine notes (1981: 9), 'far from viewing the advance of rationality as a prime source of freedom in the modern West, Weber frequently decried it as a serious threat to freedom.' In confronting this threat, Weber also rejected the prophetic role for science advocated by the positivists, insisting that sociology remain 'value-free.' To understand Weber's position on the modern threats to reason and freedom and Berger's contributions beyond Weber, we need to examine their respective discussions of these threats as they are translated into 1) empirical issues, 2) political issues, and 3) vocational issues for the social scientist.

Modern rationality and options as empirical issues

As categories of philosophical discourse, neither reason nor freedom is empirically available for scientific study. Accordingly, Weber focused on the empirical realities of rationality as a characteristic of action and rationalization as an historical process. Similarly, Berger (1981d: 98ff) suggests that we adopt the term 'options' instead of freedom as an empirical concept. So translated, much of the empirical work of Weber and Berger has concerned the relationship between modern rationalization and options for social action.

Weber argued repeatedly that ' "rationalism" may mean very different things' (1946: 293) at the subjective level of consciousness and at the objective level of social institutions. Of the types of rationality identified by Weber, the threats to freedom come primarily from one: the objectified, formal rationality of rules and regulations (Levine, 1981). The threats are largely found in two institutional spheres: 1) the bureaucratization of the state which 'restricts the importance of charisma and of individually differentiated conduct' (1968: 1156), and 2) 'the technical and economic conditions of machine production which today determine the lives of all the individuals who are born into this mechanism . . . with irresistible force' (1958: 181). The rationality embodied in both the state bureaucracy and in machine production conspires to limit the possibilities of individual choice. It would be inaccurate, however, to associate Weber with the various forms of faith in irrationalism that were fashionable in his day (Green, 1974). On the contrary, at the subjective level, Weber (1949: 124) insisted that '. . . we associate the highest measure of an empirical "feeling of freedom" with those actions which we are conscious of performing rationally . . .'

Though he is no less concerned about the potential threats to freedom from modern rationality, Berger presents a substantially different picture of the possible options for action. Berger and his associates (1973b; Luckmann, 1978) argue that technologization and bureaucratization have consequences at the micro-level that are more complex than Weber realized with his macro-historical focus. By removing work from the home, modernization has divided experience between public and private spheres. As these spheres were separated, the public sphere of technological production and bureaucratic management became increasingly rationalized while the private sphere relied increasingly on traditional and emotional bonds. Berger largely accepts Weber's analysis of the formal rationality of the technological and bureaucratic 'megastructures' of the public sphere. Individuals must conform to the formal demands of these megastructures since there is little room for 'individually differentiated conduct' on the production line or in dealing with the 'animated machine' of bureaucratic rules. Megastructures are typically experienced as alienating because they cannot bend to the demands of particular individuals (1977e). Concomitant with the growth of megastructures, however, has been a tremendous growth in options for private sphere life styles. If the public sphere stifles individual differentiation, the private sphere has seen an explosion of differentiation. Berger argues that the unstructured nature of private life in modern societies demands choices, creating an 'heretical imperative' (1979a: 16) where 'What previously was fate now becomes a set of choices. Or: Destiny is transformed into decision.'

In short, Weber and Berger come to very different conclusions in their analyses of the impact of rationalization on options for individual action. Weber painted an unrelentingly gloomy picture of growing bureaucratization and technologization that restrict 'the importance of charisma and individually differentiated behavior.' Berger, on the other hand, argues that modernity has created unprecedented options – particularly in the private sphere. He warns, however, that such an array of choices can be psychically destabilizing. He portrays the modern individual as a 'very nervous Prometheus' for whom the move from fate to choice is an ambivalent experience: 'On the one hand, it is a great liberation; on the other hand, it is anxiety, alienation, even terror (1979a: 22).' This 'anxiety, alienation, even terror' create their own threats to freedom which become more apparent through an examination of the politics of rationalization.

The politics of rationalization

Perhaps Weber's sharpest break with the optimism of the Enlightenment was on the nature of politics. Instead of viewing the state as the embodiment of reason as Kant and Hegel had, Weber emphasized its claims to 'the monopoly of the legitimate use of force' (1946: 78). His methodological writings stressed the meaning of social action, but these meanings are classified in terms of their 'legitimations' of material and ideal power interests. Politics is an arena of conflict among interest groups, the historical resolution of which is determined by the relative power of the institutional carriers of various legitimations and not by any metahistorical ideal of reason. There is an historical trend toward greater rationality because it is more effective in manipulating power (1946: 214–16, 230–44) – not because of the reasonableness of its legitimations. Power is increasingly concentrated in the bureaucratic state and technologized production because their efficiency gives them a competitive edge. Faced with these carriers of rationalization, Weber concluded that ' "individualists" and partisans of "democratic" institutions [are up] "against the stream" of material constellations;' the rationality embodied in state bureaucracies and mechanized production is producing 'a certified caste of mandarins' ruling over a new kind of 'benevolent feudalism.' Gloomily, he predicted a decline in individual freedom as 'everywhere the house is ready-made for a new kind of servitude' (1946: 71).

For Weber, the only hope for escape from the 'iron cage' of bureaucratic and technocratic domination lay in the emergence of an alternative power source. He saw this alternative in a strong leader who could claim charismatic authority. As a result, when he crossed the line from empirical analysis to political advocacy, Weber supports a 'leader democracy' (*Führer-Demokratie*). Claiming a charismatic mandate by way of the plebiscite, the strong leader is able to overcome formal rational domination (1968: 266ff; 1946: 105ff). As Mommsen points out, Weber's defense of democracy is a far cry from the classical defense that it reflects 'the will of the people,' embodying the progress of reason (1974: 86ff). Weber expressed no such faith in the will of the people, advocating democracy as the best means for producing charismatic leadership with which to challenge the 'mechanized petrification' (1958: 182) of rational domination.

The relationship between Weber's ideas and those of the Nazis who took power after his death has been much disputed (Turner and Factor, 1984). Some have unfairly saddled Weber with responsibility for events over which he could have no control. It is fair to say, however, that for Berger the idea of a strong charismatic leader ruling as a 'plebiscitary dictator' over the compliant masses is akin to a primordial nightmare, the horrible reality of which was a formative experience as he grew up in Nazi-dominated Vienna.

While he accepts Weber's analysis of the threats from bureaucratic and technocratic domination and the political need for an alternative power base, Berger's distaste for totalitarianism leads him to seek the base of this power outside of the state.

Berger also differs with Weber over the nature of meaning in human action. For Weber, meanings are of interest to his macro-historical studies primarily as they are attached to power interests as legitimations. There is little analysis in his works of the subjective experiences or social psychological consequences of types of meaning. By adding this subjective dimension Berger makes some of his most important contributions to Weber's analysis of social action. Based on Gehlen's theory (1963; 1980), Berger elevates meaning to the level of an anthropological need, filling the void of our biologically incomplete natures. The importance of this shift of focus can be illustrated by contrasting Weber's concept of 'legitimation' with Berger's concept, 'plausibility structure.' From a subjective perspective, the notion of legitimation is turned on its head. Meanings are not experienced simply as legitimations of objective power interests – rather, objective structures are important as they give plausibility to meanings that are a fundamental need of everyday life (1967c: 45). Berger urges a dialectical understanding of these levels of analysis – objective structures provide plausibility structures for subjective meanings at the same time that meanings provide legitimations for objective social structures (1966e).

Berger's political analysis may, therefore, be viewed as a search for structures that meet the needs for objective legitimacy and subjective plausibility as alternatives to totalitarianism. He locates an alternative in the division between public and private spheres, an alternative Weber overlooked because of his macro-historical focus. This division represents an implicit deal in the 'cognitive bargaining' of modernity that has served individuals rather well. In exchange for the rationalization of the public sphere with its attendant alienations is a vast amount of goods and services that only modernity can supply. Moreover, the surrender of the ability to engage in 'individually differentiated behavior' in the public sphere is compensated by time off when individuals have considerable control over their lives to pursue activities that are meaningful to them. This deal works, says Berger, because of the pivotal role played by 'mediating structures' such as families, neighborhoods, churches, and voluntary associations. These institutions mediate between megastructures and the individual, providing plausibility structures for the lives of individuals, on the one hand, and moral sustenance, on the other hand, to megastructures which would otherwise be experienced as hostile, alien forces without legitimacy.

Berger maintains that modernization has unleashed social dynamics that have weakened mediating structures and created anomie at both the objective and subjective levels – a situation which he sees as fraught with dangers. The threat to freedom from modern rationality comes not from the demise of individually differentiated conduct, as Weber feared, but from the undermining of mediating structures. Looming large on the horizon of this discussion of mediating structures is the threat of totalitarianism. With nothing between them and the state to provide meaning for their lives, anomic individuals turn to totalitarian political structures. Without moral legitimacy, democracy is endangered:

> Without institutionally reliable processes of mediation, the political order becomes detached from the values and realities of individual life. Deprived of its moral foundation, the political order is 'delegitimated.' When that happens, the political order must be secured by coercion rather than by consent. And when that happens, democracy disappears.
>
> The attractiveness of totalitarianism – whether instituted under left-wing or right-wing banners – is that it overcomes the dichotomy of private and public existence by imposing on life one comprensive order of meaning (1977e: 3).

The threat to mediating structures comes from three 'camps' any of which, if taken to an extreme, increases the possibility of totalitarianism (1983e). The first camp includes a disproportionate number of intellectuals who are committed to an ideology of individual liberation. They demand the recognition of 'the equality of all life styles' in law and policy. Freedom is seen as liberation from traditional mediating structures – especially family and the church – in order to increase the ranges of choice for individuals. Extremists in this camp demand the elimination of traditional structures which are seen as inherently oppressive. Moderate members are content with a broader range of options with some government help to mitigate the oppressive aspects of traditional mediating structures. The demands of feminist, gay rights, and other civil libertarian organizations indicate the agenda of this camp – an agenda that is highly modern in its secularity and support of individual rights. At its extreme, however, this position tends to become its opposite, leading to a relativism which is psychologically unbearable because of the human need for meaning. In contrast to Weber's association of subjective rationality with freedom, Berger fears that the 'hyper-rationalization' and 'hyper-individualization' of this position create strong pressures for authoritarian, counter-modernizing ideologies of right or left which are typically totalitarian:

> Individual freedom pushed to an extreme inevitably changes its initial quality. It becomes self-absorption once it is separated from the moral principles that initially both inspired and restrained it. It brings with it a sense of disorientation and loneliness. The individual in this condition comes to turn against the very ideal of freedom that first motivated him. Freedom itself becomes an oppression. In Erich Fromm's apt phrase, the individual now seeks an 'escape from freedom' and in consequence becomes ready for any new authority that promises him a feeling of belonging and stability. In other words, the individual becomes ready for totalitarian movements or ideologies, which 'repress' him far more effectively and comprehensively than any of the authorities he first encountered as oppressive (1983e: 178–79).

A second camp represents a 'new class,' a 'stratum in modern society deriving its livelihood from the production and distribution of symbolic knowledge rather than material goods' (1981d: 164). Because these people make their money by providing services and information, they have a vested interest in expanding these services. They disguise the vested nature of their interests with arguments about the alleged superiority of the professional services that they provide over the unprofessional practices provided by mediating structures. Programmatically, they argue for the expansion of government support for professional services in education, child care, health care, care for the elderly, care for the abused, and so on. These services not only supplant mediating structures, but are often provided by people who see mediating structures as irrelevant at best and as the direct enemy at worst.

Often the more moderate members of the critical camp are allied to this new class and its interest in expanding services. Desiring liberation from the responsibilities associated with private sphere relations, moderate members of the critical camp characteristically call for more services – calls the professional camp is only too happy to oblige. The functions and authority of mediating structures are progressively eroded while atomized individuals seek themselves, forming only temporary and shallow commitments to others. The specter of hyper-individualists seeking more government services so that they can maintain ever more desperate searches for self-liberation sets the stage for a kind of creeping totalitarianism. Worst of all, such an ethos is being transmitted in socialization patterns that no longer emphasize the virtues of strong, autonomous judgment, but instead self-centered, 'other-directed' personalities 'appropriate to a "welfare-bureaucratic" society' (1983e: 157; 169ff).

A third camp is a reactionary group that sees modernity itself as a threat. These people have an intense need for meaning and authority which they feel are lacking in modern society. This 'neo-traditional' camp is strongly anti-modern and anti-libertarian, counting as members both those from strong traditional backgrounds who are reasserting that tradition and converts from the other camps who cannot face the relativity that characterizes their position. These counter-modernizating backlashes may emerge under the banner of ideologies of the right or the left (1973b). Both are opposed to the formal rationality of the public sphere and the libertarianism of the private sphere. Indeed, the very split itself is rejected in favor of a world-unifying nomos of a totalistic ideology. In a traditional society, such a unity is taken for granted. In a society, however, which has tasted the fruits of modernity, a totalistic ideology must be coercively reimposed, ushering in some variant in revolutionary totalitarianism. If the material conditions of modernized societies strengthen the coalition of liberationists and new class professionals, leading toward a creeping totalitarianism, conditions in the Third World are more likely to lead in the direction of revolutionary totalitarianism (1974f). Like Weber,

Berger argues that the resolution of the conflicts among these camps has much less to do with reason than it does with the relative power each group is able to muster.

Not surprisingly, when Berger steps over the line from sociological description to moral advocacy, he argues for policies that will strengthen the mediating structures that are essential for freedom in the modern world. Appeals are made to each of the camps in an effort at 'capturing the middle ground' as a foundation for modern freedom. He calls on all sides to reaffirm the implicit deal of modernity. Modern technological production and the modern welfare state will provide the goods and services that we desire. At the same time, these alienating megastructures must respect and strengthen the mediating structures that provide both plausibility structures for the meanings of individual lives and the moral foundation upon which their own legitimacy rests. Freedom does not lie in adopting rationalistic, universalistic ethical imperatives as Kant urged, nor in being freed from commitments to mediating structures as individual liberationists have argued. Rather, freedom is found in the plurality of 'particularistic,' mediating structures available from which one may choose one's commitments (1977e: 43): 'Liberation is not escape from particularity but discovery of the particularity that fits.'

The problem of rationality as a vocational issue

The empirical and political analyses of modern rationalism presented by Weber and Berger raise important questions about the 'calling' of sociology for the individual practitioner. As Weber rhetorically asks (1946: 152–53), 'What shall we do, and, how shall we arrange our lives? . . . Which of the warring gods should we serve?' He paints a picture in which the charismatic leader appears to be the only hope of breaking through the 'iron cage' that seems to make the triumph of the 'specialists without spirit' (1958: 182) inevitable. But in answering his own rhetorical questions, he suggests that those who truly have the calling for science will not 'tarry for new prophets and saviors' but will 'set to work and meet the "demands of the day" in human relations as well as in our vocation.' He adds that 'This, however, is plain and simple, if each finds and obeys the demon who holds the fibers of his very life' (1946: 157).

Weber notwithstanding, finding and obeying demons is hardly a 'plain and simple' task, especially for highly rational scientists. To understand the full ramifications of this position, we must look once again at the division between science as the empirical exploration of what 'is' and morality as the espousal of what 'ought to be.' It is a matter of some curiosity that this position has been identified as 'positivistic,' especially by its detractors from the left (see Turner and Factor, 1984). Berger notes (1981d: 11–12) that the early positivists in sociology, especially Comte and Durkheim, advocated exactly the opposite. For them, science was the new authority for truth and for what 'ought to be,' replacing the earlier functions of religion.

In sharp contrast, Weber denounces such claims to moral authority by science as either self-serving attempts at 'academic prophecy' (1946: 155) or attempts by 'the complacent' to avoid the responsibility for their own decisions. Science can contribute to political debate by critically analyzing the options in terms of goals, the possibilities of achieving those goals, and the consequences of actions to achieve those goals. Each aspect of action is subjected to the most thoroughly rational analysis. But at the time of action, moral authority cannot come from science. The moral responsibility of an individual who has been through the 'disenchantment' of scientific rationalism is that each individual must bear the responsibility for the 'decisive choice' (1946: 152) among 'warring gods' – without the certainty provided by an 'ethic of ultimate ends.' There is a strong connection between the scientific position of 'value-neutrality' and the ethical position of an 'ethic of responsibility' (see Roth and Schluchter, 1979; Loewith, 1970) in Weber's conclusion that:

> The fruit of the tree of knowledge, which is distasteful to the complacent but is nonetheless, inescapable, consists in the insight that every single important activity and ultimately life as a whole, if it is not to be permitted to run on as an event in nature but is instead to be consciously guided, is a series of ultimate decisions through which the soul – as in Plato – chooses its own fate, i.e., the meaning of its activity and existence (1949: 18).

In this conclusion one hears a vague echo of Kant's Enlightenment commitment to reason, to a life that is 'consciously guided' and not simply an 'event in nature.' Levine argues (1981: 22–3) that Weber's heroic affirmation of the rational, autonomous individual indicates that he 'remained in some deep sense a child of the Enlightenment.' But he does so without Kant's identification of the reason of the individual with the ultimate reason of the social order and without optimism that such reason will lead to 'perpetual peace' and freedom. Indeed, Turner and Factor (1984) make a convincing case that Weber's insistence on the irrational grounds of all values, his endorsement of a 'decisionist' ethic in which the individual simply must choose between rationally irreconcilable options, and his hopes for a strong charismatic leader to break the power of rational domination show more influence from the nihilism of Nietzsche than from the rationalism of the Enlightenment.

Berger's ideas on the moral role of sociology have undergone considerable evolution in the emphasis made and the imagery used. In his earlier works (1961c; 1963c), society is portrayed as a comedy toward which the sociologist may adopt a detached, playful, even naughty, attitude – an attitude that shows more of the influence of Sartre (1956) than of the stoic, tragic position of Weber. Berger portrays a sociology as a liberator from the 'bad faith' of habit and the irrationality of social forces by raising them to consciousness. He celebrates (1963c: 175) the subjective liberation by sociology as a form of consciousness which is 'justified by the belief that it is better to be conscious than unconscious and that consciousness is a condition of freedom.' While it may make us feel initially like puppets dangling from social strings, sociology also provides the realization that:

> Unlike the puppets, we have the possibility of stopping in our movements, looking up and perceiving the machinery by which we have been moved. In this act lies the first step towards freedom. And in this same act we find the conclusive justification of sociology as a humanistic discipline (1963c: 176).

The evolution in Berger's thinking since he wrote these words might be illustrated by contrasting the playful Pinnocchio song 'I Got No Strings' to the somber Protestant hymn 'Blessed Be the Tie That Binds.' In contrast to the earlier celebration of sociology as liberator, Berger admonishes that 'It is all the more important to see the *limits* of such liberation' (1981d: 110, his emphasis). These limits are reached when they come up against the anthropological needs for meaning and order. He worries that the debunking motifs of sociology have a nihilistic tendency where 'sociology itself might be seen as a contributor to decadence and social disintegration – the diagnosis that is itself part of the disease' (1981d: 161). To recognize that the social order is socially constructed may, indeed, be psychically liberating. But a world in which everything was a matter of choice would not be a state of liberation but a state of chaos. In contrast to the playful naughtiness that characterized his earlier work, Berger urges a 'specific form of humility' that recognizes that:

> In the end, every society can be seen as a precariously put together fabric of meanings by which human beings seek to find guidance for their lives, to be consoled and inspired, in the face of finitude and death. It is only one short step from this vision to the explicitly moral judgment that all human meanings of this kind have great value and should not be lightly discarded (1981d: 74).

Berger's call for 'a militant commitment to reason' (1977e: xix) is not, therefore, a call for a renewed commitment to the utopian visions of sociology inspired by the Enlightenment's optimistic faith in reason. Politically, such faith often implies 'a totalistic conception of science' (1981d: 102–105) where a 'cognitive elite' rules in the name of reason, a faith shared by Comte's positivism and Marx's revolutionary socialism. Berger also criticizes reformist variants of this positivistic theme that ally sociology with this or that social agenda in the name of liberation (1981d: 114–20). Sociologists should be wary of the unintended totalitarian possibilities of such liberations and humble in pronouncing their opinions on 'what is to be done.'

If Berger rejects these optimistic visions of sociology as a promoter of freedom, he also rejects the profound pessimism that is found in Weber's work for two reasons. In the first place, Weber's pessimism is due, in large part, to the fact that his political analyses leave freedom with no institutional base and little psychic support. Freedom's scant hope rests on the precarious base of support by heroic individuals who struggle against the psychic costs of relativity and the material constellations of modernity. Berger, on the other hand, argues that the autonomy of individuals as well as the legitimacy of democratic political structures rests upon institutions that, while under attack, are not inevitably destined to disappear. His support of the particularity of mediating structures is a far cry from Kant's optimism over human reason as a universal principle governing the affairs of individuals and nations. But Berger remains guardedly optimistic that, as a vital fulcrum in maintaining freedom in the modern world, mediating structures have substantial support because they address some deeply rooted needs for order and meaning in life.

Berger also remains more optimistic in a second way by out-relativizing Weber's theory of modernity. As noted earlier, Weber contributed a great deal toward understanding the historical relativity of modern rationality, undermining the faith in modernity as the realization of reason and freedom. Weber may not see modern rationality as the end of history, but his images of an 'iron cage' seem to leave him 'no exit.' In contrast, Berger sees no reason to view modernity as anything more than 'one moment in the historical movement of consciousness.' He calls for a relativizing of modern relativity, a relativity where sociology represents both an extreme point and a possible way out:

> Modern consciousness . . . has a powerfully relativizing effect on all worldviews . . . An empirical understanding of the situation making for this cannot deliver anyone from the vertigo of relativity. It may even, for a while, increase the vertigo. Yet it also points to a way out – by relativizing the relativizing processes. But modernity itself is a relative phenomenon; it is one moment in the historical movement of human consciousness – not its pinnacle, its culmination or its end (1979a: 10).

The differences between Weber and Berger on this point lead to subtle but important differences in their understandings of an 'ethics of responsibility' for social scientists. Weber argued that the 'value freedom' of the sociologist leads to a highly relativized view of ethics in which the individual is faced with the 'warring gods' of various ethical positions. The ethical position for the individual is to confront this relativity head on and to bear the responsibility of the 'decisive choice' among ethical possibilities. This is a responsibility that many cannot bear because the full weight of the relativity of such decisions must be borne by the individual. Weber sarcastically invites those 'who cannot bear the fate of the times like a man' to make the 'intellectual sacrifice' and return to the 'arms of the old churches' (1946: 155).

Berger also notes the intimate relationship between value freedom as the cognitive position of the sociologist and ethical relativity as a moral position (1981d: Chapter 3). Intellectual honesty requires the sociologist to confront directly the problem of relativity – even the relativity of his own relativism. But Berger is betting that the 'will to believe' is stronger than the 'will to power.' Ethical responsibility, therefore, leads to a more benign view of those who decline to make a decisive choice in heroic struggle with 'warring gods.' Given his theoretical emphasis on the powerful need for meaning, the implication is that the fewer who are troubled by the woes of relativism the better, since relativism on a mass scale sows the seeds of totalitarianism. Berger urges the sociologist to 'think daringly but act prudently,' to recognize the 'social limits to freedom – the very limits that, in turn, provide the social space for any empirically viable expression of freedom' (1977b: xvii–xviii). More affirmatively, he urges support for the particularism of mediating structures and issues 'a call for authority in the Christian community' (1977b: 182ff; 1976a) as a way to transcend the dangerous moral and cognitive relativism of modernity.

Prometheus bound?

The ways in which Berger has built upon the Weberian legacy of a humanistic sociology must be evaluated separately for the empirical, the political, and the moral implications. By adding the subjective dimension through Schutz's phenomenology, Berger has enriched empirical studies of the peculiarities of the modern experiences of self and social world. Just as important have been his insights into the role that institutions play as plausibility structures for those experiences. His analysis of the bifurcation of modern experiences into private and public spheres adds to Weber's theory of rationalization an understanding of the psychological consequences of increasing choice and an appreciation for the mediating structures that make the attendant uncertainty bearable.

There is more reason to question, however, the empirical basis of the argument that ties this uncertainty to totalitarian political solutions. Relying on Gehlen to argue that humans have an anthropologically constant need for meaning, there is a tendency to overlook the empirical variability in the amount of certainty needed. It is not clear to what extent most people can live with modern uncertainty and doubt and under what conditions. Thus, while Berger adds important dimensions to our understanding of the social-psychological appeal of totalistic ideologies of various stripes, the actual political impact of these ideologies is open to dispute. One can point to small groups of disaffected individuals who have joined various religious cults and revolutionary terrorist groups but this is not unique to modern societies. The Flagellators of the fourteenth century who ran around naked, beating each other and burning Jews, certainly represented a fanaticism and a threat to the public order that was far greater than a few Hare Krishnas in the airports.

Indeed, there has as yet been no example of a modernized society in which the libertarian critics have established a totalitarian system to fill the void of meaning in their lives. There is, however, no empirical example of a coalition of this camp and the bureaucratized professionals establishing totalitarian control through a gradual process of usurping power over all aspects of private life. The welfare states of the modern West hardly resemble totalitarian states. Indeed, one might note that 'individually differentiated conduct' and 'democratic institutions' are most protected in these welfare states. There have been, of course, revolutionary movements of backlash against modernity, especially in the Third World. Such movements should suggest strategic caution to those advocating agendas for modernization – with particular attention to the social and economic factors that give rise to counter-modern revolutions. The ranks of these revolutionary movements, however, have not been made up primarily of critics and bureaucrats who could not stand their own relativity.

Differences on the dangers of choice have been reflected in discussions of the mediating structures idea from the beginning, resulting in what might be termed left and right revisionist versions. Both versions are united in their distrust of bureaucratic professional control of services. The leftist version, a spin-off of the critical camp, wants to see government support opened to a wider variety of mediating structures. This group is committed to expanding the areas of choice available to the individual and is prepared to live with the pluralism and uncertainty that results. The rightist version, a spin-off of the neo-traditionalist camp, sees choice and the moral uncertainty that it brings as a danger. This camp wants to get the modernizing, secularizing arm of government out of the provision of services so that traditional mediating structures can be revived. These two groups have sometimes been united in coalition as when, for example, the Congress of Racial Equality joined forces with Christian academies to support vouchers for a privatized education system. More often than not, however, these groups are at odds over issues such as day care, abortion rights, gay rights, and other issues that affect mediating structures.

In this dispute, Berger appears to have come down solidly on the rightist side. As junior author with Brigitte Berger in a recently published major statement on mediating structures and policy, he defends the bourgeois family – 'father, mother, child' (mother at home) – as necessary to democracy (1983e: 178) and, therefore, worthy of government support. Feminists (the demons of this book) may choose alternative life-styles but 'they should not expect public policy to underwrite and subsidize their life plans' (1983e: 205). Critics from other camps are, moreover, unlikely to be convinced by the implication that gay rights and day care centers are the first steps toward the Gulag.

A final controversy concerns the ethical responsibility of the sociologist. Berger argues for humility on the part of sociologists acting as advocates and rejects the notion that they should be part of a cognitive elite which rules by virtue of superior knowledge. Certainly, sociologists have more than enough to be humble about, but is there not a different kind of elitism in the implication that only a few can stand the psychic turmoil into which the relativizing consciousness of sociology leads? One can appreciate a measure of sensitivity to the psychic instability of the freshmen who enter the classroom after leaving home for the first time, but some of Berger's statements seem to go further. Whereas Weber's ethical ideal is the individual who has tasted 'the fruit of the tree of knowledge' and takes responsibility for the decisive choice of action, Berger's recent writings seem to echo the ethical (though not the political) elitism of Dostoevsky's 'Grand Inquisitor' who argued (1952: 129–30) that, 'Without a stable conception of the object of life, man would not consent to go on living . . . [M]an prefers peace, and even death, to freedom of choice in the knowledge of good and evil.' One suspects that Weber would have been willing to argue not only that 'Fundamental doubt is the father of knowledge' (1949: 7) but that it is the 'mother of morality' as well. In short, the threat to freedom comes not from the relativized consciousness of the 'nervous Prometheus' but from the jealous gods who would chain him to the rock of certainty.

The Enlightenment theme of the relationship between reason and freedom continues to demand the attention of each succeeding generation which would not permit life 'to run on as an event in nature but is instead to be consciously guided.' Berger's call for 'a militant commitment to reason' is all the more necessary the more isolated and anachronistic it sounds. One does not have to accept his variant of a Christian theology or his particular political agenda to note, as Durkheim had insisted (1951: 386ff), that freedom does not rest on the shoulders of rationalized, relativized individuals alone but on the constellations of institutions that grant moral authority to the objective structures of a society, on the one hand, and that socialize succeeding generations to bear the responsibility for moral reason and freedom, on the other. An ethic of responsibility demands that we evaluate institutional arrangements as they promote or detract from the moral authority that gives birth to freedom. It also demands that sociologists lift their heads occasionally from their computer print-outs to address the larger issues that gave birth to the discipline. In maintaining the dialog of the humanistic tradition of sociology, Berger has expanded our understanding of the nature of human freedom and of the possibilities for preserving this precious legacy.

PART III

Religion

CHAPTER 5

Religion as sacred canopy

Robert Wuthnow

The task of this chapter is to reconsider the theoretical and empirical adequacy of Peter Berger's formulation of religion as 'sacred canopy.' The relation of this chapter to the overall purpose of the present volume consists of re-examining Berger's approach to religion in light of the task of an interpretive sociology. Has he raised questions about religion which transcend the usual bounds of positivist sociology? And does he 'make sense' of religion in a way that provides a critical perspective on modern times?

At the outset it needs to be stated that Berger's formulation of religion as sacred canopy has been widely used in the social sciences. As with his other work, writers have often drawn on his treatment of religion for conceptual purposes and as a kind of philosophical justification for the study of religion. Perhaps more than in other areas, his work on religion seems to have provided an interpretive sociology that writers and students alike have found challenging. Yet Berger's formulation of religion is not intended simply as a metatheoretical perspective with no empirical base and no empirically testable hypotheses. Its validity as an interpretive framework in many ways hinges on the empirical claims it makes. Thus, to an important degree, an assessment of Berger's approach to religion requires an evaluation of its empirical claims as much or more than of its broader perspective.

A great number of studies have been done in the sociology of religion during the past two decades since *The Sacred Canopy* was written. Often stimulated by Berger's own work, contributions have appeared in relevant areas of inquiry, including cultural anthropology, sociology of knowledge, sociolinguistics, and textual analysis. Some of these contributions have drawn sympathetically from Berger's work, thus casting it in ways that further illuminate the significance of its original insights. Other contributions have provided empirical evidence which buttresses some of

Berger's theoretical claims. Still other work has raised questions about biases or limitations in the Bergerian perspective which at least need to be understood. In addition, the corpus of Berger's own work has grown enormously over the past two decades, providing new angles from which to interpret his basic perspective on religion, while at the same time increasing the frustration which the beginner student is likely to feel in attempting to grasp the core ideas underlying this perspective. For all of these reasons, the time seems ripe for a review and evaluation of Berger's discussion of religion as sacred canopy.

There is, as well, another important reason for reconsidering Berger's concept of religion. In an ironic sense perhaps, this concept remains to be fully appreciated in the social science literature. Despite its wide familiarity, the idea of religion as sacred canopy seems not to have been grasped in more than a superficial way in much of the literature. Empirical studies often refer to it almost in ceremonial obeisance while failing to incorporate it into the research design in any meaningful way. And theoretical discussions often praise it for philosophical grandeur without providing any firm guidelines for empirical testing. The result is that much of the broader significance of the original contribution has been missed. Religion tends to be understood in ways narrower than Berger would have had us recognize, while behaviorist and reductionist conceptions of the individual which discount the importance of religion continue to hold sway in many of the funding agencies and major journals. As in other areas which Berger has addressed, the study of religion stands to gain both in theoretical breadth and in humanistic depth by looking anew at his insights.

Core arguments

It is inevitably a matter of oversimplification to take the rich prose in which Berger's formulations are phrased and reduce them to basic assertions. Berger is a highly skilled theorist who knows how to present a compelling example but also how to provide the necessary caveats and qualifications for his arguments. To make matters more difficult, Berger's formulations flow from a rich web of theoretical deduction which takes many of its own predecessors for granted and has been spelled out at length in three or four of his more basic book-length treatises. At the risk of oversimplification, then, it seems necessary to attempt a brief summarization of the core arguments which, at the bare minimum, must be grasped in order to understand Berger's view of religion.

The first of these is that reality is socially constructed. Like most other sociological theoreticians, Berger holds that the world we live in is essentially a world of our own design. This is not a way of acknowledging the simple fact that we live among people as well as things, that we choose our own associates, or that even much of the material world is now the product of human construction. It is rather a more fundamental insight about how we perceive reality.

According to Berger, there is a selective process at work in the reality we experience. In brute form the actual world is infinitely complex, even chaotic, making it much too rich to experience meaningfully without some filtering process. That process involves the use of symbolic categories. The words we know, the pictures and mental images we share, all help to reduce the raw world to a 'reality' that has order and meaning.

The profound extent to which our experience is shaped by symbolism has been amply demonstrated by empirical research. Studies comparing different languages, for example, suggest that some languages are better than others at sensitizing us to certain kinds of experience. Some Native American languages fail to distinguish clearly between past, present, and future verb tenses and thus make the linear progression of history difficult to experience. With more than twenty words in the Eskimo language to describe 'snow,' some observers suggest that Eskimos actually experience snow in a richer and more variegated form than most non-Eskimos. Along similar lines, physiologists believe that the human eye is capable of distinguishing among more than 6 million hues of color; yet, because we typically use only about a dozen words to describe colors, we apparently see them much less richly than we are capable of doing (Farb, 1973). The role of words and symbols has also been emphasized by child psychologists. The reason children require a number of years to develop mastery of certain basic concepts, according to some child psychologists, is not that they are slow in learning the words – they actually know the words quite early – but that they have to start *experiencing* the world in a new, more simplified way that corresponds with the classifications suggested by these words (Bruner, *et al.*, 1966). The conclusion suggested by all of these studies is that the very world we experience is shaped by symbols. We tend to experience what we have symbols for; the remainder is filtered out of perception.

Recognizing the importance of symbolism – words, utterances, ritual, language, culture – is obviously an important building block in the edifice on which Berger constructs his arguments about religion. He rejects Marxist, behaviorist, and instinct theories which reduce human processes to sheer economic or physiological needs. For Berger, the symbolic realm is both prior to and constitutive of our very experience of the world.

A second core argument is that everyday reality is paramount. If reality is socially constructed rather than simply being 'there,' then we must ask, What kind of reality do people construct? Do we create worlds that are purely idiosyncratic to ourselves as individuals or do we construct reality according to some common principles that make communication, and hence social life, possible? The answer Berger gives is an integral feature of his argument about religion. His answer, derived partly from the writings of German phenomenologist Alfred Schutz, is that we construct a mutually shared world that can be termed 'everyday reality.'

Everyday reality is constructed according to several distinct principles. First, primacy is given to the 'here and now.' That which intuitively seems most real to us consists of those things closest to us in time and space – our immediate family and friends obviously seem more 'real' than persons in distant Tibet, and our immediate activities consume our attention in a way that memories of our childhood do not. Second, this here and now world is usually defined in terms of standard time and space. Time is linear, progressive, historical, inescapable, irreversible; space is three-dimensional, measurable in distances. We cannot in everyday reality have 'flashbacks,' escape our bodies, or occupy two places at the same time. To do any of these things requires adopting a different mental framework (such as fantasy or daydreaming).

Third, everyday reality tends to be a highly pragmatic world. It is the world of work, where things have to get done – the 'real world,' as we call it. Objects and persons in everyday reality tend to be evaluated instrumentally, in terms of 'utilities' for accomplishing our tasks. Closely related, as a fourth characteristic, is what Berger calls 'wide-awakeness.' Everyday reality commands our full attention – not to the exclusion of boredom and daydreaming, but as a matter of basic existential involvement – because it is the world in which we live and die, the world of real time where our purposes have to be accomplished.

Fifth, we 'willingly suspend doubt' in everyday reality. Haunting suspicions that things may not be what they seem are pushed from the forefront of our minds so that full attention can be given to the tasks at hand. Finally, everyday reality is compartmentalized into 'spheres of relevance.' That is, we define certain aspects of our daily world as being relevant to the accomplishment of a specific task (say, driving a car), and other aspects as being relevant to different activities. This compartmentalization reduces the inevitable complexity of the world by 'bracketing out' everything that is presently irrelevant. Thus the pragmatic objectives of everyday reality can be more effectively fulfilled.

Together, these features of everyday reality make it a highly efficient world in which to live. It is a routine world, an orderly world, in which things have their place. Deeper questions, longer-range goals, memories of the past, fundamental values, ambiguity and complexity – are all minimized relative to the pragmatic considerations that govern us in the here and now. It is also a safe, secure world in which we know our place and can largely take for granted the objects and persons in our immediate environment. Furthermore it facilitates social interaction: since time and space are standardized, we know what to expect; and since the norms governing this world make for familiarity and routine, we can interact with others on a common basis.

Some of Berger's characterizations of everyday reality can be questioned, of course. For example, it might be asked whether 'everyday reality' in ancient India was constructed according to these principles as much as everyday reality in the contemporary West. Even in the contemporary West, it might be asked whether the high degree of emphasis given to long-range planning is fully compatible with Berger's description of everyday reality in a world of the here and now. Nevertheless, the idea of everyday reality seems to have enough intuitive appeal to at least support Berger's use of it as a starting point for further theoretical considerations. Certainly the world of work, as most of us know it, tends to encompass a great deal of our waking hours, absorbs much of our immediate attention, and imposes a kind of pragmatic calculus on much that we do. It is for these reasons that Berger considers it the 'paramount reality' – the world in which we spend most of our time and to which we must inevitably return after brief excursions into the alternative realities of fantasy, sleep, or philosophical reflection.

A third major argument Berger makes is that 'symbolic universes' supply broader meaning. Although we live mostly in everyday reality, Berger is quick to point out the limitations of this reality. We need periodic escapes from the here and now; questions about longer-range values need some way of informing our day-to-day activities; pragmatic interests give way at least on occasion to concerns about basic truths, aesthetics, and human relationships; the 'wide-awakeness' of our existential world is persistently haunted by the prospect of our own death; experiences of grief – or of ecstasy – shatter the willing suspension of our doubts and raise questions about the deeper meanings of life; and the compartmentalized spheres of relevance in which we perform our tasks require some means of broader integration if we are to function as whole persons. In short, Berger posits a requirement for meaning that goes beyond the confines of everyday reality.

Following Weber, Berger recognizes that some of the lingering experiences of human existence on the face of it 'make no sense.' Innocent suffering, tragedies, injustices inevitably raise 'why' questions. When these events are experienced personally, Berger argues, they seem to occur on the fringes of everyday reality, thus forcing individuals to reckon with broader questions about the legitimacy of that reality. The same can be said, albeit in a positive way, about experiences of play, beauty, or ecstasy which open up vistas of reality that seem to transcend daily life.

Berger also perceives a requirement for meaning which integrates the separate spheres of relevance in everyday life. Implicit in his approach is the assumption that meanings are contextually determined. Thus, the meaning of any specific activity (say, cooking dinner) is given by the broader sphere of relevance in which it occurs (e.g. being a parent). But these spheres of relevance, in turn, have meaning only in relation to some broader context; and they, in still broader contexts, etc. The solution, as Berger sees it, is to posit a kind of hierarchical series of symbols which give meaning and integration to ever-widening segments of life. Within this logic, questions about 'the meaning of life' itself represent the broadest type of symbolic integration.

Berger uses the term 'symbolic universe' to refer to symbols or symbol systems that are concerned with providing meaning to reality in the most encompassing sense: 'These are bodies of theoretical tradition that integrate different provinces of meaning and encompass the institutional order in a symbolic totality' (1966e: 95). They differ from explanations, maxims, proverbs, propositions, and theories, all of which pertain to more limited spheres of reality. Symbolic universes thus occupy a prominent place in Berger's overall conceptual framework: they provide integration and legitimation at the highest level, which in turn is necessitated by the limited character of everyday reality.

Following from this is a fourth argument, namely, that religion is a type of symbolic universe. The necessity for some overarching symbol system can be fulfilled in a variety of ways – through personal philosophies of life, scientific world-views, secular philosophies such as Marxism or nihilism, or commonsensical ideas about luck and fate. Religion is also a type of symbolic universe. Berger defines it as 'the establishment, through human activity, of an all-embracing sacred order, that is, of a sacred cosmos that will be capable of maintaining itself in the ever-present face of chaos' (1967c: 51). Elsewhere he elaborates by pointing out that religions provide legitimation and meaning in a distinctly 'sacred' mode, that they offer claims about the nature of ultimate reality 'as such,' about the location of the human condition in relation to the cosmos itself.

Seeing religion in Berger's larger theoretical schema as a type of symbolic universe helps to illuminate its typical functions. Religious teachings characteristically serve to shelter the individual from 'chaos' – from a reality that seems to make no sense – by providing explanations for suffering, death, tragedy, and injustice. They integrate the individual's biography by providing an overarching frame of reference that applies to all of life, that locates the individual ultimately in space and time, that specifies an ultimate purpose for the individual's life, and thus permits daily activities to be organized around the fulfillment of this purpose. In addition to religious teachings, religious rituals provide mechanisms for containing the potentially disruptive experiences of mourning, on the one hand, or of transcendent joy, on the other. Funerals, weddings, and other religiously orchestrated rites of passage therefore maintain the stability of everyday life by providing occasions on which the non-ordinary can be experienced. And for society at large, religion legitimates institutionalized life by relating its existence to the 'nature of things,' to the gods. As Berger writes, 'Religion legitimates social institutions by bestowing upon them an ultimately valid ontological status, that is, by *locating* them within a sacred and cosmic frame of reference' (1967c: 33).

In his definition of religion Berger stresses that religion is established 'through human activity.' This assertion is not meant to imply that religion is either false or ultimately nothing more than the fabrication of human minds – indeed, Berger argues in other of his writings that the transcendent seems to break through humanly constructed worlds, as it were, from the outside. However, the social scientist must recognize the degree to which religion, like all symbol systems, involves human activity. Religion is a reality that inevitably draws on cultural materials, that is filtered through the symbolically constructed reality of personal experience. Moreover, it is maintained through the social interaction of individuals. Thus, despite the fact that Berger gives prominence to religious symbolism, he also recognizes the importance of churches, worship services, and religious communities for the perpetuation of any religious system.

In *The Sacred Canopy* Berger articulates the relation between religious symbolism and social interaction by suggesting a kind of dialectic interplay between the two. Starting with a hypothetical individual who experiences a requirement for some form of all-embracing meaning, Berger imagines the emergence of a religious symbol system as a result of this individual interacting with others in similar circumstances. This phase of the dialectic he terms 'externalization.' Next, the emergent symbol system becomes 'objectified;' that is, through further interaction it ceases to be the creation of any single individual but rather becomes something 'out there' which may even be codified in formal creeds and sacred writings. Finally, this reality is 'internalized,' becoming once again part of the individual's subjective identity.

To speak of religion in dialectical terms is done only for analytic convenience, of course. No assumptions are necessary about the actual origins of religion for the dialectic to be useful. What it highlights is simply that religion can be viewed from several different angles: as discourse and practice through which the individual expresses religious convictions (externalization), as a formalized cultural system or sub-system (objectification), and as the beliefs, sentiments, and experiences of the individual (internalization).

Berger does, however, introduce one additional concept in his discussion of the dialectic that must not be neglected. That is his idea of 'plausibility structures.' Any religious system remains plausible only as people articulate it in their conversation and dramatize it in their social interaction. The conversation and interaction that maintains religion, then, becomes its plausibility structure. For many, participation in religious institutions such as churches or synagogues serves as the plausibility structure for their religion. Kinship, friendship networks, and local communities may also serve the same purpose.

Some empirical evidence

Of the numerous empirical claims on which Berger's theory of religion rests, perhaps the most crucial is his assumption that people seek broader forms of meaning than those supplied strictly by everyday reality. Only if people register concern for questions about the meaning of life, the causes of suffering, and so forth, does it make sense to emphasize the role of symbolic universes of any kind, let alone religious examples. Put differently, religious beliefs may be empirically evident, but unless a more universal quest for overarching meaning exists Berger's approach may be the wrong way of going about understanding these beliefs.

There is in the social sciences a rather well-established tradition that disputes the idea – as a theoretical proposition – of some intrinsic requirement for an all-embracing conception of meaning. According to this view, personal meaning does not somehow depend on the individual being more than a 'sum of the parts,' but results exclusively from the discrete roles an individual performs. Thus, well-being could be said to derive simply from the sum of responsibilities performed in everyday life, quite apart from broader questions about the purpose of one's life. In a highly secularized society this argument naturally seems compelling.

Nevertheless, much empirical evidence has been amassed over the past decade which supports Berger's contention that people are concerned with broader issues of meaning and purpose. A cross-sectional survey of adults in the San Francisco Bay Area in the early 1970s (in which only 30 per cent at the time listed themselves as being church members) showed, for example, that 70 per cent claimed to think a lot or to some extent about the question of what the purpose of life is; 73 per cent said they thought about the existence of God; and 83 per cent indicated thinking about why there is suffering in the world. Fewer than one in twenty claimed to have never thought about these questions and to have dismissed them as unimportant (Wuthnow, 1976).

In-depth interviews with people in the Bay Area study also demonstrated a high degree of willingness to discuss broad questions of meaning and purpose in life. A 39-year-old public relations worker remarked, for example, 'The meaning of my life is to remember that there are goals that everyone should set and goals that give meaning to everything else you do.' A 42-year-old social worker responded, 'The purpose of life is to be in tune with all the forces and causes in the universe.' In a similar vein, a 27-year-old secretary commented, 'I think there is harmony in the universe and this harmony gives me meaning.' Using more traditionally religious language, another respondent volunteered, 'We are like co-workers with God to help his will be done; so when we help people to know God, it gives our lives meaning and purpose.'

None of this is to suggest the *unimportance* of everyday reality as a source of meaning. On the contrary, most people seem to think immediately of daily activities as sources of meaning. For example, a 28-year-old mother in the Bay Area, like many other respondents, pointed to 'my family and my children primarily, and my career.' Another respondent answered, 'My child, my friends, my hobbies, and mostly my work; they give me a sense of achievement.' More quantitatively, the same results were evident in a 1982 Gallup survey which asked people to say how important various things were to their 'basic sense of worth as a person.' Heading the list was 'family' (93 per cent listed it as 'very important'), followed by 'close friends' (63 per cent), 'financial well-being' (57 per cent), and 'work' (54 per cent).

Despite the high importance attached to everyday activities, however, most persons continue to reflect, as Berger suggests, on more cosmic questions. Another 1982 Gallup survey, for example, showed that 90 per cent of the public claimed to have thought about 'living a worthwhile life' at least a fair amount during the preceding two years; 83 per cent said they had thought this often about their 'basic values in life'; 81 per cent gave the same response for 'your relation to God;' and 70 per cent gave similar answers for 'developing your faith.' The same study found that eight out of ten people believe that 'everything that happens has a purpose' – seemingly in vindication of Berger's claim about people wanting to shield themselves from chaos by imputing order to the universe. And on a question directly related to Berger's idea that discrete spheres of relevance in everyday reality need to be integrated by some broader framework, respondents were asked, following a set of items dealing with family, friends, work, etc., as sources of meaning, if they 'try to keep all these areas separate or tie them all together?' Seventy-one per cent said they tie them all together.

Another aspect of Berger's discussion that has been directly affirmed by empirical research is his idea that experiences at the margins of everyday reality tend to be an important source of reflection about broader questions of meaning and purpose. In the study just cited, respondents were asked first to indicate which among a list of such experiences they had ever had and then whether or not each experience had affected their thoughts about the meaning and purpose of life a great deal. Generally speaking, those who had had each experience were also prone to say it had deeply affected their thoughts about the meaning and purpose of life. For example, of those who had ever had a deep religious experience, 83 per cent said it had affected their thoughts about meaning and purpose a great deal; the corresponding proportion for those who had experienced having a child was 75 per cent; and for those having experienced the death of a close relative or friend, 64 per cent.

Other research has explored the question of whether the actual *content* of different sacred canopies tends to be important. Berger's own discussion suggests that overtly religious symbolic universes and more secular symbolic universes may perform much the same functions and thus may compete with one another for adherents. He also suggests that in a pluralistic culture elements of several different symbolic universes may be combined to form an individual's world-view. Several studies have sought to address these claims.

The Bay Area study mentioned previously gave respondents opportunities to apply different symbolic frameworks to broad questions such as how they understood the forces shaping their own life or how they explained the presence of suffering in the world. The results demonstrated a relatively high degree of pluralism among the responses. Most respondents were prone to perceive multiple influences and causes, ranging from supernatural intervention, to social and cultural forces, to the functioning of heredity and will-power, to economic conditions and luck. Several factor analyses of the responses revealed some clustering around religious, social, and individualistic ideas, but the results also suggested a high degree of 'mixing' among different thematic traditions. About half of the respondents could be classified according to the thematic tradition on which they drew most heavily, but the remainder were genuinely eclectic, drawing equally from several traditions for their understandings.

Another study, also conducted in the San Francisco area, demonstrated that symbolic universes tend not to be applied with high degrees of consistency to different types of questions. On average, about half of the responses given to such questions as why racial differences exist, why someone might be killed in an airplane crash or die young, and why suffering in general exists were consistent with one another; the remaining half drew from different thematic traditions (Apostle, *et al.*, 1983: 207).

Thus the evidence tends to support the idea that in a pluralistic culture individuals are likely to draw on several different symbolic universes to cope with broad questions of meaning and purpose. Some evidence also suggests that eclecticism may be prominent even in less pluralistic settings. A national study of commune members, for example, showed that many individuals in these settings held assumptions which differed from the official ideologies of their communes (Aidala, 1984).

The fact that individuals do not draw consistently from a single symbolic universe in constructing their personal world views has been taken, on occasion, as evidence of the non-existence of symbolic universes (for example, Bainbridge and Stark, 1981). This criticism, however, mistakenly confuses consistency with coherence. Berger's point is not that symbolic universes impose substantive consistency on a person's attitudes; only that symbolic universes lend coherence to the reality they experience by linking it together and giving it overarching meaning (cf: Smith, 1979; Wuthnow, 1981).

Research has also explored the question of whether the content of different symbolic universes tends to predict differences in more specific attitudes or life-style attributes. The Bay Area study which asked questions about personal meaning, for example, suggested that the content of different meaning systems was a good predictor of propensities to become involved in or to abstain from various social reform activities and alternative life-styles. Persons whose symbolic universes emphasized the role of supernatural forces tended to disbelieve that society could be reformed through human action and refrained from experimenting personally with alternative life-styles. Those who thought the world's problems were mainly the fault of individuals (that is, blamed the victims) were also reluctant to favor social reform efforts. In contrast, persons who recognized the role of social arrangements as part of their broad explanatory frameworks tended to be supportive of reform efforts, including personal involvement in experimentation. And those who devalued the 'givenness' of reality through mystical and other transcendent experiences also seemed willing to countenance reform and alternative life-styles. Much the same patterns were evident in the previously mentioned study of commune members and in a study concerned with predicting racial attitudes (Apostle, *et al.*, 1983). Despite difficulties in conceptualizing and measuring the idea of broad meaning systems or broad explanatory frameworks, the studies seemed to demonstrate the importance of such cognitive perspectives. The assumption behind all these studies was that general overarching frames of reference set the context in which more specific activities have meaning and thus are likely to shape the salience and direction of these activities. In so far as this assumption seems to be empirically validated, Berger's emphasis on the importance of sacred canopies gains additional support.

His idea of 'plausibility structures' has also been employed in several research studies. One that was based on a survey of mainline church members, for example, suggested that identification with the local community served as an important plausibility structure for traditional religious tenets (Roof, 1978). Accordingly, those who held such localistic identities were considerably more likely than 'cosmopolitans' to espouse traditional religious beliefs – controlling for a variety of other factors – and to allow these beliefs to influence their thinking on racial and social questions as well. Another study examined the effect of social networks on components of symbolic universes among college students (Bainbridge and Stark, 1981). Arguing that social networks among like-minded students constituted a kind of plausibility structure, the study demonstrated that traditional Christian world views seemed to be both more salient and internally more consistent than other worldviews, in large part as a result of the fact that Christian students were more likely to have cultivated social ties with other Christians.

More recently, the idea of plausibility structures has been employed in several studies concerned with the question of how American evangelicals are able to maintain their traditional religious beliefs amidst the secular, pluralistic context of modern culture. One study, drawing on national survey data, demonstrated that evangelicals tend to be relatively isolated from the main sources of secular influence (such as higher education, professional careers, urban/suburban residence), thus permitting them to retain their plausibility structures more or less intact – although other modes of cultural accommodation were also evident (Hunter, 1983). Another study sampled students at nine evangelical colleges in an attempt to determine how effective these institutions were in providing plausibility structures for evangelical beliefs. By comparing the six campuses that required statements of faith from all entering students with the three campuses that did not, the study was able to see whether a more 'insular' setting actually served better to protect the plausibility of traditional beliefs. The results tended in part to confirm this supposition: evangelical beliefs were both higher and remained stronger over the four years of college in the more insular settings. However, a comparison sample of students drawn from a secular university showed that, although evangelicalism was much rarer, evangelical students were able to maintain their convictions in this setting as well. They did so mainly by adopting a more defensive stance toward the secular culture and by developing a relatively strong social and political ideology which protected their religious beliefs. Thus the general importance of plausibility structures was affirmed, but the study suggested that religious plausibility can be upheld amidst a secular context as well as in isolation from it (Hammond and Hunter, 1984).

On the whole, the idea of religion as sacred canopy has not yet been tested sufficiently to suggest that its merits outweigh those of several other contending approaches to the sociology of religion. Indeed, the basic ideas tend not to be at a level of specificity which would allow such tests to be made. But Berger, perhaps along with three or four other theorists of his stature, has made an important general contribution to reorienting research in the sociology of religion over the past two decades. He has specifically raised questions that go well beyond the study of conventional religious practices such as church attendance and prayer. His emphasis on meaning systems has placed the study of religion in a broader cultural context, such that matters of private experiences of the sacred, as well as functional trade-offs between religion and secular symbol systems, can be addressed. It is perhaps not surprising that his orientation has been particularly valued by scholars interested in new religious movements and other alternatives to conventional faith. In this, Berger has done much to make sense of religion in its distinctly modern setting.

Critical considerations

The Bergerian view of religion is broadly informed by theoretical tradition, generally supported by empirical research, sufficiently sophisticated to embrace the major variants and components of religious expression – and, perhaps ironically, an ingenious blend of social science and theological philosophy that has found favor with both the detractors and defenders of modern religion. Those who deny the validity of religion point enthusiastically to Berger's call for 'methodological atheism,' to his argument that religion is a socially constructed view of reality, and to his claim that religious beliefs depend on social interaction for their plausibility. Friends of religion, in contrast, find support in Berger's criticism of the limitations of everyday reality, in his argument for the role of overarching canopies of meaning, and in his openness to the possibility of 'signals of transcendence,' as he calls them in *A Rumor of Angels*, which break through the sheltering humdrum of everyday reality. On balance, Berger has provided a modern apologetic for the value of religion, arguing not from theological tradition but from the secular premises of social science that man cannot live by the bread of everyday reality alone. In so far as meaning is contextual, the meaning of life ultimately depends on a different kind of symbol – not amenable to empirical falsification – which evokes a sense of the ground of being. Berger acknowledges the tendency of social science, including his own, to debunk religion, but he has in a sense also saved religion from this scourge by the very perspective in which it is cast.

For all its flexibility, however, Berger's approach is not simply amenable to any interpretation. It contains its own distinctive perspectives – biases that account for both its strengths and weaknesses. These built-in biases need to be understood and evaluated in order to gain a proper appreciation of what Berger's approach can do best as well as a greater degree of sensitivity to its limitations. Three particular issues merit consideration: the role of plausibility structures, the role of subjectivity, and the role of rational cognition.

The idea of plausibility structures has provided sociologists with their best entrée to the study of religion within the Bergerian framework, since this is the concept that gives an influential role to social factors. Those who wish to see religion as an emergent or ultimate truth, or as an autonomous cultural system shaped strictly by its own inner structure and meanings, will inevitably charge that the idea of plausibility structures opens the door for a type of sociological reductionism which explains away the reality of religion by attributing it to social conditions. There is some basis for this charge, given the fact that Berger seems to treat plausibility structures as somehow prior to, or more basic than, the religious beliefs they make plausible. That is, religious beliefs seem to be treated as if they need to be explained; plausibility structures are introduced into the discussion without questioning their origin or the conditions maintaining them. Obviously one could also ask where plausibility structures come from, whether certain symbols encourage interaction more than others, whether the type of interaction possible depends on the type of discourses available, and so forth. Berger ducks these questions.

Yet in contrast with many classical approaches to religion in the social sciences – Marx, Freud, even Durkheim – Berger seems to give greater autonomy to the functioning of religious symbols and, indeed, suggests an insightful means of circumventing the problem of reductionism while giving social conditions a legitimate role. By posing his discussion in the context of a dialectic he has, in effect, stressed the importance of social interaction for the production and maintenance of religion, but at the same time recognized the independent capacity of religion to exist as a cultural system and to shape individual thoughts and attitudes.

What sociologists can more tellingly object to is the possibility that plausibility structures do not go far enough in specifying the importance of social conditions in shaping religion. Social interaction – 'conversation' – is surely important in maintaining religious realities, but that leaves the influence of social conditions largely indeterminate. For example, when research finds that Christian friendships reinforce Christian convictions, the question still remains of why some people choose Christian friends and others do not. Ideally, theory would suggest which kinds of social contexts are likely to be the most or least supportive of certain beliefs. Berger's approach is, in short, a 'weak' form of sociology of knowledge reasoning in that it specifies only the most general connection between social conditions and beliefs. One gains the impression from Berger that any kind of conversational setting can sustain *any* kind of belief. Perhaps so – but that conclusion certainly flies in the face of a long tradition of sociological research which has shown relationships between specific types of beliefs and variations in social class, region, family structures, political system, etc.

In addition, sociologists can object that Berger's description of plausibility structures as exchanges of discourse and interaction misses the importance of other kinds of social *resources* in maintaining religion. In a strict 'free market' of ideas among autonomous and relatively equal individuals, discourse may be the decisive factor in shaping beliefs. But most religions have long histories as established organizations in which money, power, and professional expertise play a prominent role. Behind the scenes – making possible the situations in which religious discourse happens – are massive ecclesiastical bureaucracies, hours and hours of administrative labor, vast fund-raising efforts, complex bookkeeping schemes, training programs, patronage and other distribution agencies, all of which play their part in maintaining religious realities. Berger himself is not unmindful of these institutional arrangements and has devoted more attention to them in recent treatments of policy issues. But much of the secondary literature on plausibility structures has failed to consider the broader role of social resources.

The question of subjectivity raises a second set of issues. Part of the intuitive appeal of Berger's approach to religion is that it begins with the individual and stresses the individual's subjective requirement for meaning in life. Unpersuaded by rational–logical argument for the existence of God, the student can find in Berger an existential basis for seeking broader meaning in life, one solution to which may be the sacred cosmos of religion. At the heart of this approach are the individual's concerns with questions about suffering, purpose in life, coping with grief, ecstacy, etc. Indeed, the emphasis on reality construction itself stresses the perspective of the individual and the manner in which the outside world is filtered through the individual's world view to become meaningful. This emphasis provides a refreshing contrast to sociological approaches concerned with broad generalizations about culture and society in which the individual as actor seems to have been lost. Yet there are costs associated with attaching this much emphasis to the individual.

The most obvious cost is that broader social arrangements may be neglected. To Berger's credit, discussions of individual meaning are always balanced with discussions of the legitimation of social institutions and in his writings on modernization he has been chiefly concerned with these large-scale institutions. However, the focus is often more on the ways in which individuals perceive institutions than on questions of institutional relations themselves.

No theory need cover the entire array of social life to have value, of course. But sociologists seem generally to have found more mileage in the Bergerian framework for considerations of individual beliefs that for more macroscopic levels of analysis.

Another potential limitation that hinges on emphasizing the subjective has to do with developing empirical generalizations. Critics of Berger's work have sometimes pointed to its lack of testable hypotheses as well as its apparent failure to have produced a more substantial body of empirical research. In part, these criticisms may be misdirected due to the fact that Berger's intention seems not to have been one of specifying testable 'middle range' hypotheses but of providing a meta-theoretical perspective from which to approach religion as a social scientist. At the same time, it does appear that Berger's work has probably received more usage for *appreciating* religion than for studying it – certainly no mean achievement, of course – and this reception may be associated with the work's basic emphasis on individual meaning. Thus research studies, such as the ones cited earlier, which have sought to operationalize questions about meaning have often been stymied as to how such an inherently private, idiosyncratic topic can be studied effectively. Few would doubt that little has been accomplished in this area other than demonstrating that typical individuals have an interest in the topic of meaning and that they draw on a host of thematic traditions, including both religious and secular ideas, in attempting to construct meaning. It is perhaps not surprising that many, expressing dissatisfaction with these results, have turned away from a focus on individual meaning and have begun to investigate more seriously the attributes of language and discourse (cf. Lindbeck, 1984). In an ironic sense, of course, Berger himself anticipated this problem-shift in *The Sacred Canopy* in stressing the integral importance of discourse for the maintenance of religion.

What an emphasis on discourse offers is a way of identifying observable, objective materials for analysis. The subjective emphasis on reality construction and personal meaning has pointed decisively toward inner moods and motivations in the study of religion – phenomena that seem to elude the usual methods of documentation and verification of the social sciences. Moreover, the idiosyncratic and fluid character of personal meaning has defied the very logic of seeking social scientific generalizations. Focusing on language and discourse, in contrast, has already paid high dividends in fields such as linguistics and artificial intelligence and seems to be capturing the interest of an increasing number of theologians and sociologists of religion (cf. Brummer, 1982; Taylor, 1984).

Finally, the role of rational cognition in religion presents issues of concern, especially when Berger's approach is contrasted with that of other theorists. The issue here is difficult to pin down precisely, but has to do with the general impression one comes away with, from reading Berger, that people somehow act like amateur philosophers when it comes to religion. For example, we find people approaching tragedies and grief, not so much by grieving, but by raising abstract questions about the causes of suffering in the world. And, while religious experiences and rituals are mentioned, emphasis is clearly given instead to a sort of broad philosophical system – the 'sacred canopy' – that answers one's questions about life. Perhaps this is a misreading of Berger, or perhaps it is the Austrian Lutheranism in his background coming out, but one cannot help wonder if his emphasis is not overly rational and cognitive.

One way of sharpening the issue is by contrasting Berger's approach with that of sociologist of religion Robert Bellah. The comparison is a natural one since both start with much the same presuppositions about symbolism, everyday reality, and the need for meaning. Yet when it comes to religion, Bellah seems to draw a distinction between rational–logical discourse and the more intuitive, 'ikonic' symbolism he believes to be characteristic of religion. These, he writes, 'are non-objective symbols that express the feelings, values, and hopes of subjects, or that organize and regulate the flow of interaction between subjects and objects, or that attempt to sum up the whole subject–object complex or even point to the context or ground of that whole' (1970: 252). Like Berger, Bellah has in mind the need for an overarching sense of meaning, but the symbols Bellah discusses seem not so exclusively to consist of 'theoretical tradition,' as Berger describes them, but of anecdotes, images, pictures, connotatively rich names and places, rituals, and personal experiences. Zen Buddhism seems to fit in Bellah's discussion, not in Berger's.

The problem is not one of deciding in favor of Bellah's emphasis or Berger's – plenty of evidence exists to support the importance of both types of symbolism in religion. But there is a fundamental ambiguity in Berger's discussion of symbolic universes which has perhaps made his view of religion seem more rationalistic than it should. In defining symbolic universes Berger contrasts them with simpler levels of legitimation, such as proverbs, maxims, and theories, not along a single dimension, however, but along two dimensions. On one dimension, symbolic universes are distinguished as the most *encompassing*: embracing and integrating all segments of reality, all institutional or biographic sectors, rather than being limited to a single, narrow aspect of reality. On another dimension, though, symbolic universes are distinguished as being the most theoretically *elaborate*: consisting of whole systems or traditions rather than single theories or even simpler, more discrete statements such as an explanation or proverb. Obviously these are distinct dimensions and it may be useful to draw a sharper contrast between the two.

Thus it would appear that a relatively simple statement which leaves unsaid much of what it implies (for example, 'Jesus loves me'), or a word like 'luck' that exists in the absence of any sophisticated theoretical tradition, could evoke a sense of the meaning of life as much as an elaborate philosophical system. Even an ikon or mandala might evoke a sense of encompassing meaning. In any of these cases cognition is involved, of course. But the meaning evoked may not consist so much of an orderly, systematic accounting of life, only an intuitive sense that life as such has meaning.

Looking backward

Returning then to the question of how *The Sacred Canopy* is to be evaluated, given the advantage of twenty years of hindsight, it seems evident that the perspective it provides still contains much that speaks to the modern situation. Written at a time when it appeared to many that the churches and synagogues were becoming increasingly irrelevant to the major questions facing modern society, it nevertheless offered an argument which explained why religion – in some form – would remain vital in modern times. That prediction has proved accurate again and again since the late 1960s. A whole generation reared on campus unrest in which religious experimentation played a vital part, then the phenomenon of an avowedly 'born-again' President, followed by religious resurgences from Tehran to Lynchburg, with a rising crescendo of constitutional concerns about the mixing of religion and politics – all underscore the abiding relevance of modern religion.

But if Berger's diagnosis was largely accurate, the social sciences have nevertheless moved subtly away from the assumptions on which his analysis was founded. There is in Berger's discussion of religion and culture a sort of courageous optimism, despite the existential despair in which humanity is assumed to live, that the social sciences will reshape and reinvigorate our very understanding of ourselves, giving us hope and increasing our sense of mastery over our own quest for basic values. That optimism no longer seems to characterize the social sciences in any prominent fashion. Rather, it seems, technical concerns have increasingly set the agenda, replacing the quest for basic values. As the editors of this volume have pointed out, much of what passes for social theory today deals hardly at all with fundamental questions but focuses instead on internal debates about one theorist's interpretation of another. Rather than attempting to rethink the nature of modern social life and identify problems of basic human importance, social theorists all too often seem to be engaged in technical controversies over their own tradition. Methods and data also accumulate at a rapid pace, but the enthusiasm for the broader vision of the social sciences that fired its leaders' imaginations as recently as the 1950s and 1960s seems to have waned drastically. It is as if the social sciences have been captured by their own version of everyday reality.

Berger, of course, would be the first to point out the limitations of that reality and assert its need for a broader vision – a 'sacred canopy.'

CHAPTER 6

Religion in the modern world

Phillip E. Hammond

It is certain that when assessments are made of sociology in the second half of the twentieth century, Peter Berger's work will have a prominent place. Moreover, it will occupy a category with few other occupants because, while general theorists have never disappeared altogether, few if any do their theorizing with Berger's palpability. He is remarkably close to his data, even as his focus is unabashedly abstract. Nowhere is this unusual perspective more apparent than in Berger's sociology of religion.

There can be no doubt that Peter Berger is one of the liveliest and most insightful analysts of the contemporary religious scene. Even when he turns his attention elsewhere – as he claims to have done in the 1970s with his work on modernization – he still deals with such themes as 'tradition,' 'authority,' 'plausibility,' 'sacred,' 'secularization,' etc. In other words, religious questions are always lurking in the background even when his ostensible focus is somewhere else.

Nor could it really be otherwise, given Berger's theoretical style; he naturally gravitates to the 'soft' end of the sociological spectrum. While adamant that his agenda is scientific because empirically based and value-neutral, he nevertheless pays little attention to 'hard' variables like births, deaths, migration, or income, but instead analyses those aspects of social life in which what is problematic is precisely the various and changing 'meanings' people assign to objects, persons, and processes around them. The consequence is a far greater attention to the way people go about 'constructing' their surrounding social reality than to the way they merely react to already-agreed-upon constructions. Berger knows, of course, that the number of mouths to feed, as a concrete fact, necessarily and everywhere influences social behavior; what interests him, however, are not changes in the number of mouths but changes in notions of responsibility to feed, for example, or in notions of adequate nutrition. In other words, Berger seeks out for analysis those features of social life in which 'meaning' is most fragile, most open to change, and most likely therefore, to vary through time and from one person to another according to social background and present location.

This perspective thus locates Berger in the tradition of sociology's founders, but with a distinctive modern twist. Like the founders who, faced all around by the crumbling state of feudal society, began to ask how society is even possible, Berger too is awed by the sheer existence of ordered social life. But at the same time (and more than those earlier theorists), Berger investigates the meaning of these larger social forces as they get played out on the microscopic level. Whether the subject is the passing of traditional society or the onslaught of modernity – whether, in other words, society is seen as going or coming – the perspective of Peter Berger both follows orthodox models and adds to them by attending to individual experiences. To put it succinctly, there is more social psychology in Berger than in classical sociology; not only do Marx and Durkheim and Weber inform his views, but Freud, Mead, and Cooley inform his views as well.

If there is one overarching image of the human in Berger's work, it is that of an animal, filled with genetic urges and surrounded by social conventions, forced none the less to make his/her path by accepting, discerning, modifying, and creating 'sense' out of all that. Reality is there, but it must also be discovered; it is fixed but ever-changing; people do not and cannot start fresh, but neither can they assume immutability. What really intrigues Berger is the question of how, under these circumstances, persons attach 'meaning' to their behavior.

So it is that religion – a major and ultimate way by which meaning, plausibility, and 'reality' are established – commands the attention of Peter Berger. And, it is perhaps correct to say, secularization in the modern world receives the lion's share of this attention. Beginning his writing career with analyses of the precarious and vulnerable position of the church in modern society, Berger has never strayed far from this dilemma, even as he has modified somewhat his portrait of it. The consequence is that, for a quarter of a century now, he has provided a continuing, theoretically consistent, and engaging commentary on religion in the modern world. A review of Berger's position on religion in a modern and secular society is the central focus of this chapter. As we shall see, the picture he gives us results in not just enormously interesting analyses of churches and church-related behavior. It also reveals that the Bergerian view of religion in the modern world is narrower than the view generally found in the sociology of religion. This later fact is due in large part to his particular conceptualization of 'religion.' A brief review of this conceptualization, then, is my starting point.

The role of religion generally

It is well-known, of course, that Berger's most basic theoretical argument is that culture is continuously being produced and reproduced through an on-going dialectical process – it is a human construction. Yet, even though people create culture, they are neither free to create it at will, nor are they obliged to be creating it all the time. Much meaning (of persons, instructions, events, processes, etc.) remains fairly constant. It is accepted as true, as real. For most people most of the time, in fact, the world is taken for granted. It is neither challenged nor even thought about. 'Through most of human history,' Berger writes, 'individuals lived in life-worlds that were more or less unified' (1973b: 64). All of this is to say that the world we live in is, for the most part, 'legitimate.' It is of human creation, but, operationally, 'we' do not so much create it as encounter it and what we encounter, we accept as normal and right.

The analysis thus shifts to the *source* of this order, this legitimacy, and here is where religion enters the Berger scheme in its most general form. While the legitimacy attributed to order is not necessarily religious, religious legitimacy is especially effective (that is, stable) because 'it relates the precarious reality constructions of empirical society with ultimate reality' (1967c: 32). Meaning and order ('nomos-building'), though, is possible without religion. In fact, the only ingredient that *is* necessary, Berger asserts, is 'conversation' with 'significant others' who will uphold one's own views. But if those views are not just *socially* supported but believed to be *sacredly* endowed as well, then their degree of legitimacy is extraordinarily high. According to Berger, past cultures that can be described as having been highly integrated were typically *religiously* integrated (1973b: 64).

> Particularly in modern times there have been thoroughly secular attempts at cosmization, among which modern science is by far the most important. It is safe to say, however, that originally all cosmization had a sacred character. . . . Viewed historically, most of man's worlds have been sacred worlds (1967c: 27).

Berger continues: 'It can thus be said that religion has played a strategic part in the human enterprise of world-building.'

I point out these passages (and their context, 1967c: 25ff) because in them Berger clearly equates 'religion' with the 'sacred' – which is, of course, perfectly reasonable to do but which, as we shall see, is not the position Berger consistently takes. His inconsistency leads him, I think, into a trap, though this trap does not become apparent until the 'undoing' of religion, that is, until secularization starts to occur.

Religion and secularization

Secularization, for Berger, is 'the process by which sectors of society and culture are removed from the domination of religious institutions and symbols' (1967c: 107). The parallel construction here ('society *and* culture,' 'institutions *and* symbols') is important because Berger clearly wants to emphasize both the objective and the subjective aspects of secularization. Not only do churches lose clout but so also do people generally think less about religion. Not only does education cease to be a religious responsibility and become instead a task for the state, for example, but so does the curriculum lose its religious content and parents fail to notice. Clergymen lose prestige and economic position, but so also are people less inclined to turn to religion for help. In the extreme, subjective secularization becomes 'invisible' secularization, a situation in which the erosion of religion takes place without people's awareness. Such invisible secularization is what Berger says occurred in the 1950s with record-setting church attendance; while more bodies were going to more churches, the meaning of that act had changed – become less religious – and church-goers were blithely unaware of their altered motivation.

The implication of this last point is that religious institutions themselves may secularize. Secularization, in other words, not only involves the removal of domination *by* 'religious institutions and symbols' over society-at-large; it also involves the decline of the sacred *within* those religious institutions and symbols. The reason is simple: Religious traditions are embodiments of religious experiences, which, however real they may be, are not continuous or equally distributed. Thus even religious virtuosi must institutionalize into ritual and symbol their subjective encounters with the sacred. Once this happens, however, the religious institutions may themselves lose their original meaning and consequently secularize (1979a: 46).

The question then becomes: How does secularization take place? Berger offers two answers. One source of secularization is subjective – whatever replaces religious explanation in people's thoughts about their lives. Science leads the way here, as we have already noted, as more and more of the natural world is understood to operate not at God's whim but according to laws which God either cannot or will not influence. In the process, God may be left out altogether. High also on Berger's list of secularizing influences is social science, perhaps psychotherapy above all, which in the extreme is:

> capable of doing just what institutionalized religion would like to do and is increasingly unable to do. . . . Thus the symbols of psychologism become overarching collective representations in a truly Durkheimian sense – and in a cultural context singularly impoverished when it comes to such integrating symbols (1977b: 32f).

Berger also nominates 'the Western religious tradition' itself as a secularizing influence. In doing so, he joins Weber in seeing the Protestant Reformation as a watershed period in human consciousness; by removing 'magic' from the world, Protestantism placed more and more responsibility on people themselves.

The second answer Berger offers to the question of secularization's source is pluralism, the presence of multiple reality-defining agencies. Where the first answer is subjective, taking place in the mind, pluralism is objective, taking place at the social structural level. Berger seems to attach increasing importance to this second aspect of secularization in accounting for modern behavior. Having noted that to maintain certainty about anything people must have social support, Berger observes that pluralism erodes certainty just as secularized consciousness does. 'Increasingly, however, it has seemed to me that, of the two phenomena, pluralism is more important than [subjective] secularization' (1980: 43).

Berger, then, recognizes not only subjective secularization but also the objective condition of pluralism or structural complexity generally. Whatever their *relative* causal importance – and Berger, I'm sure, would readily admit that no single metric exists for deciding on all occasions – the consequence of both pluralism and subjective secularization is the relativizing of outlook, hence the loss of certainty, and thus the 'crisis of credibility' or 'homelessness.' Interestingly, this homelessness of modern social life

> has found its most devastating expression in the area of religion. The general uncertainty, both cognitive and normative, brought about by the pluralization of everyday life and of biography in modern society, has brought religion into a serious crisis of plausibility. The age-old function of religion – to provide ultimate certainty amid the exigencies of the human condition – has been severely shaken. . . . This is very difficult to bear. . . . In one way or another, religion made meaningful even the most painful experiences of the human condition, whether caused by natural or by social agents. Modern society has threatened the plausibility of religious theodicies, but it has not removed the experiences that call for them (1973b: 184f).

The crisis of credibility leaves religion in a most difficult situation in the modern world. Secularization, both subjective and objective, forces religion to be largely a private matter since no single religion will be credible to everybody in any society. The public face of religion, therefore, largely disappears. Moreover, even a credible religion is plausible to believers only if social support serves to 'insulate' them from the corrosive forces of secularization, which results in 'pockets' of religious persons who, though perhaps aware of each other's beliefs, remain oblivious to the religions of other groups and to the agnosticism of non-believers. Publicly, then, religion is a patina. It 'manifests itself as public rhetoric and private virtue. In other words, insofar as religion is common it lacks "reality" and insofar as it is "real" it lacks commonality' (1967c: 130).

From this double-barreled perspective on secularization, Peter Berger has discussed a number of aspects of religion in the modern world, providing analyses unsurpassed for currency, wit, and theoretical consistency. These analyses can be conveniently presented in two categories: those based on Berger's 'market model' understanding of religion in modern society – corresponding to his notion of 'objective secularization' – and those based on the problem of plausibility – corresponding to his notion of 'subjective secularization.'

The market model of religion

The decline of religion in the West (as indicated by the loss of 'established' status for churches, removal of education from their administration, emergence of 'civil' methods of demographic book-keeping, the 'separation' of church from state, voluntary organizational status, etc.) has meant that religious groups are forced to see themselves as units in a market, competing for the time, loyalty, and money of a limited clientele. In this situation, they very much behave as secular, commercial units behave in *their* markets: with an eye to mass appeal, advertising, sensitivity to competition, 'profit,' innovation, and so forth. Such a market model has permitted Berger to understand a variety of features of contemporary churches.

For one, pressures toward ecumenism are, significantly, pressures to gain some measure of control over ecclesiastical cost/benefit ratios. Whatever its theological rationale – and Berger does not dispute its authenticity – the ecumenical movement among mainline Protestant denominations is also an effort to 'rationalize' a very competitive market (1963d).

These same market pressures also lead to the ecclesiastical equivalent of 'marginal differentiation,' an effort to set one's own product off from its competitors – but only slightly, not to the degree that it loses the attractions all competitors share. Thus various churches rediscover their various creeds, their rituals, and their 'histories', but it is precisely because these are insignificant differences that they can be emphasized.

So, too, do churches in these circumstances become unabashedly commercial by offering almost anything they think the public might want. For example, the *Los Angeles Times*, June 23 1984, reported:

> The athletes, organizers, vendors and visitors aren't the only ones warming up for the 1984 Summer Olympics. From Baptists to Buddhists, from the Sikhs to the Salvation Army, most of the world's organized – and not so organized – religious groups have targeted Los Angeles as a prime place to spread their variegated forms of faith. . . . One of the most visible, 1984 Outreach, has been girding up to do the Lord's work in Southern California for nearly two years. A coalition of 70 religious organizations representing about 2,800 area churches, 1984 Outreach plans to blitz the Olympics crowd with an army of 13,000 young volunteer evangelists brought in from around the world. . . . A cross-country torch relay . . . is already off and running 'to claim this nation for God.' . . . a billboards for Jesus campaign has contracted to place 605 posters on transit buses proclaiming 'Peace for the World Through Jesus Christ' in three languages. . . . The Baptists, Methodists and Lutherans . . . are all offering bed and breakfast accommodations in church members' homes to visiting out-of-towners. The Methodists and the Lutherans are charging $30 per night per guest, and the Southern Baptists, $20. . . . The major Olympic emphasis of the Episcopalians is financing and staffing the . . . telephone help line . . .

While it is clear from this near-parody that denominational differences remain, it is just as clear that a market mentality underlies this activity, along with whatever other motives may be present. Berger would recognize this market aspect immediately; indeed, he helps us to see it.

Still a fourth feature of church life Berger understands with the help of the market model is the relationship between church growth/decline and the appeal to youth – and through youth to their families. Thus churches followed the population movement to the suburbs, mounted programs attractive to youngsters, and thereby added many families to their rolls (cf. 1962a; 1962b).

A final arena on which Peter Berger shines his market-model spotlight is theological education. He sees seminaries as naïvely trying to be 'trendy' while seeing themselves as academic/theological, when in fact they are neither – very much at least. Why is this?

> If we look at it [American Protestantism] in 'wholesale' terms, we find a limited number of large organizations competing with each other on a free market. On the other hand, looking at the 'retail' picture, we find an immense number of local establishments economically controlled by loose associations of laymen, which actually constitute consumers' cooperatives that enjoy considerable autonomy as against the afore-mentioned large organizations. The minister finds himself in a very odd position between these two quite dissimilar groups. On the one hand, he is an officer of the organization, commissioned by it to be its representative in a particular locality. On the other hand, he is employed by the lay association and, if only for economic reasons, is compelled to pay serious attention to its wishes (1962c: 179).

Sensing this squeeze to exist, seminaries give over increasing curricular space to 'practical' matters such as pastoral counseling and church management, and what emerges is 'the religious organization man . . . that middle-management type who has the same face, the same smile and behind these the same mind no matter what the organization is' (1962c: 186) The comparison of church with corporation is well-nigh complete in this analysis; the market model is in high gear.

The problem of plausibility

Pluralism contributes to subjective secularization even as the reverse is also true. Subjective secularization, however, is more often manifested as a problem of plausibility – how to *believe* religiously – and from this perspective, too, Berger has given us several cogent analyses.

Foremost of these, no doubt, is his notion that religious organizations must choose either to accommodate their beliefs to cognitive standards external to their tradition or else defensively isolate themselves from those standards in order to remain theologically plausible. The first option leads to a disappearing boundary between religious beliefs and other beliefs, thus rendering religion irrelevant because they are indistinguishable from a secular viewpoint. The second leads to a boundary so rigid as to make religion irrelevant because of its withdrawal from the rest of life (cf. 1967c: Chapter 7).

Related to this difference in organizational style is Berger's understanding of different theological strategies – whether to proceed reductively (by accommodation), deductively (by defensive isolation) or inductively, a method Berger advocates as one avoiding the pitfalls identified above, associated with the accommodation/isolation dilemma (cf. 1979b, 1969a).

A third, quite different, arena in which the plausibility problem shows through is theological education. In the preceding section this arena was analyzed organizationally in terms of the market model, but here the analysis is cognitive, and the differences between the two analyses provide helpful insight into Berger's thinking. He writes:

> the present trend in theological education is oriented towards people for whom Christianity has already become meaningless, and is inspired by the absurd notion that this can be remedied by meeting various non-religious needs of these people under a Christian label (1968c: 135f).

Berger here is castigating seminaries for too readily accommodating their instruction to external, that is, 'non-religious,' standards. Very little courage is needed to break with the orthodox tradition, he says in the same essay, because so much makes that tradition implausible: Rather:

> courage is needed to deviate from the taken-for-granted reality-assumptions of secularized culture, as defined by shifting coteries of intellectuals with access to the mass media. . . . I think that theological existence today ought to include the readiness . . . to be in a cognitive minority and to accept the social consequences of this position . . . (1968e: 130)

From this analysis alone, one might infer that Berger would join the entrenched conservatives, choosing sharply etched isolation over indistinguishable interchange. His involvement, moreover, in the 'Hartford Declaration' in 1975 might suggest the same. It is clear, however, that, as much as he might admire intransigent theology, Berger advocates not that strategy but another – identified above as 'induction' (cf. 1979a).

More, however, can be said about Berger's preferences when it comes to theologizing in the modern world. As a frequent contributor to *Christian Century*, *Worldview*, and *Commentary*, as well as to the more specialized religion and sociology journals, Berger permits us to see what he fears even more than religion's irrelevance brought on by isolation. It is irrelevance brought on by having nothing *distinctively* religious to say to the world: 'Thus, what Christianity is "really all about" turns out to be this or that set of values that are perfectly consonant with the prevailing secular consciousness' (1979a: 140). Instead, Berger wrote in 1962, 'our situation demands more than anything else that Christians be able to penetrate *intellectually* the consciousness of this age' (1962c: 190, emphasis in the original). And in a letter to a young man who has asked him if the Protestant ministry was not irrelevant, morally ambiguous, even absurd, Berger allowed as how it was all of those things, and the minister might therefore be compared to a clown:

> who dances through the world, incongruous in the face of the world's seriousness, contradicting all its assumptions – a messenger from another world, in which tears turn to laughter and the walls of man's imprisonment are breached (1964b: 549).

Needless to say, clowns, too, need to be surrounded by other clowns if their clownishness is to remain plausible, but Berger has less to say about how this is to be accomplished.

A final topic to be discussed here under the plausibility rubric is Berger's focus on psychologism in modern religion. Already in *The Sacred Canopy* (pp. 78–80) he had alerted us to the tendency of 'the problem of theodicy' to become 'the problem of anthropodicy,' so that the question of evil shifts from 'How could God permit this?' to 'How could men act this way?' Underlying this shift is the more general change brought about by religion's loss of plausibility and thus of authority:

> individuals are forced to become more reflective, to ask themselves the question of what they really know. . . . Such reflection, just about inevitably, will further compel individuals to turn to their own experience (1979a: 32).

Any religious certainty one might feel is thus 'dredged up from within . . . since it can no longer be derived from the external, socially shared and taken-for-granted world' (1967c: 152f). Experienced most acutely in Protestantism, because of its emphasis on the individual's unmediated relationship to God and its distrust therefore of the church, this reliance on subjective emotionalism as the basis for religious truth made common cause – and still makes common cause – with Enlightenment rationalism or 'scientific common-sense.' Berger notes this feature of modern-day religion in the 'positive thinkers' of the 1950s and 1960s, much as William James (1958) did before him and Richard Quebedeaux (1982) has since. Surely one does not comprehend the resurgence of Evangelicalism in America today without this window Berger has helped to construct. Not 'What is its independent truth status?' but 'How do I feel about it?' has become the hallmark of religious reality today.

A concluding commentary

Some of Berger's work on the problem of religion in the modern world is first-rate, some of it is brilliant, but none of it, exceptionable. It little behooves a reviewer, then, to be negative about anything reviewed, and I will not be. None the less, there runs through Berger's analysis of religion and secularization in modern life an element separating him from most of the rest of sociology of religion, and this difference, it seems to me, is worth discussing. This element can be seen in his unusual use of the terms 'sacred' and 'supernatural' – and thus his very definition of religion – which takes him on a tangent not followed by most other theorists. This peculiarity shows up also in discussions of secularization, for, as Larry Shiner puts it, 'It is evident that part of the difficulty in measuring the decline of religion is the definition of religion itself' (1967: 211).

My point of departure is a notion expressed by Berger in several contexts:

- the present religious resurgences not only indicate a possible reversal of the secularization trend, but can be understood as a particular manifestation of the demodernizing impulse (1973b: 199).
- In the last few years, I have come to believe that many observers of the religious scene (I among them) have over-estimated both the degree and the irreversibility of secularization (1974h: 14).
- There is one more possibility: a reversal of the long-standing trend of secularization in the Western world generally, and particularly in its cultural elite. . . . The possibility of such a revival is nowhere more relevant than in America (1977b: 68).

As we have seen, secularization for Berger is 'the process by which sectors of society and culture are removed from the domination of religious institutions and symbols.' But what is the reversal of this process he refers to in the above remarks?

It bears repeating that secularization, for Berger, comes through the twin forces of pluralization and subjective secularization. Is Berger, in contemplating the reversal of secularization, suggesting a reversal in either or both of these forces? This is unlikely since little or no empirical evidence would support such suggestion; society is not becoming less pluralistic nor is religious explanation of events on the upswing. Instead, Berger seems to have in mind something else, a more primitive variable.

A clue can be found in Berger's discussion of 'religious experience.' Putting aside for the moment the question of pluralization and subjective secularization, we see that secularization, when viewed in terms of religious experience, now might mean something else. Secularization, he says:

> could imply two things. One, people are having fewer religious experiences. Or, two, they still have these experiences, but, under social pressure, they deny them. . . . I suspect that both these things are true to some extent, but I am increasingly inclined to think that the second is more important (1974i: 132; 1979a: 54f).

The reversal of secularization may then be indicated by an *increase* in religious experiences or, more likely, by an increasing willingness to *acknowledge* such experiences as religious.

Now, this viewpoint works splendidly as long as the experience is expressed through the beliefs or rituals of one or other of the historic religious traditions. One can note, for example, a decrease in orthodox 'God talk' and call the result secularization; one can then observe an increase in such 'God talk' and say that secularization is reversed. But what if there are *new* encounters with the sacred? What if *new* language is being used to express such encounters? How, to put it plainly, would Berger recognize a religion-in-the-making?

This is no mere quibble but goes right to the heart of the meaning of secularization. We saw earlier that Berger dismissed the so-called religious revival of the 1950s as inauthentic, calling it 'invisible secularization.' In doing so he adopted a position widely shared and best expressed by Bryan Wilson (1966) that the very freedom people have, to join or not join this or that old or new religion, is itself a measure of secularity. On what basis, then, does Berger look upon Solidarity in Poland, the Baptists in Russia, or evangelical Protestantism in America and declare them to be potential reversals in secularity?

I do not want to be misunderstood here. Whether these contemporary religious movements are or are not evidence of a religious revival is not at issue here – as important as that question is in other contexts. What *is* at issue here is how secularization and the sacred are to be conceived. Despite all of his attention to this issue, Berger, I am arguing, is nevertheless led by his conceptualization to recognize as religious only those encounters with the sacred that come clothed in orthodox, traditional guise. Solidarity celebrates with the Mass, so it is a reversal of secularization; the suburban parish celebrates with a barbeque, so it is a furtherance of secularization.

How could this anomaly come about? Because, I contend, Berger departs from most of the rest of sociology of religion at his starting point. Where most see the supernatural as a subset of the sacred, Berger sees the sacred as a subset of the supernatural. Put another way, most sociologists of religion operate with a functional definition: Whatever results from encounters with the sacred, if it is systematic and institutionalized, is religion, whether or not it is expressed in supernatural terms. Berger operates otherwise. For him, the experience of the supernatural is indispensable to religion, and 'the sacred is a phenomenon *within* the reality of the supernatural' (1978c: 40; emphasis in the original). Moreover:

> there are non-supernatural *surrogates* of the sacred, such as, for example, the nation as a symbolic entity. These *surrogates*, at least up to a point, allow a continuation of the social and psychological functions of religion without access to the primary experience of the sacred in a supernatural context (1978c: 41, emphasis added; cf. 1979a: 43f).

Here is a rather different approach; Berger, in the above quotation, might even be suggesting that non-supernatural encounters with the sacred are only 'surrogate' encounters, that is, not even truly sacred.

Now, Berger has long contended his position on this definitional issue (1976: Appendix one; 1974i). It is not my purpose here to change his mind, or even to argue with his position. But I do argue that his position, no less than the functional definitions he 'militantly' opposes, carries its own ideological freight. This is most clearly seen in the 1974 article, 'Some Second Thoughts on Substantive Versus Functional Definitions of Religion':

> My thesis is this: The functional approach to religion . . . serves to provide quasiscientific legitimations of a secularized worldview. . . . The specificity of the religious phenomena is avoided by equating it with other phenomena. The religious phenomena is 'flattened out.' Finally it is no longer perceived. Religion is absorbed into a night in which all cats are grey. The greyness is the secularized view of reality in which any manifestations of transcendence are, strictly speaking, meaningless, and therefore can only be dealt with in terms of social or psychological functions that can be understood without reference to transcendence (pp. 128f).

This charge may be correct, but Berger's strategy also pays a penalty. *His* consequence is the exclusion from the sociology of religion of all study of the sacred that is *not* transcendent (supernatural). Given these self-imposed limitations, Berger can study neither religion-in-the-making nor realms of the sacred that do not now, and may never, achieve the status of 'religion' in his scheme.

By insisting on the substantive characteristic, 'transcendence,' Berger keeps a clear focus on what he *does* study, it is true; but it is a focus – because of secularization – on a smaller and smaller category. For example, all twenty-two essays in *The Sacred in a Secular Age: Toward Revision in the Scientific Study of Religion* (Hammond, 1985), grapple with how to understand the sacred in societies clearly continuing to secularize. In most if not all of these essays, the notion is expressed that traditional, transcendent, and supernatural language is often not involved. Traditional rituals and institutions may be even less involved. And yet, these essays insist, something of religious significance is occurring. The conceptual problem is by no means solved in this volume, but it is addressed. Berger, I have to assume, is not very interested in such stuff – at least not as a sociologist of religion.

In fact, this last point may be the crux of the matter. Berger fashions himself to be changing hats when he moves from the study of traditional religion to other issues, while most sociologists of religion do not. He therefore refers to the 'ersatz religions of secularism' (1974h: 15) while most of his colleagues look for what is religious rather than what is artificial in such phenomena. On balance, this is hardly a devastating difference, but it *is* a difference; perhaps under his hat as a sociologist of knowledge, a hat he also wears superbly, Berger could tell us what and so what.

All things considered, however, the above is not a substantial flaw. Berger has, more than any other sociologist in this century, developed a serious audience among 'religionists.' His capacity to speak to this audience is only partly attributable to his theological and ecclesiastical sophistication, however. Another factor is his persistence in addressing big questions in accessible terms. He deals with experiences we all might have had, but he casts them in conceptual terms enabling us to see more than the unaided eye can observe.

Religion in the modern world qualifies exactly as such an experience. The naïve find it easy to dismiss, but Peter Berger helps us to see that religion remains a major force in society.

Excursus: The problem of truth

S. D. Gaede

The purpose of this excursus is to ruminate on the interaction of sociology and theology in the works of Peter Berger. Congressional speculation is always a risky business, however, especially when the putative intercourse involves religion and science, and its supposed chamber is the mind of Peter Berger. Discerning such activity is difficult enough in an academic brothel, where the house publicizes its intent and participants are prone to full disclosure. In this case, however, the house purports to be, if not a purist's cloister, at least the handmaiden of chastity – in the business of protecting the virtue of its inhabitants. The practical question, then, is how does one ruminate on an affair which, if it takes place at all, does so behind closed doors?

Given Berger's philosophy of science, this question would be a daunting one if it were not for a singularly important fact: though Berger may be the guardian of disciplinary chastity, he does enjoy temptation. Indeed, he seems to revel in it. Thus, he is the author of numerous manuscripts which, though manifestly sociological in design, nevertheless delight in whispering sweet nothings in the ear of the theologian. Here, however, one must depart from the metaphor since it shall be my argument that these whispers are anything but 'sweet nothings.' In fact, they are the outward expression of an internal dialogue between Berger-the-sociologist and Berger-the-theologian. And although Berger may view this as a dialogue between two distinct frames of reference ('relevance structures'), the conversation itself reflects a significant degree of theoretical interaction. Returning to the metaphor, the dialogue provides strong support for the assertion that this is a consummated affair.

The problem of truth

Every text requires a pretext and ours shall be the 'problem of truth.' It is an artificial setting for the ensuing discussion, not because it is foreign to Berger's repertoire, but because it is not the primary problematic of the works to be discussed. Nevertheless, given the objectives of this paper, the use of such a device seems altogether proper. For one thing, it is a useful vehicle for gaining entrée to Berger's presuppositions, and that is something that must be accomplished if this venture is to be anything like a success. The problem of truth, moreover, though subliminal at points, has remained a haunting presence in the sociological tradition. Thus it is not a disservice, either to Berger or his intellectual heritage, to accept it as the framework for our analysis.

How do we know that something is true? Few questions are more problematic or consequential. Regardless of whether one considers truth to be a primary objective (as might the scientist or theologian), or a secondary need (as might those involved in a business transaction), the desire for truth is a ubiquitous phenomenon. Though most operate as 'naïve realists,' assuming truths appropriated through experience, serious reflection reveals the inadequacy of such naïvety (Hodges, 1983). It is difficult enough to adjust the reliability of one's senses (witness the mirage, for example); it is infinitely more difficult to adjudicate between competing theories (Kuhn, 1962) or transcendent beliefs (Wolfe, 1982; Wolterstorff, 1976). Truth is not tame.

The sociological version of this problem becomes apparent when we observe that it is an especially modern issue. That is, the problem of truth, though existent since the serpent's assurance of longevity in the Garden of Eden, becomes a pervasive existential and intellectual dilemma in the modern era. This is the case, not because of the mental inferiority of our ancestors, but because of their social location. Aside from the few who were permanently engaged in the procurement and distribution of knowledge, the majority of pre-moderns did not live with a vast array of competing truth claims. Moderns, by contrast, must select from a smorgasbord of ideologies and veridical assertions. As Berger himself has argued (1967c: 127–54), such pluralism mitigates against the credibility of any exclusivistic truth claims. Though truth may be 'out there' among the plethora of offerings on the menu of modernity, the variety of possibilities makes the selection process more difficult, and confidence in one's selection harder to cultivate.

Such a sociological observation, though substantively interesting, is not the significant issue, however. More importantly, by putting the problem of truth in sociological perspective, we have raised the sociological version of the problem of truth. Though this may sound like verbal gymnastics, it is nothing of the sort. In fact, the problem of truth is sociologically relative. It is more likely to occur, be debated, and considered existentially salient in some societies than in others. In other words, knowledge, which in this case is the 'problem of truth,' lives within a social context which provides it with meaning and plausibility. Modernity, therefore, offers an ideal plausibility structure for the problem of truth.

With surgical precision, Berger articulates the sociological dimension of the problem of truth in *The Sacred Canopy*. 'Society is a product of man,' he begins. 'It has no other being except that which is bestowed on it by human activity and consciousness' (1967c: 3). Humans must build and maintain their social worlds of meaning and institutions. Religion, as with all other institutions, is a socially constructed reality. It serves as an agent of social control and solidarity, providing a coherent set of meanings which legitimate and preserve the institutional order. In the same way that one becomes a delinquent, a Republican, or both, natural processes of socialization, identity formation, and so on, move one to accept certain forms of religiosity. Whether Baptist, Buddhist, or Bug-a-booist, whether 'true' religion or a 'fraud,' the conversion process and its consequences are the same. The content may vary, but the forms and dynamics of religiosity are predictable, natural, and scientifically explainable.

Berger concludes his work with a question that frames precisely the problem of religious truth from a sociological perspective: 'if all religious plausibility is susceptible to "social engineering", how can one be sure that those religious propositions (or for that matter "religious experiences") that are plausible to oneself are not just that – products of social engineering – and nothing else?' (1967c: 184). In other words, if what we believe to be true (religious or otherwise) is dependent upon our social context, then how can we say that it is Truth in some broader, universal sense? Are not religious beliefs simply human projections which readily conform to our social circumstances? And, if so, how can we have any confidence that they are ultimately true?

The self-inflicted wound

The sociological version of the problem of truth, of course, is in no sense novel to the works of Berger. Marx (1867, 1959; Abercrombie, 1980), Mannheim (1960, 1971; Simonds, 1980), Scheler (1980; Becker and Dahlke, 1973), along with numerous other scholars who take the sociology of knowledge tradition seriously (Merton, 1968; Remmling, 1967; Stark, 1958a, 1958b), have all struggled with this issue. My interest in the topic has nothing to do with its novelty, however, and everything to do with the manner in which Berger attempts to deal with, and move beyond, the problem of truth. For it is in the midst of this struggle that important metaphysical insights can be gained.

Though Berger touches upon this issue in many of his works, he launches his most direct assault in *A Rumor of Angels*. The book itself was designed as a personal follow-up to *The Sacred Canopy* from the perspective not of scientific disinterest but of one who is religiously curious. The picture of religion which emerged from the earlier work was an essentially melancholy one, especially concerning the future of religiosity in modern societies. The artist, however, took great pains to point out that the tapestry was composed with a sociological brush, and should not be considered the final statement on the future of religion. He attempts to demonstrate that fact in *A Rumor of Angels*, where a slightly different picture of religious possibilities is developed, one less dependent upon the insights of sociological relativism and more reflective of the author's philosophical anthropology.

One issue, among many, which he confronts in *A Rumor of Angels* is the inherent relativism in the sociological perspective. This is precisely the sociological version of the problem of religious truth raised at the close of *The Sacred Canopy*: How can we have any confidence in the veracity of our beliefs if they are merely a function of our social location? Berger's approach to this problem is to assume the role of traitor, and critique the implied logic in a consistently relativistic position. He notes that it is quite unfair to apply the insights of sociological relativism exclusively to religion; all knowledge, not just transcendent varietals, must be brought within this relativistic vision. When this is done, one suddenly discovers (with a tinge of Bergerian 'ecstasy' (1963c: 136–52)) that the sociological perspective is itself sociologically relative. That is, sociological relativism is not immune from the relativizing process. It too is a product of a particular social context, subject to the explanatory power, or debunking motif, of the sociological vision. In the end, the one who asserts that all religious truths are relative must assume as well that his own assertion is similarly relative. Alas. The relativist is relativized and the radical sociologist is hoisted on his own petard.

At this point, of course, Berger is not only attacking the problem of truth, but also the disguised foundationalism of many sociological critics of religion. In their attack upon the legitimacy of religious ontologies, such critics often assume that their own world-view is immune from the same critique. Marx appears to do this, for example, when he considers religion to be a self-serving product of the social conditions of capitalism, and therefore false, while his own perspective, which could be similarly explained in terms of his social location, remains untainted. Berger takes the 'secular' theologian to task for the same tendency:

> The 'past', out of which the [religious] tradition comes, is relativized in terms of this or that socio-historical analysis. The 'present', however, remains strangely immune from relativization. In other words, the New Testament writers are seen as afflicted with a false consciousness rooted in their time, but the contemporary analyst [read 'secular' theologian] takes the consciousness of 'his' time as an unmixed intellectual blessing (1969b: 41).

The possibility of relative truth

If the logic of sociological relativism undermines its own critique, how does one proceed in the search for truth?

> Any such method will have to include a willingness to see the relativity business through to its very end. This means giving up any 'a priori' immunity claims. . . . It seems, however, that

> when the operation is completed a rather strange thing happens. When everything has been subsumed under the relativizing categories in question . . . the question of truth reasserts itself in almost pristine simplicity. Once we know that all human affirmations are subject to scientifically graspable socio-historical processes, 'which affirmations are true and which are false?' (1969b: 40).

In other words, according to Berger, one must first give up any hope of a foundation of beliefs which remain aloof from the relativizing process. Only then can one honestly reapproach the search for truth.

Still, this is only a statement concerning how not to approach the problem of truth; the crucial question remains, how does one tackle this issue 'after' relativization has been assumed? At this point, Berger is not as clear as he should be (though, in his defense, it ought to be noted that his primary objective in *A Rumor of Angels* is not epistemological). Nevertheless, from this and other works, one can construct a reasonable Bergerian response.

One possible option, of course, is to give up the search for truth altogether. That is, one might conclude that given the relativity of human knowledge, the desire for truth is a vain hope which cannot be realized. Berger rejects this option as both unnecessary and inappropriate. For one thing, it gives too much weight to the vision of sociological relativism. It assumes that the relativistic argument is so credible that all knowledge is *ipso facto* incredible. Such a deduction, however, not only falls into the self-referential fallacy (Dixon, 1980), it also presumes that sociological relativism is the only adequate foundation for knowledge. Such an error can be averted, according to Berger, if one remembers that the sociological perspective is only one perspective among many which must be taken into account in any search for understanding. It is one 'relevance structure' (1981d: 17–55) among a number, and from it we cannot infer to the whole of reality.

A corollary argument, which Berger makes at various times, is that a belief may be both relative and true. In other words, the discovery that a belief is relative to its social context does not bear on the truth or falsity of the belief. He makes this point in the second appendix of *The Sacred Canopy*:

> The case of mathematics is rather instructive in this connection. Without any doubt mathematics is a projection onto reality of certain structures of human consciousness. Yet the most amazing fact about modern science is that these structures have turned out to correspond to something 'out there'. . . . What is more, it is possible to show sociologically that the development of these projections in the history of modern thought has its origins in very specific infrastructures without which this development is most unlikely to have taken place. So far nobody has suggested that 'therefore' modern science is to be regarded as a great illusion (1967c: 181).

Although Berger's last sentence is debatable, his point nevertheless stands: ideas may be both relative and truthful.

The yearning for universals

Although this thought may provide some degree of existential relief, it still only pertains to the 'possibility' of truth and not to its actual location. In order to discover the substance of truth, one must first define what kind of truth it is that one is pursuing, and secondly, devise a method which comports with one's relativistic assumption.

Regarding the generic issue, though there is theoretically a vast panoply of possibilities, Berger chooses to content himself with one: religious truth. This choice is intriguing, if not surprising. It is not unexpected, of course, since Berger has often chosen to draw a certain amount of nourishment from a theological brew. His first two monographs, *The Noise of Solemn Assemblies* (1961a) and *The Precarious Vision* (1961c), were significantly concerned with theological issues, as were many of his initial journal publications (for example, 1955, 1958a, 1959a). Since that time, however, Berger has become a connoisseur of numerous other social phenomena. But it is only in the area of religion that he tackles precisely the problem of truth. This fact remains intriguing because the sociological version of the problem of truth is every bit as vexing in science (for example) as it is in religion (Wolterstorff, 1976).

Assuming the problem to be addressed is 'religious' truth, the question still remains: Given the assumption of socio-historical relativism, how shall the problem be approached? Once again, though Berger plays with this issue in quite a number of his excursions, it is first in *A Rumor of Angels*, and then later, in *The Heretical Imperative*, that this matter receives its fullest development. His conclusion about method, however, is most succinctly stated in *Sociology Reinterpreted*:

> Minimally, a sociologically sensitized theologian will have to reckon with the 'constructedness' of religious systems – and, minimally, this will preclude certain forms of theological fundamentalism that are unable to acknowledge this. And, as with the ethicist, the theologian who understands sociology [read: 'understands the social relativity of religious beliefs'] will be propelled to search for those universally valid criteria of religious truth that will transcend the relativities of time and space (1981d: 89).

In other words, according to Berger, the sociologically enlightened religionist must look for truth among the universals – those religious projections which present themselves most often and with greatest clarity. Berger's statement that such truths must 'transcend the relativities of time and space' does not imply that they are free of sociological influence, however. They are still human 'projections' which reflect their social location. Nevertheless, they are not historically spasmodic or particularistic projections, but those which exhibit commonalties and universalistic tendencies. It is here that Berger thinks the sociologically informed theologian will discover those 'ejaculations of meaning' (1967c: 180) which are most likely to correspond to 'truth.'

The sexual overtones of the previous sentence are not accidental. For whatever the merits of Berger's argument, it is here that we begin to uncover the clandestine affair between Berger-the-sociologist and Berger-the-theologian. What is presented in the above quote from *Sociology Reinterpreted* as a dialogue, is nothing of the sort. When Berger notes that the sociologically sensitized theologian ought to look for truth among the universals, it comes not as a mere suggestion (or bit of data) provided by the sociologist to the theologian, but as a philosophical imperative. In this case, of course, it is a requirement imposed upon Berger-the-theologian by

Berger-the-sociologist. It is so, not because Berger-the-sociologist is some kind of intellectually bully, but because his sociological assumptions (for example, that religious understandings are socially located projections) obviate the possibility of certain theological conclusions ('certain forms of fundamentalism') and point logically to others ('universally valid criteria'). In other words, at this point, Berger's sociological presuppositions delimit his theological options. One might say that his ontological assumptions concerning the nature of reality are here fashioned by his sociological vision.

Placing his order

The effect of Berger's sociological vision upon his theological proclivities, of course, is not especially important to the vast majority of modern sociologists. (Paradoxically, such nonchalance vanishes when Berger applies that same vision within the political arena – an anomaly which speaks volumes about the devotional inclinations of the modern sociologist). For these, the more poignant concern is the antithetical possibility, in which case Berger's religious proclivities might shape the method and substance of his sociological thought. To ponder this – the more *obviously* salient issue – we must continue to follow the path which Berger has blazed in his search for religious truth.

One might say that Berger initiated this aspect of his quest in the third chapter of *A Rumor of Angels*, for it was here that he began to stalk ontological truths within the context of his sociological paradigm (developed in *The Sacred Canopy*). He commences his search on a somewhat apologetic note, picking up an argument which he developed earlier in Appendix II of *The Sacred Canopy* (1967c: 179–86) – that religious projections are not necessarily fabrications and may in fact correspond to some transcendent reality. He asserts, moreover, that if there is such a correlation, we ought to be able to find traces of transcendent reality in the *common* projections of religious man. He concludes that there are 'prototypical human gestures' which are empirically observable and which might be 'signals of transcendence' (that is, because of their implied faith, point to a reality beyond the natural environs of man). These are: the propensity to order and believe in an orderly universe; the disposition to play, hope, and use humor, in spite of the absurdity of doing so in a wholly naturalistic universe; and the desire for an eschatological judgment of those whose evil goes unpunished in this world. Of the last 'signal,' he even wrote a novel entitled *Protocol of a Damnation* (1976b).

Now, an important question here is what has Berger demonstrated by this argument? For example, are these 'prototypical human gestures' really 'signals of transcendence'? Quite possibly. The fact that a vast preponderance of human beings assume order and engage in play may suggest that these proclivities emanate from a much grander Cosmic Reality. On the other hand, it may merely suggest that human beings believe and act 'as if' there is a reality beyond the material. Since we know that people often act 'as if' things are true even though they are false (for example, for years, sailors would not venture too far out to sea because they were afraid they might fall off the edge of the earth), we know that the faithful act does not demonstrate the reality of the object of faith. This point does not undermine Berger's empirical assertion that such gestures imply a certain degree of faith, but it does question the apologetic value of the assertion. Finally, it could be argued that the human gestures detailed by Berger do not correspond to transcendent reality at all. A naturalist, for example, would argue that Berger is imputing meanings to these gestures which they do not necessarily have; the fact that the hope of some is informed with transcendent qualities, for example, does not mean that hope *must* be so informed, nor does the fact that Berger understands hope in this way make it so.

None of this suggests that Berger's argument is without merit. Indeed, I find it personally appealing. But – and this is one of those crucial 'but's' – it is attractive, in part, because it comports well with my own world-view. If my assumptions were less engorged with transcendence, however, I am confident that my enthusiasm for Berger's argument would wane considerably. This observation is crucial because it points to the fact that Berger considers these 'prototypical human gestures' to have faithful qualities and to be 'signals of transcendence,' not because that is unarguably the case, but because he *believes* it to be the case. In other words, the linkage between these gestures, faith, and transcendent reality is a Bergerian metaphysical assumption.

This assumption is important from a sociological perspective because it is an 'empirical assumption.' That is, the linkage between gesture and transcendence is based upon, first, Berger's observations concerning the existence of hope, play, order propensity, and so on, and second, his assertion that such gestures imply a faith which transcends the material world. Both of these are empirical statements, the first because it is based upon induction from empirical phenomena, the second because it is rooted in a deduction about the relationship between the empirical phenomenon of faith and the empirical experiences of everyday life.

At this point, some will no doubt be asking: How can the conclusions of the last two paragraphs both hold true? How can Berger's assumption be termed both metaphysical and empirical? The answer is that it is an observation about empirical phenomena that cannot be demonstrated to be true. In fairness, it ought to be noted that I hold to the position that *all* empirical observations fall into this category. But leaving that sticky wicket aside, it should be fairly clear that in this case 1) Berger is making a patently empirical observation (that is, he perceives the existence of these human gestures) which 2) can be both contravened (for example, we might argue that most people do not hope, order, and so on) and differently interpreted (for example, that their hope does not imply transcendent faith).

The significance of this is that here is a point at which Berger's religious metaphysic has informed his sociological understanding. His assumed social world is one which contains a human being full of the need for meaning, order, and faith. This assertion can be readily confirmed by a quick reading of the introductory chapter in any one of his major treatises in sociology. Of course, he is by no means unique in employing these assumptions; some of his acknowledged masters make similar assumptions, as do many others within the classical sociological tradition. This being the case, one could argue that his metaphysic results more from sociological inheritance than religious inclination. Such an argument raises the question: was Berger attracted to this particular sociological tradition because of his theological proclivities, or did he fall naïvely into a sociological tradition that just happened to correlate with his religious interests? While many adulterers justify their behavior in terms of uncontrollable passions, few there be who plead ignorance.

The hermeneutics of heresy

The discovery of these 'signals of transcendence' did not end Berger's search for religious truth, of course. Indeed, by his own admission, it did nothing more than raise the possibility of transcendent reality and suggest an approach by which the empirically minded might uncover the nature of that reality. The question still remained: How does one go about the business of discovering the content of religious truths? Once again, following Berger on this trek is instructive for those wishing to understand the interaction of theology and sociology in his thinking.

In *The Heretical Imperative*, Berger argues that, in the modern era, three different methodologies have been employed in an attempt to understand religious truth. The first, he terms 'deduction.' It involves the reaffirmation of the authority of a religious tradition, in spite of the difficulties of doing so in the context of modern pluralism and within the assumptions of socio-historical relativism. An exemplar in the use of this method would be Karl Barth. He labels the second method 'reduction' and considers the work of Rudolf Bultmann to fall into this category. Here, the religious tradition is reinterpreted via modern, secular categories in the hope of making aspects of the tradition meaningful to the modernist mind. The last method, 'induction,' involves an attempt to uncover and retrieve essential experiences embodied in the religious tradition. It is both empirical and comparative, in that it takes all religious experiences seriously in its search for transcendent reality. Friedrich Schleiermacher achieves paradigmatic status relative to this approach.

It is important to note that all of these methods are non-foundationalist in theory, since none of them assumes the possibility of demonstrating religious truth with certitude. Even deduction, which affirms the essential truth of religious orthodoxy, does so only 'after' acknowledging the impossibility of proof (and, indeed, distancing itself from any such attempts). This is why each of these methods are 'heretical;' none assumes that one can come to orthodoxy directly, and most assume the impossibility of orthodoxy altogether. Berger argues, moreover, that in a modern pluralistic society, heresy of this kind is unavoidable, since the warp and woof of everyday life compels the citizen to make religious choices. Whether he is correct in this assertion is, of course, debatable (Gaede, 1981), but his point is nevertheless important: In a religiously heterogeneous society, traditional orthodoxy is an anomaly at best, and more than likely, a sociological impossibility.

Now, of the three articulated options, Berger favors the one he has labeled induction. His reasons for this choice are both interesting and metaphysically revealing. The problem with deduction, he argues, is that in a world of religious truths (plural), it asserts a religious Truth (singular) without providing empirical evidence to support its exclusivistic claim. Indeed, it asserts religious Truth despite contrary evidence and eschews the need to defend its position on empirical grounds. While Berger admits that such a 'leap of faith' may be heroic, it is not especially convincing – especially to those, such as the author, who are rather phenomenologically minded. In other words, Berger rejects deduction because its approach is a priori and non-empirically grounded.

Note Berger's line of reasoning. Society is pluralistic; it evidences a heterogeneity of religious experiences and truth claims; we must take all of these empirical phenomena seriously; therefore, we cannot accept as a prior claim an exclusive truth. Thus the starting point of Berger's critique is an empirical statement about the nature of modern social conditions, from which he draws an epistemological conclusion about method, out of which he will derive (one must assume) some ontological assertions about religious truth. In other words, here once again is evidence of the impact of his sociological conception of reality upon his theological endeavor.

Something a little different happens, however, when he turns his artillery on the method of reduction. The problem with this approach, he argues, is not its exclusivity, but quite the contrary, its nearly uncritical acceptance of modern hermeneutical categories. Thus, in the process of translating the religious tradition into a modern, secular frame of reference, it tends to undermine the *raison d'être* of religion itself. What begins as a translation of the tradition, ends up in self-liquidation. The reason, Berger argues, is not difficult to discern. Why should someone wish to affirm a totally secularized, demythologized religion? If modern categories are so compelling, why bother with religion at all? Cannot a secular understanding of reality be found, in much purer form, outside of religion? The answer, for Berger, is clear.

In this argument we once again see the interaction of sociological and theological assumptions, albeit in a somewhat more subtle fashion. In his critique, Berger assumes the inadequacy of both a secularized religiosity and a purely secularized conception of truth. The first assumption is most obvious, since he clearly states that there is no compelling reason to imbibe a wholly demythologized religious tradition. But his argument also assumes that a naturalist understanding of truth is inadequate because the argument itself is located within the context of a broader search for religious truth. This is not as difficult to understand as it may at first appear. When Berger states that one can find a purer form of secularism outside of reductionist religion than within it, he does not conclude that 'therefore, we should all become secularists.' Rather, he continues to search for transcendent meaning which is not wholly reductionistic. If, on the other hand, he thought that a purely secularized conception of truth was adequate, he would have set his manuscript aside and returned to sociology.

But he does not return to sociology at this point, in part because sociology (as a secular conception of reality) is an inadequate relevance structure to encompass the matter of truth. This should not come as a surprise to those who have followed Berger's sociological career, because he often cautions his readers about the limited perspective that one receives via sociological lenses. That is the reason for his incessant use of 'bracketing;' he wants his readers to comprehend the perspectival nature of the discipline. What may come as more of a surprise, however, is that this understanding of sociology does not result simply from a particular philosophical tradition, but also from a conviction concerning the existence of transcendent reality. Thus his use of brackets is not only a mode of protecting sociology from the incursion of religious (or other) value judgments, but also of protecting religion from the incursion of sociological reductionism. Whether this procedure is effective – or even possible – is not the issue at hand. What is important is that, once again, we can see that Berger's religious assumptions do bear on the manner in which he engages in the sociological enterprise.

Finally, then, Berger chooses the method he calls 'induction,' in part, because it avoids the pitfalls of reduction and deduction. Unlike deduction, it takes human experience as its starting point;

unlike reduction, it takes transcendently pregnant experiences at face value, without attempting to explain them away through secularist categories. Its goal is, first, to discover the essential experiences in all religions – where the infinite encounters 'the finite phenomena of human life' (1979a: 13). Secondly, it seeks to describe and analyze the 'essence' of such experiences. And, finally, it attempts a comprehensive investigation of all religious truth claims, wherever they may be found, through comparative and historical analysis. It is an approach, he believes, which appreciates the plurality of religious traditions without undermining the authenticity of religious phenomena itself.

Quite clearly, here is a method which comports well with both Berger's theological and sociological assumptions. It is, at once, empirical, phenomenological, and transcendentally suggestive. Thus, within the rubric of this approach, Berger is able to bring together strands of thought which only remain disguised in other discussions. In it one may find the most explicit expression of his metaphysical base and his most overt attempt at the interweaving of theology and sociology. Though it is still couched in the language of epistemology, it nevertheless attempts the use of a sociologically informed method to bring about a theological end. A more 'vulgar' declaration from Peter Berger we shall not find.

A concluding thought

The reader is left hanging, however, with the question of merit: How successful is this wedding of theology and sociology? Such a query can, of course, be asked at many levels. For example, we might ask about the adequacy of his ontological conclusions: How compelling are the results of his methodology and what insights into truth emanate from its implementation? Less overwhelming, but no less important, is the question concerning the internal validity of his approach: Within the context of Berger's own parameters, how successful is his inductive method? Does it live up to its own billing?

While a thorough discussion of either of these questions would require a treatise of some magnitude, it is appropriate to conclude with a few comments on the issue of internal adequacy. Taking such a tack, of course, plucks us out of the role of interpreter and places us in the realm of the critic. Though somewhat out of place in an investigative study of this kind, we hope it generates sufficient insight into the metaphysical debate to justify its inclusion.

The single most important question to be asked of Berger's inductive methodology is whether or not it does indeed overcome the failings of reduction and deduction (as per Berger's own critique). For example, is his inductive approach any less of a capitulation to secularist categories than reduction? Certainly, it is true that the author's use of induction does not rule out the possibility of religious truth a priori, but neither is that the intent of Bultmann (his reductionist exemplar). Bultmann wishes, it should be remembered, to make the religious tradition *more* meaningful and credible to the modern mind. Berger understands this, of course, and thus his critique of reductionism is leveled not at its intentions, but its results. Similarly, therefore, we must hold Berger to the same standard and judge his inductionist approach by its fruit. Unfortunately, Berger's methodology has only been planted (and substantially fertilized); we await the coming of both roots and branches.

We do not need to wait, however, to compare his method with reduction, and here there appear to be difficulties by Berger's own standards. Is it not true, for example, that both reduction and induction are inspired by the same objective, namely, to derive a method of religious understanding that is palatable to the modern mind? And are not those assumptions which are acceptable to the modern mind the categories of naturalism, regardless of whether they are described as secularist (as per reduction) or empirical (as per induction)? And if one assumes such categories, does it not lead one to the same conclusions, regardless of how 'open' one is to 'other possibilities'? In *Rumor of Angels*, Berger seems to think so:

> The theologian who trades ideas with the modern world, therefore, is likely to come out with a poor bargain, that is, he will probably have to give far more than he will get. To vary the image, he who sups with the devil had better have a long spoon. The devilry of modernity has its own magic: The theologian who sups with 'it' will find his spoon getting shorter and shorter – until that last supper in which he is left alone at the table, with no spoon at all and with an empty plate. The

devil, one may guess, will by then have gone away to more interesting company (1969b: 22).

The approach which Berger uses, moreover, necessarily assumes a diversity of religious truths. Such an assumption is perfectly legitimate, but automatically rules out the veracity of any exclusivistic truth claims (such as those in the orthodox versions of Judaism, Islam, and Christianity). Thus, while his approach does not exclude the possibility of transcendent reality, it does exclude specific understandings of that reality in certain religious traditions. From the vantage point of those who participate in such religious communities, therefore, Berger's approach does not appear empirically inductive at all, but rather quite deductive – and the deduction which emanates from his presuppositions arbitrarily precludes the possibility that their version of religious truth is correct. For these, Berger is no less deductive than Barth (and much farther from the 'truth').

What this suggests is not simply the relativity of labels such as deduction and reduction, but also the extent to which such methods are relative to their metaphysical moorings. It reminds us anew that we do not go about the business of truth gathering – whether in sociological or theological garb – in an assumptive vacuum, without regard to the truth we seek. Instead, in our quest for understanding, we must necessarily assume some of the understanding we pursue.

The nagging question that always haunts the reader is: What forms of presumed truth lie behind the author's assertions? It has been that question which has motivated our discussion of the alleged cohabitation of sociology and theology in the mind of Peter Berger. Admittedly, our success has been limited; deciphering the graffiti on the door of the honeymoon suite rarely captures the full flavor of what is therein occurring. Hopefully, however, it has laid to rest the rumor, perpetrated by the management, that the occupants' intentions are merely discursive. Though discreet, the cohabitants are not inert. Indeed, to those of us who love to roam the halls, it appears to be a rather robust *tête-à-tête*.

Part IV

The method and vocation of sociology

CHAPTER 7

The place of politics

James P. O'Leary

A great part of the considerable scholarly contribution of Peter Berger deals in one way or another with the ethical implications of sociological investigation. There are moral and ethical challenges posed to the 'value-free' social scientist by the perverse fact that his work inevitably contributes to the practical political dialogue. The social scientist may legitimate or delegitimate governments, corporate directors, religious elites, or entire academic fields of inquiry. He may inspire a new religiosity or encourage the collapse of cherished human myths and traditions. Perhaps more than any other profession, the sociologist's vocation entails a continual and unavoidable tension between the aspiration to objective, *value-free* science and the equally obvious need to scrutinize the *value-laden* uses to which the sociological enterprise is inextricably tied. As Berger himself put it;

> History is not only a succession of power structures but of theoretical edifices, and every one of the latter was first *thought up* by somebody. This is so regardless of who conned whom at any given moment – whether it is a case of intellectuals convincing the wielders of power to carry into practice some particular theoretical scheme, or power wielders hiring intellectuals to concoct theories that will legitimate that particular exercise of power ex post facto. In either case, there are intellectuals in the woodpile (1974f: 4).

As this relationship of the social scientist to the practical political realm pervades Berger's writings, it is not feasible to attempt a detailed textual explication in the compass of this chapter. Instead a number of discrete albeit interrelated aspects of Berger's work will be analyzed in so far as they illumine his evolving position on these questions.

The chapter begins with an analysis of Berger's methodological views. It will be argued that his particular understanding of the methods appropriate to social scientific investigation derive from an understanding of the historicity of human reality which, in turn, has direct implications for the understanding of the proper relationship between the social scientist and political activity. In this section the importance of Berger's grounding in the 'sociology of knowledge' will be particularly stressed, and his unique contributions in this area will be highlighted. Particularly important are the conclusions about each individual's biographic development towards which he is led, and the relevance of these conclusions to the relationship between science and political commitment.

The implications of methodological modesty

There is a mutually reinforcing relationship between an investigator's methodological presuppositions and his attitude toward the realm of practical political commitment. Methodological modesty encourages political prudence. For Berger, sociology is the *modest* science *par excellence* and one consequence is a cautious, often skeptical attitude toward political uses of sociological investigations. To the degree that one regards sobriety and modesty as inherently *moral* qualities, he sees an affinity between methodology and morality (1981d: 73). Sociology properly conducted demands a continuous, sustained attention to the immensely diverse variety of meanings by which people live. Such immersion in the historical drama of unfolding human meanings – always tenuous and precariously fragile – can inspire a poignant humility which may in fact be the specific form of humility appropriate to authentic social science.

The method of attentive listening appropriate to sociological inquiry thus encourages a 'cognitive respect' for the beliefs, opinions, and idiosyncrasies of wildly diverse individuals, groups and cultures. Such attentiveness discourages a wide range of political involvement which would strive to 'uplift,' 'reform,' 'educate' and otherwise 'raise the consciousness' of people who are judged to be insufficiently aware of their own 'true' needs and potential. A common denominator, indeed a defining characteristic, of all political movements whether of the right or the left, has been the conviction of the 'True Believers' that their unique access to 'truth' justifies a proselytizing mission that may justifiably run roughshod over the most cherished beliefs and traditions of those less cognitively privileged. Such arrogance, institutionalized in political movements and, in extreme cases, couched in revolutionary rhetoric, has provided a measure of intellectual respectability to 'causes' in whose name millions have been slaughtered.

By contrast, Berger's estimation of the sociologists' method and vocation militate against all but the most humane of political commitments. Indeed, in his estimation, *compassion* is the only legitimate motive for such activist commitments:

> The only political commitments worth making are those that seek to reduce the amount of human suffering in the world. Much of politics, of course, is too ordinary to evoke commitment of any depth. Most of the rest is crime, illusion or the self-indulgence of intellectuals . . . Intense political commitment is usually bad (1970a: 13).

For Berger, then, the method appropriate to sociology may be summarized as that of attentive listening and cognitive respect. The sociologist must ground his concepts and his observations in the experiences of everyday life. Social science cannot *deduce* concrete events from universal laws. To do so risks losing *meaningful* reality which is our proper field of study. Our search for causal explanations must ground itself within the world of human meanings and this requires a relentless attention to those structures of human meaning in which people live. Only scrupulous cognitive respect can ensure that sociological concepts and explanatory schemes avoid the bloodless aridity of positivism and its grand deductive schematics.

Berger stands clearly in the Weberian tradition in his rejection of the positivist position on the uses to which social science can and should be put. Paradoxically, positivists endow value-free social scientific findings with moral authority. Despite their professed ideal of scientific detachment, the actual tendency of positivist social science is precisely to provide instruments for manipulation of ordinary people by the enlightened scientific community who are allegedly better able to judge the true interests of 'society.' On the contrary, Berger's interpretive social science aspires to the ideal of value-freeness while grounding its very *raison d'être* on the bedrock of the immensely diverse richness and pluralism of values which infuse and govern everyday human coexistence. Sociology in this view should strive for acts of 'pure perception' in so far as this is humanly possible. But such an ideal of value-freeness does not imply that the sociologist himself has no values (a patent absurdity), *nor* does the approximation to such pure perception equip the sociologist to adjudicate scientifically among competing values. He is in a sense a 'spy:'

> The good spy reports what is there. Others decide what should be done as a result of this information. The sociologist is a spy in very much the same way. His job is to report as accurately as he can about a certain social terrain. Others, or he himself in a role other than that of sociologists, will have to decide what moves ought to be made in that terrain (1963c: 6).

It is crucial to note that this Weberian conception of the nature of value-free inquiry in no way precludes the sociologist from asking serious questions about the uses to which his work is put in the realm of practical politics. On the contrary, Berger repeatedly insists that his *method* and his notion of the *vocation* of the sociologist are intimately connected. His method, grounded as it is upon the interpretive injunction that social science concepts must be *Sinna d'equat* (that they must be comprehensible and resonant with the everyday world of living human beings) enjoins a rejection of positivist social engineering and a resigned acceptance of our inevitable 'cognitive nervousness' – a nervousness that stems from the limits of our knowledge and the consequent dangers of arrogance.

The quest for a social science which satisfies the Weberian criterion that concepts must be grounded in the actual meanings which real individuals hold and share leads to a dawning appreciation of the inescapable, exhilarating, and sometimes frustrating inevitability of *pluralism* in social life. Indeed, a defining characteristic of modernity for Berger is precisely the *pluralization* of life-worlds which markedly distinguishes modern life from pre-modern traditional worlds. Modern man is a restless player of roles. Personas are shed as frequently and easily as clothes by modern men and women accustomed to the diversity of roles – family member, worker, citizen, church member, political actor –

which are typical of contemporary life. A radical consequence of sociological attentiveness to the diversity and pluralism of modern man is an incipient *relativization* of life and values. Our interpretive method incessantly forces us to confront the inherent conflicts and marked diversity of beliefs and values which comprise the milieu of modern (or modernizing) society. 'Reality,' both theoretical 'ideas' and commonsense everyday 'knowledge,' is to a large degree *situational* and *constructed*. Diverse roles yield diverse perspectives on 'reality.' What we see may depend upon where we stand. Geography, chronology, material circumstances, and nurturing shape our understanding and mould our meaningful world view to yield a remarkable wealth of attitudes and understandings only dimly captured in the concept of a 'pluralization of life-worlds.'

It is the *political* implications of this methodologically induced immersion into the pluralistic, near-anarchical milieu of modern society which are the proper focus of this chapter. Does the 'sociological imagination' as construed by Berger entail any consequences in so far as political involvements or commitments by social scientists (*qua* social scientists) are concerned? Can a sociological sensitivity be linked, either logically or empirically, with any easily generalizable implications for practical political actions by the social scientist? The branch of sociological investigation which has perhaps the most to say on this matter is, not surprisingly, the sociology of knowledge, the sub-field which has most crucially advanced Berger's understanding of the properly 'debunking mission' of the sociological enterprise.

The sociology of knowledge and political relevance

The sociology of knowledge constitutes the most relentlessly relativizing activity of modern social science. By pointing out the situationally fixed constructedness of human thought it operates as a continuing, nagging reminder of the limits of human knowledge and, logically, of the limits of all *political applications* of the 'knowledge industry.'

The inherent limitations of what we can 'know' with any degree of 'certainty' is of course a familiar theme of philosophical–epistemological speculation. Max Weber's classical methodology was grounded upon the Kantian denial that our knowledge can ever faithfully copy reality. All 'knowledge' (whether of the 'generalizing' or 'individualizing' type, in Weber's sense) entails an unavoidable abstraction from reality in pursuit of the elusive goal of conceptual clarity. Social 'laws' are at best tenuous aids which assist us in an ever-closer *approximation* to understanding causal relationships in the cultural sciences. The nature of this abstraction is always affected by the values of the investigator, as is the very choice of the problems and phenomena which are to be investigated. 'Presuppositionless' investigation of empirical data is never possible because segments of reality only are of interest to us to the extent that they have relevance to our own values (Weber, 1949: 68–84; Berger, 1966e: 17ff).

A critical consequence of this appreciation of the social–cultural rootedness of 'knowledge' in the human sciences is the perception of the ineradicable subjective element of our 'knowledge' and the resulting emphasis on 'perspectivism' (to use Jose Ortega's formulation). Weber notes:

> All knowledge of cultural reality, as may be seen, is always knowledge from *particular points of view*. When we require from the historian and social research worker as an elementary presupposition that they distinguish the important from the trivial and that they should have the necessary 'point of view' for this distinction, we mean that they must understand how to relate the events of the real world consciously or unconsciously to universal 'cultural values' and to select out those relationships which are significant for us (1949: 18f).

Of course this understanding of the subjective nature of the criteria of significance in social science did not lead Weber into an anarchical denial that cumulative knowledge is possible, nor have more recent investigations in the tradition of the sociology of knowledge. Weber's own 'solution' – the construction of 'ideal types' – has guided subsequent investigators, including Peter Berger, through the potential minefield of relativism and subjectivism.

Ideal–typical constructs do not describe reality. Rather, they afford an investigator even closer *approximations* of adequate conceptualizations of reality. Their construction proceeds by means of a process of selective accentuation of certain elements which comprise social reality, those elements which the investigator himself deems most essential and 'typical.' Because these analytical tools are constructs, *abstractions*, which assist us in groping toward causal explanation, the greatest danger confronting the social scientist is that he will mistake his constructs for 'reality.' This fallacy of 'reification' becomes particularly acute whenever a social investigator turns his attention to practical political programs and translates his intellectual constructs into blueprints for political reform or social engineering. This modest unpretentiousness of the Weberian 'interpretative' tradition infuses all of Berger's works. Once again, the moral and ethical implications derived from the type of methodological caution appropriate to sociological investigation become counsels to prudence in undertaking all manner of political commitments and social 'reforms.'

This sort of methodologically grounded conservatism, of course, need not translate necessarily into rock-ribbed resistance to change in support of any *status quo*. This is not a conservatism borne of faith in some sacrosanct *status quo* hallowed by prescription and tradition. It is rather a conservatism borne of *lack of faith*; that is, a skeptical conservatism which is constantly alert to the 'irony of history' and the unintended consequences of human actions. With Weber, Berger is sensitive to the historical evidence that most social institutions are typically the result not of deliberate human design but of accidents and unintended results. In one of his most explicitly political testaments Berger lays claim to a conservatism which 'does not derive from a philosophical or psychological commitment to immutability, but rather from empirical insight into the nature of socio-political reality' (1970a: 22).

Such a conservative 'accepts the messiness of history and is suspicious of the idea of progress;' he is skeptical of innovation and 'doubly skeptical of violent innovation;' a conservative 'accepts human beings as they are' and 'values order, continuity and triviality in social life' (1970a: 23f). The upshot of this humane and modest conservatism is a predisposition toward courses of action in political life which are sensitive to those human realities which are precisely the proper focus of the sociologist's investigatory enterprise: the world of human beings as they are, not as they might be or as they have been envisioned in the vast array of Utopian schemes for 'progress' and 'reform' of the race. It is a world view which accepts that order is 'the fundamental social category' and which is *ipso facto* repelled by those political ideologies – *whether of the right or the left* – which prescribe and proselytize *disorder* as necessary for desirable societal change. In short, his is a conservatism which could never serve as the foundation of a movement, nor does it propose deliberate programs of political action.

Thus, to use the arguments against certainty as arguments against any and all variety of 'reform' or consciously pursued social change is, as we have seen, to misread fundamentally the import of Berger's (and Weber's) message. If we are, in a sense, condemned by our epistemology to a lifelong 'debunking' skepticism (Nietzsche's 'art of mistrust'), we are not, thereby, condemned to sterile passivity. What is proscribed is not political commitment *per se* but rather those sorts of political commitments which are impelled by a blind indifference to the limits of our unique 'perspective' on reality. In short, an appreciation of the implications of the sociology of knowledge can lead consistently to a position best characterized as an 'ethic of responsibility' and a continuing vigilance against the tempting self-assurance and smugness typical of the 'ethic of ultimate ends.'

Although he consistently advances the Weberian case for value-freeness in sociological investigation, Berger repeatedly reminds us that aspiring to this methodological ideal can never absolve the social scientist of *responsibility* for the political uses to which his findings may be put. As he argued in *Pyramids of Sacrifice*:

> 'Value-freeness' is an ideal for theoretical understanding. It does *not* imply (and was never intended by Weber to imply) that the social scientist who aspires to it is himself free of values, is unaware of the values operative in the situation he is studying, *or has the option that one can engage in policies devoid of value consequences*. . . . In essence, 'value-freeness' means that one tries to perceive social reality apart from one's hopes and fears. This does not mean that one has no hopes or fears, nor does it mean that one refrains from acting to realize what one hopes for or to avert what one fears. 'Value-freeness'

> in science is, therefore, perfectly compatible with the most intense value commitments and with intense activity springing from these commitments (1974f: 135).

Interpretive sociology thus counsels not passivity but informed, prudential, responsible action continually attentive to the probability of unintended outcomes with potentially high human costs. The elementary *compassion* which is in part a result of our method of 'cognitive respect,' and which equally and mutually reinforces our methodological canons, dictates a sober ethic of responsibility rather than the intoxication of an ethic of ultimate ends. There is plenty of room in this conception of political change to accommodate the charismatic political figure. Indeed for Weber such charismatic leaders are central moving forces for social change. The possibility of charismatic 'breakouts' from received tradition are empirically demonstrable. They provide in turn a source of continued hope that man can shape history and society and that he is not a helpless pawn confronting the solidity and immovability of received social practice. The potential for voluntarism and freely undertaken political action in pursuit of change is a critical element of the Weberian tradition in reaction against the oppressive stolidity of the Durkheimian view of 'society' as all-encompassing and stifling. Berger has frequently averred that the possibility of political praxis ('ex-stasis') to change (or support) society is not necessarily ruled out by acknowledging the omnipresence of social constraints and roles. Indeed, these constraints and roles are themselves fragile and in continual need of reaffirmation by individuals (1963c: 128f).

Thus political praxis is not ruled out by the interpretive sociological understanding. In fact we are positively encouraged to perceive the fragility of all established orders, rules and regulations. The debunking motif is itself inherently *revolutionary* while paradoxically, a continual council to *moderation*. It is constantly alerting us to the *limits* of responsible, compassionate social change which are rooted both in our own personal biographies and in the empirical 'real-world' environment of bureaucratic policy formulation and implementation.

The sociology of knowledge, and the interpretive sociological consciousness more broadly construed, thus have the effect of alerting the investigator to the precarious and transitory nature of his own beliefs. It is clear then that the counsel to modesty and moderation implicit in the 'sociology of knowledge' derives not merely from the revelation that all ideas, ideologies and political 'theories' are spatio-temporally bounded and necessarily suspect as grounds for any degree of human engineering or social reform. We are as well forced to confront and (it is hoped) to acknowledge the boundedness of our own lives, our own everyday taken-for-granted predispositions, and our own intellectual (and emotional) 'growth.' The 'vertigo' of which Berger speaks is one which should at least temporarily stun the reflexive urge to 'do something' to solve 'social problems' through political interventions, however well-intentioned. Indeed, the marked dichotomy between intentions and consequences ('unintended outcomes') is in part rooted in the inevitable boundedness of both our everyday unreflective notions and of our most carefully constructed theoretical edifices: neither can ever grasp reality from any but a partial perspective. This is, indeed, a sobering antidote to the urge toward large-scale programmatic pursuit of social change.

Institutions and political life: bureaucracies and mediating structures

The insights of Berger's sociology of knowledge concerning the flux and tenuousness of each individual's biography encourage a circumspect attitude toward politically-directed social change and reformism. This micro-level investigation encourages a healthy skepticism about ambitious programs of political change, reform, and social engineering. To this micro-level insight we may now incorporate Berger's *macro*-level understanding of the dynamics of *large-scale* public institutions. The study of the sociology of knowledge and more recent investigations into the impact of 'modernization' upon human consciousness comprise a coherent analysis of the deadening effect of such powerful political agencies.

The entire thrust of Berger's analyses of institutionalization and bureaucratic inertia is of course inimical to certain functionalist tendencies – notably that social persistence is evidence that useful social functions are being served. Rather, he suggests that institutions may persist long after they have lost their practicality or functionality simply because such things have been legitimized as *right* in terms of the symbolic universe promulgated by intellectuals and other 'universal experts.'

In part as a direct result of the impact of the Vietnam War, Berger has turned his attention increasingly to the problem of the political relevance of sociological thought (1970a: 7–9, 1977b: 130f). This has involved, among other concerns, a focus on the effects of increasing politicization and bureaucratization of modern secular life upon the individual, both in advanced industrial society (particularly the United States) and in the modernizing nations of the 'Third World.' A proper, indeed a vital, mission for contemporary sociology is the investigation of the process by which modernization dichotomizes human life into that part dominated by the immense, impersonal institutions of the public sphere and the residual, 'underinstitutionalized' preserves of the private sphere. Contemporary society is characterized by those 'megastructures' of bureaucratic domination – principally, but not exclusively, political arrangements (1977b: 133).

Berger's explication of the predicament of modernity stresses that programs for political governance are invariably institutionalized in structures which grow increasingly remote from the meaningful lived realities of the everyday world. This would include, of course, the lived reality of the bureaucrats themselves. As Weber pointed out, charismatic leaders and revolutionary programs alike are susceptible to the effects of this routinzation and inertia.

That revolutionary movements invariably become institutionalized and take on all the conservative trappings of a new *status quo* follows directly from the notion that all social reality is constructed. All meaningful definitions of reality must be objectivated by social processes. Hence any practically successful revolution will require continued sustenance and support both from within the subsociety of revolutionaries and the broader society itself. The social career of revolution thus leads to consolidation and official entrenchment of the once-deviant ideology as the new legitimized (and continuously legitimizing) *status quo*. Berger thus provides a phenomenological and sociological explanation, at the level of the individual's own constructed definition of reality, which helps to explain the familiar phenomenon of the 'natural history of revolution' observed by Brinton (1938), Edwards (1927), and many others (cf. Janowitz, 1977).

Nevertheless, this proliferation of bureaucratic impersonal megastructures still leaves a substantial scope for private life in all but the most totalitarian of political orders. This reserved private sphere is in fact a potential source of anomie and alienation to the extent that the individual is incapable of discovering meaning and identity in his private life. The very fact that his private life is (in Gehlen's terminology) 'underinstitutionalized' means precisely that the threat of anomie and disintegration is ever-present.

Drawing upon the classical tradition, Berger maintains that a politically relevant role for the modern sociologist is to illuminate the contours of contemporary alienation and to identify those 'mediating structures' – such as those of family, church, neighborhood, voluntary associations, and subcultural groups – which provide degrees of identity, meaning, and stability in *private life* (1977e). Public life itself is only possible if the individuals who comprise a collective order retain a degree of shared moral values, what Durkheim called the 'collective conscience.' Political life at the collective level rests upon these lower and intermediate orders of moral authority. If these intermediate levels of order are undermined by the progressive eradication of mediating structures through unbridled political coercion or cooptation from the top, private life collapses into anomie and the political order will lose its moral ground of legitimacy and authority. Chaos or brutal repression are likely consequences of such a scenario of 'disintermediation' (to appropriate the economists' terminology). Indeed, the totalitarian phenomenon is a perversely promising solution to the dichotomization of the public and private spheres: it solves the problem by absorbing the private into the public!

Berger has pointed out that most mainstream ideologies are insensitive to the important role of mediating structures. Classical *laissez-faire* liberalism and modern welfare-state liberalism alike betray a faith in *rationality* (whether the rationality of economic man in the free market or the rationality of public policy designs for social improvement) and a disdain for the 'parochial' and anti-rational allegiances of church, family, neighborhood, etc. Left-socialist schemes similarly acknowledge the alienating tendencies of capitalism but fail to see the equal or greater degrees of alienation attendant upon socialist state planning. Ironically, only classical Burkean conservatism and New Left anarcho-synderalism reveal an appreciation of the role of mediating structures in resisting anomie.

The sociological investigation of bureaucracy is thus supplemented logically by the sociological study of the private sphere and the mediation effected by certain types of structures between these two poles of human existence. Without this mediation, meaningful political order becomes impossible. Herein lay a crucial agenda for a politically relevant sociology the outlines of which Berger has quite effectively delineated. The specific implications for public policy which have issued from the 'mediating structures' project (1977e) are squarely in the tradition of 'cognitive respect' enjoined by the methodological considerations outlined above. Public policy, according to Berger, should encourage the survival and growth of mediating structures. This implies minimal official interference with sub-cultures, family authority, the texture of neighborhood life, and First Amendment guarantees of religious freedom. On the other hand, legitimate official party objectives should be pursued by means of methods which encourage, or at least do not damage, the same mediating structures. In this regard, voucher systems in education, tax incentives to encourage private voluntary solutions to social problems, and other measures of decentralization (but not wholesale governmental retreat) should typify public policy in the future.

The intellectuals and 'development'

The problematic relationship of the social scientist to the realm of practical political action is perhaps best encapsulated in the postwar experience of 'development' studies. The conventional wisdom that global poverty is a problem largely attributable to the prosperity of the more advantaged nations (principally the United States, the ex-colonial powers, and a handful of successful non-Western states such as Japan) is largely a product of the liberal and left intellectual establishment. That a certain sense of guilt has accompanied and reinforced this conviction has been frequently pointed out, often by Berger himself. Western intellectuals and Third World leaders educated in Western institutions (or taught with Western texts) have constructed a vast edifice of theory and practical political prescription. This enterprise reveals strikingly the dangers of wholesale programs of reform and progress promised upon the limp abstractions of scientific theories. It violates at least five of the major theses which Berger has advanced to guide the relations between social scientists and public policy:

1) The definition of the 'problem' of development has itself been a product of the intellectual imagination. It is a recent postwar phenomenon which largely derived from the disenchantment with the old colonial system and the left-liberal desire to ensure not only political autonomy but also economic independence in the wake of the rapid and unexpected decolonization experience of the 1950s and early 1960s. For these coteries of intellectuals whose principal occupation is thought rather than action, development is a problem which they have defined largely in complete ignorance of the perspective of those who actually are poor. In Berger's view, the injunction to *cognitive respect* has been ignored.

2) Intellectuals, and those policy makers who utilize their ideas to legitimize their own preferred political programs, invariably arrogate to themselves the role of spokesmen for the masses who are judged incapable of understanding their own situation. As Berger notes, such claims are 'usually spurious.' In fact each individual knows his own situation better than anyone else. Therefore, they should be integrally involved both in the process of defining the nature of the problem and in the processes set in motion in pursuit of 'development.' The existing developmental enterprise thus violates the injunction to '*cognitive participation*.'

3) The developmental enterprise has consistently violated the injunction to ground their intellectual constructs upon a 'postulate of ignorance.' Instead, a variety of nostrums have been proffered which promise a quick transition from poverty to prosperity. Whether the particular 'quick-fix' is that preferred by the right (*laissez-faire* free market capitalism) or the left (extensive state planning and control), the starting point is a 'presumption of certainty' as to the proper course of action to take. A faith in rationality and in the limitless potential for social engineering in pursuit of *consciousness raising* is endemic to the developmentalists' schemes for change.

4) In part as a result of the abstract, disembodied definition of

the problem and the arrogance of certainty which typified the developmental ethos of the past, the 'calculus of pain' has been ignored. Schemes of the capitalist right and socialist left have alike brought wrenching social disruption, growing inequalities of income and wealth maldistribution, urban misery, rural stagnation, inflation, and mounting external problems of indebtedness and dependency.

5) Perhaps most importantly, 'developmentalism' represents the latest manifestation of the mythic potential of modern science. 'Development,' to borrow from Voegelin, has 'immanentized the eschaton,' promising a secular, salvific transformation which has made it the operative myth among many Third World and Western intellectuals (1983c). Whether it takes the form of a capitalist 'myth of growth' or a socialist 'myth of revolution' (the more virulent variety today, in Berger's estimation) the result is that the abstractions of disembodied social science become the focus of redemptive hope. Science, and by definition the scientist, acquire mythic potency. Minds rendered 'homeless' by the anomic virulence of social change escape from alienation by embracing the promised parousia of 'development,' 'high mass consumption,' 'proletarian solidarity' or 'equality' with the West. As major 'carriers' of the myth of developmentalism, the intellectual/scientific cadres acquire a power and legitimacy which is heady brew for such normally 'marginal' societal figures.

Intellectuals and the appeals of socialism

The developmentalist reveals in particularly striking relief the proclivities of the intellectuals to embrace socialism *precisely* because of its unique *mythic* appeal to the intellectual mind-set.

One of the defining features of contemporary Western society is the vast expansion in numbers and influence of that stratum of the population – the 'intellectuals' – whose principal activity is the production and distribution of ideas. While this notion is neither new nor a cause *per se* of concern, Berger has emphasized the peculiar affinity of modern intellectuals to embrace the socialist 'myths' of anti-capitalism, anti-bourgeois cultural arrogance, egalitarianism, redistributionism, and consciousness raising. The sociology of knowledge has sensitized him to the awareness that 'ideas have consequences,' less because of their intrinsic truth or validity than because of their appeal to particular configurations of social forces and powers. It is precisely his perception that moral passions, values, hopes, and interests in large measure fashion intellectual constructions and commitments that lead him to speak of the 'socialist myth' and its appeal to intellectuals (1976d). There are specific characteristics of this 'socialist myth' that explain its resonance with intellectuals of the left. Most importantly, socialism incorporates not only the familiar litany of progressive, rational themes (history as progress; human perfectibility; the triumph of scientific reason over prescientific illusions) but also promises to preserve or create *community*. In other words, socialism integrates into its myth a uniquely potent synthesis of the principal modernizing and counter-modernizing themes which represent the dominant trends and ideas of contemporary history. Socialism promises modernization without alienation. It promises a reintegration of the traditional order shattered irrevocably by modernizing forces, a reintegration of communal 'we-feeling,' and an end to the 'homelessness' typical of modernity. Socialism promises a future redemptive community which will be grounded upon scientific reason *and* which will include all the benefits of the modern secular order to boot. Herein lay its seductive appeal to the modern intellectual elites of the West and in the emerging Third World. The fact that the concrete realization of this myth has continually been postponed from one expected utopia to another (Soviet Union? People's Republic of China? Vietnam? The 'Third World' itself as a redemptive new order?) has not dampened the intrinsic appeal of this fusion of Enlightenment scientism and quasi-religious eschatology.

The soothing bromide of socialism thus has a particular appeal to intellectuals because it is this stratum which has proven most susceptible to the discontents of modernity (discussed in Chapter 4). The intellectuals derive from the bourgeois class which most directly experienced the dislocations of incipient modernization upon their world. While the earlier bourgeois classes could turn to the family, church, and other structures which helped to cushion the blows of modernity, contemporary intellectuals have directed their fire at precisely these remaining pillars of the older bourgeois order. As a result this class of adversary intellectuals feels the 'homelessness' of modernity with a peculiar intensity. Its attraction to the comforting myth of socialist transformation is all the more intense and potentially dangerous. Berger shares the concern of many contemporary observers that a new 'knowledge industry' has enshrined this socialist myth and given it a new, established, institutionalized base in Western society. Against this anti-bourgeois, anti-capitalist assault the West itself has failed to articulate any countervailing mythical vision which even remotely approaches the socialist counter-culture. The result of this 'mythic deprivation' is an alarming sense of drift in the West:

> With socialism as the only myth going, the political and economic elites of Western societies have become remarkably demoralized. The old rhetoric in defense of free enterprise, of the American way of life, and even of the institutions of liberal democracy, has come to sound hollow – it increasingly lacks the capacity to convince and inspire. Calls for a revival of liberalism or of the American creed, however well reasoned, will be ineffective unless they can be 'fueled' by the power of mythic plausibility. It seems unlikely that, on its own, liberalism – least of all in its social-democratic versions – is capable of regaining such powers (1983c: 58f).

Perhaps paradoxically, the mythical trappings of socialism have proven least appealing precisely in those countries in which it has succeeded. Intellectuals in the totalitarian states of the Eastern Bloc betray little affection for those ossified dogmatics which remain from formerly fiery Marxist polemics. Of course, by the time such delusion takes hold, it is too late.

Sociology as political dynamite

In Peter Berger's view, the sociologist is by nature a politically dangerous figure. His 'debunking' mission involves relentless scrutiny of all institutions and their legitimating thought patterns. The sociologist is in the business of unmasking the vested interests which benefit most from the *status quo* of uninvestigated 'taken-for-grantedness' typical of everyday life. The value-free inquiry towards which sociology aspires is profoundly revolutionary in its political implications for the entire range of established institutions, rules, norms, and customs. Sociology demystifies the 'false consciousness' upon which any existing political order must rest, and this can amount to 'political dynamite,' an unsettling experience for both the investigator and for those whom he is unmasking:

> Anyone who pursues the sociological perspective to its logical consequences will find himself undergoing a transformation of his consciousness of society. At least potentially, this makes him unsafe from the viewpoint of the guardians of law and order. It also produces unsafety, sometimes with catastrophic effects, for his own peace of mind (1977b: xiii).

At the same time that value-free sociology serves the revolutionary cause of human liberation from the routine, it is also profoundly *conservative* and inimical to revolutionary political commitment. Succinctly put, sociology reveals continually the essential imperatives of 'order, continuity, and triviality' inherent in human social life. The sociologist *qua* sociologist appreciates that

> Every social institution, no matter how 'non-repressive' or 'consensual,' is an imposition of order – beginning with language which is the most basic institution of all. If this is understood, there will then also be the understanding that *social life abhors disorder as nature abhors a vacuum* (1977b: xv).

Similarly, the simple fact of parenthood and the parent–child bond ensures that continuity will be a cherished aspect of human existence and a built-in resistor to radical social experimentation and the discontinuities of political upheavals. Finally, the truth that any man's attention span and his tolerance for emotional excitation is by nature limited reinforces the conservative proclivity toward 'normalcy' and the disinclination to pursue frenetic political programs of reform and 'consciousness raising.'

One inescapable conclusion toward which this line of thinking ineluctably leads is the debunking of the fashionable political ideal of *participation* as a major criterion (if not the *only* criterion) of the desirable polity. Berger's sociology provides a coherent brief against the creeping politicization of life and a counsel to prudential moderation in the face of the modern urge to expand the political agenda.

CHAPTER 8

The Jamesian Berger

Jay Mechling

Imagine the college freshman of 1964 reading the last few sentences of the paperback text assigned in her introductory sociology class. 'Unlike the puppets,' writes the author, 'we have the possibility of stopping in our movements, looking up and perceiving the machinery by which we have been moved. In this act lies the first step towards freedom. And in this same act we find the conclusive justification of sociology as a humanistic discipline' (Berger, 1963c: 176). Our freshman closes the book and smiles broadly. Having expected sociology to be dry and boring, full of numbers and difficult words made up for no good reason, she instead finds a highly readable, witty view of sociology full of talk of the humanization and liberation of our consciousness about society. To be sure, she needed to find this message after the shock of the assassination of President Kennedy the previous November, and she still has before her a decade of disorder and trauma, including perhaps the deaths of some of her classmates in the jungles of South-east Asia. But in 1964 the words are exciting and liberating, perhaps not exciting enough to persuade her to become a sociology major, but certainly powerful enough for her to take with her a piece of the consciousness about which the textbook author writes.

Imagine further that our freshman goes off to graduate school in 1968, where she is assigned a deceptive short paperback text bearing a familiar name. Berger and Luckmann's *The Social Construction of Reality* (1966e) now does relentlessly what her freshman text did gently, that is, radically relativizes all realities and in the process makes problematic her entire taken-for-granted world. She is a mature graduate student, however, so the message that might have struck terror in a freshman's heart now strikes her as an exciting theoretical and methodological foundation for her further graduate study in history, rhetoric, literary criticism, anthropology, sociology, American Studies, or any of the other disciplines in which she might plausibly be asked to read the Berger and Luckmann treatise in the sociology of knowledge.

It is impossible to judge how many American undergraduate and graduate students in the 1960s and 1970s passed through the 'fiery brook' of Peter L. Berger's sociology of knowledge; certainly they must number in the tens of thousands. Berger's work has always been in conversation with philosophy and history, so he inspires that small band of sociologists dedicated to the interdisciplinary project of a 'humanistic sociology.' Just as importantly, Berger's 'humanistic sociology' held then, as now, an attractiveness to some outside sociology, to scholars working in the interstices where the humanistic and social scientific study of culture converge (Kelly, 1983). It is not unfair to say that the 'interpretive social science' (Dolgin, Kemnitzer, and Schneider, 1977; Rabinow and Sullivan, 1979) that began to have impact in the 1970s was sowing its seed in ground prepared in the 1960s by Berger in sociology and by Maurice Natanson in philosophy.

Which is not to say that Berger was or is entirely happy with the practice of interpretive sociology since his 1963 invitation. His brief essay on 'Sociology and Freedom' in 1971 complained that too many sociologists were taking sociology to be a 'liberating discipline' without having any sense of the conservative implications of the discipline, and sociology was in sufficient disarray by 1981 for Berger to collaborate again with Hansfried Kellner on *Sociology Reinterpreted*, a sort of 'son of *Invitation to Sociology*' or *Invitation to Sociology Revisited* aimed at the younger colleagues and students 'in whom the future of sociology, if there is to be one, will be vested' (1981d: viii). *Sociology Reinterpreted* is unlikely to become widely adopted as an introductory text, as did its predecessor; these are different times for sociology, for the university, and for American society. But the publication of the book does pique curiosity. Has Berger held firm to the 'calling of sociology' as he defined it in 1963 for a generation of college students, or have twenty years of remarkable human history changed his tone and ideas?

My aim here is not merely to say again what Berger and Kellner say so clearly for themselves but to try to offer a modest critique and 'reinterpretation' of Berger's notions of sociology as 'method and vocation.' A consequence of my reinterpretation could possibly be that his work will be attractive again to those increasingly disenchanted with his Weberian distinction between science and politics. Quite frankly, Berger's political conservatism (often misunderstood) and his increasing focus on public policy matters have repulsed a good many scholars and general readers who originally were attracted to his humanistic, interpretive sociology of the 1960s but who cannot fathom how that radically relativizing and debunking consciousness led Berger in the 1970s to the camp of the neo-conservatives.

First I shall briefly review Berger's view of the 'calling' of sociology as a vocation, relying primarily upon *Invitation to Sociology* and *Reinterpreting Sociology* but referring also to other works as they are relevant. Second, I propose the possibly surprising notion that Berger is best understood as an inheritor of the American pragmatic tradition, specifically that of William James. Finally, I shall adopt the pragmatist's strategy and ask what are the consequences of Berger's ideas? Does Berger satisfy his own agenda for sociology in his interpretive work? The test case for this inquiry is the book, *The War Over the Family* (1983e), he wrote with Brigitte Berger.

In what follows I shall endeavor as much as possible to avoid taking long detours into the whole of Berger's thought. I wish not to repeat here matters covered competently elsewhere in this volume and in the major published exegeses of the Berger texts (for example, Mechling, 1979; Wuthnow, *et al.*, 1984). But I beg the reader's indulgence if I say again for the sake of my argument some things that by now may be commonplace for readers of Berger.

Sociology as a way of seeing

Berger carried into his earliest work a sense of the 'precariousness' of what Schutz called 'the world taken for granted.' Society and culture, the latter being the patterned systems of public signs and meanings shared by a group, are mechanisms for bringing order to the world (Geertz, 1973: 87–125). Of the three imperatives present in every human community – the imperatives of order, of continuity, and of triviality – for Berger 'order is *the* primary imperative of social life.' Moreover, Berger believes that this imperative for order is rooted in the biological constitution of human beings (1971d: 3). What Schutz (following Husserl) called 'the natural attitude' is our first form of consciousness toward the world, and as such it is predominantly an ordering form of consciousness.

The phenomenologist's project, of course, is to find a way to step outside the natural attitude, to suspend belief in the commonsense world taken-for-granted, to perform what Husserl called transcendental phenomenological reduction or 'putting the world in brackets.' This is the aim of science, including scientific sociology. For the sociologist, 'to make up his mind to observe scientifically this life-world means to determine no longer to place himself and his own condition of interest as the center of this world, but to substitute another null point for the orientation of the phenomena of the life-world' (Schutz, 1973: 137). This new, scientific attitude toward the life-world is what Berger takes to be sociological consciousness.

The genius of sociology for Berger (1981d: 5) is that it is *negative*. It is a radical form of scientific doubt and disinterestedness. 'Sociology,' writes Berger, 'is essentially a debunking discipline. It dissects, uncovers, only rarely inspires. Its genius is very deeply negative, like that of Goethe's Mephistopheles who describes himself as a "spirit that ever says no." ' (1973b: 234). Berger's analogy for the sociological consciousness is the loss of innocence upon viewing the revealed interior of a building with the facade bombed away, a chilling reference to his European childhood (1961c: 11).

Berger is well aware of the historical and social location of scientific sociology in human thought, 'as a peculiarly modern and Western cognition' (1963c: 25). He understands, as well, that the negative character of the sociological consciousness – that is, that sociology cannot legitimate anything, it can only delegitimate – probably 'contributes to the disillusion, *anomie* and normative disintegration of modern society' (1981d: 164). At its worst, the sociological consciousness can lead to desperation. 'Toward the end of his life,' notes Berger (1971d: 3),

> Max Weber was asked by a friend to whom he had been explaining the very pessimistic conclusions of his sociological

> analysis, 'But, if you think this way, why do you continue doing sociology?' Weber's reply is one of the most chilling statements I know in the history of western thought: 'Because I want to know how much I can stand.'

Even at its best, the negative character of the sociological consciousness may lead to cynicism. Indeed, the dramatistic model of social life Berger presents in *The Precarious Vision* (1961c) and in *Invitation to Sociology* (1963c) includes the possibility of role-distance and the 'confidence man' as a social type. The 'sociological Machiavellianism' Berger advocates near the end of *Invitation to Sociology* (1963c: 163) and the special sort of 'individualist' he describes near the end of *The Social Construction of Reality* (1966e: 171) are his alternatives to the cynicism lurking in the sociological consciousness.

So how is the human being with the sociological consciousness to escape the anomie, pessimism, or cynicism that seem the only responses possible to the radically relativizing, unmasking, debunking, delegitimating character of that consciousness? The key lies in Berger's notion of the sociologist's 'double citizenship.' Berger insists time and again upon Weber's distinction between science and politics as vocations. What Weber meant by the 'value-freeness' of scientific sociology is essentially what Schutz had in mind as the scientific ideal of suspending the personal bias and interest characteristic of one's natural stance toward everyday life, and as such the term 'is virtually identical with the notion that science should be objective' (1963c: 5). Berger (1974f: 135) cautions that value-freeness

> does *not* imply (and was never intended by Weber to imply) that the social scientist who aspires to it is himself free of values, is unaware of the values operative in the situation he is studying, or has the notion that one can engage in policies devoid of value consequences . . . 'Value-freeness' in science is, therefore, perfectly compatible with the most intense value commitments and with intense activity springing from these commitments.

Berger admires Weber's ability to 'bear without flinching' the tension between his passion for science and his passion for politics, between detachment and engagement (1974f: 248). This is the social scientist's 'dual citizenship,' by which Berger means the scientist's peculiar status as a citizen simultaneously of two 'republics' – one the 'republic of scholars,' the other the 'republic' of society, religion, political party, and so on (1981d: 66, 83, 168). The social scientist must be sure to specify when he or she is speaking '*qua* sociologist' (as Berger puts it) and when *qua* value-directed human being. The predicament of the sociological consciousness, then, is Weber's: 'the predicament of one who tries to see the world as lucidly as possible, who suffers from the radical "disenchantment" such lucidity almost invariably brings about – and who *nevertheless* is committed to humanizing interventions, political or otherwise, in the course of collective events' (1981d: 7).

It is only by keeping this 'dual citizenship' in dynamic tension, Berger seems to be saying, that we can be sure our scientific sociology generates knowledge of our life-worlds quite free of our bias, wishes, and fears, for we would want our choices and actions in the world to be based upon how the world actually is rather than upon how we wish or suspect it is. Berger is claiming, therefore, that the knowledge gained in the scientific attitude of the sociological consciousness is not only epistemologically *different from* but *superior to* the knowledge gained in the natural attitude toward the life-world.

It is at this point, I believe, that Berger has permitted himself to fall into a position that is not only untenable but (as I shall show) unnecessary for his larger project. By the time he and Kellner wrote *Reinterpreting Sociology*, Berger was trying to sustain an impossible mixture of a Popperian view of science and a phenomenological one (for example, Kuhn, 1970, or Feyerabend, 1975). More accurately, Berger in this most recent work is slipping sideways into a pragmatic understanding of scientific knowledge without either a) abandoning the Popperian language or b) exploring fully the phenomenological, pragmatic position on scientific knowledge. I shall devote the remainder of this section to exploring the contradiction in *Reinterpreting Sociology* before addressing in the next section the pragmatic alternative I think Berger actually is taking in his substantive work.

Berger is quite in tune with the interpretive social sciences of the 1980s in his call for a return to 'the spirit of Weberianism.' Weber understood that 'human phenomena don't speak for themselves; they must be *interpreted*. Thus a clarification of the act of interpretation was at the center of Weber's methodology' (1981d: 10). Berger distinguishes Weber's from Durkheim's more positivistic approach, admitting with Weber that 'science always views its objects in a selective, partial and *ipso facto* problematic manner' (1981d: 12). Accordingly, the model Berger develops in Chapter 2, 'The Act of Interpretation,' is meant to clarify Weberian sociological method.

That chapter uses as an example the amusing case of a young, female graduate student in sociology from the Midwest, who is attending a convention in a West Coast hotel and is invited by another graduate student to an orgy on the fourteenth floor. (Berger often uses sexual examples, not only for their intrinsic interest but because sexual experiences have a special status in 'the precarious vision.') The invitation demands interpretation, says Berger, and he proceeds to show how the act of interpretation involves placing the invitation (a communication) into a context, connecting the invitation with a 'relevance structure' that makes sense of it. The initial relevance structure will be one in the natural attitude, having to do with the existential concerns (such as sexual adventuresomeness) of the female sociologist. To interpret the communication *qua* sociologist is to connect it with a relevance structure of a different kind – namely, the relevance structure of sociological theory and knowledge. 'Put differently,' writes Berger, assuming the persona of the imaginary graduate student, 'as I interpret the situation, *sotto voce* in my role as sociologist, the entire discipline (or, rather, that segment of it that is theoretically relevant to this research material) is invisibly present in my own mind – a silent partner in the situation, as it were' (1981d: 27).

Thus far in clarifying the act of interpretation, Berger has said nothing to jeopardize his credentials in the interpretive school of social science. But the next claim does, for he apparently subscribes to Popper's view that for a hypothesis to be scientific it must be falsifiable:

> Sociological interpretation is not a philosophical enterprise. It is always subject to testing by empirical evidence. Sociological propositions are never axioms, but empirically falsifiable

> hypotheses. In that they are similar to propositions in all sciences. But evidence and falsification in sociology are not the same as in the natural sciences – precisely because they always involve meanings (1981d: 46).

Berger seems to hedge the falsifiability claim in the last sentence of this passage, but it is not at all clear from this section on 'evidence' how it is that evidence in sociology 'must always be framed in terms of meanings' or how 'the falsification of the sociologist's hypotheses must also be framed in terms of meaning' (1981d: 45). Nor is it clear, from the phenomenologist's point of view, how philosophy is any more or less responsive to the 'empirical evidence' of our everyday lives.

Berger's next discussion, on 'objectivity,' offers an elaboration of the scientific relevance structure without solving the falsifiability question. The scientific relevance structure brings with it both a set of concepts and 'a body of empirical knowledge that must be taken into account in any specific interpretation.' The act of interpretation apparently consists of 'bringing the new to-be-interpreted phenomena into a *meaningful relation* with comparable phenomena previously interpreted by other sociologists' (emphasis added). Scientific objectivity, therefore, 'does *not* mean that the sociologist reports on "raw facts" that are "out there" in and of themselves. Rather, objectivity means that the sociologist's conceptual scheme is in a dialectical relationship with the empirical data' (1981d: 49). Moreover, the scientific relevance structure is institutionalized in Peirce's 'community of investigators,' so that objectivity 'is a result of this ongoing interaction between the individual sociologist and the community of sociologists' (1981d: 51). 'Summing up on this issue,' Berger concludes, 'we agree with the positivists that there is such a thing as scientific objectivity (even if in practice it is often difficult to achieve). We disagree with the positivists in insisting that the objectivity of an interpretive science cannot be the same as the objectivity of the natural sciences' (1981d: 52–3).

I see at least three major problems with this statement of the meaning of objectivity in the act of interpretation. First, Berger's language in this chapter is rather vague. What, for example, does it mean to bring 'to-be-interpreted' phenomena into a 'meaningful relation' with the corpus of sociological concepts and data? Surely he is not proposing a correspondence theory of truth, but what is he proposing? The second problem with the statement about objectivity is that Berger needlessly blends essentially incommensurable positivistic and phenomenological philosophies of science. He sees Popper's ideas about the falsification of hypotheses as a 'crucial safeguard against dogmatism in science' (1981d: 52), but it is not at all clear what he gains by adding Popper's positivistic epistemology. Thomas Kuhn (1970) demonstrates that 'falsification' itself is no unambiguous, binary event, that historically scientific communities are capable of interpreting a great deal of anomalous data as 'counter-instances' and 'puzzles' rather than genuinely falsifying anomalies. In philosophy, Paul Feyerabend (1975) has launched the most complete critique of Popper's view, and the debate continues.

My point is not that Berger is obliged somehow to accept the phenomenological critique of Popper's version of the history and philosophy of science. Clearly he is not. But his zeal for defending Weber's value-free sociology against sociological ideologues has led him, in my opinion, to embrace a rhetoric of scientific method incompatible with the rest of his epistemology. If, as he wrote, 'the objectivity of an interpretive science cannot be the same as the objectivity of the natural sciences' (1981d: 52–3), then why insist that sociological propositions be falsifiable? Especially when a viable alternative is available?

His silence about an alternative view of objectivity in interpretive social science is the third problem I see in Berger's formulation. He does not mention the ways in which those who call themselves 'interpretive' social scientists take on the problem of objectivity. Rabinow and Sullivan (1979) use the 'Introduction' to their reader of essays in interpretive social science to discuss the range of such responses. Charles Taylor's contribution to the Rabinow and Sullivan volume takes the most radical position, denying that there are available to us any verification procedures for our interpretations. Fellow contributors Clifford Geertz and Robert Bellah 'clearly hold a modified notion of social science in which there is advance, contribution and refutation of one sort or another which a community of researchers could agree on, if they agreed on starting points.' Paul Ricoeur, say Rabinow and

Sullivan, prefers a 'dialectic of guessing and validation:'

> He holds out a hope for a new form of confirmation and refutation which would not be either based on a propositional model or one of falsifiability. For Ricoeur a method of mediating and judging between conflicting interpretations would look rather more like a transformed version of textual criticism in the humanities (1979: 7–8).

My view is that this, not Popper's, is the conversation about interpretation and validation in which Berger should be taking part. The Rabinow and Sullivan crowd rely much upon the same philosophical tradition (for example, Weber, Mead, Habermas) as does Berger, and the former's reliance upon the intersubjective agreement of an interpretive community is compatible with Peirce's 'community of investigators,' though without Peirce's certainty that confirmation in the social sciences would operate as it did for the natural sciences. And Berger can be quite at home with the hermeneutic approach outlined by Ricoeur and others.

Perhaps most importantly, Berger arrives finally at something like Geertz's answer to the question of how the social scientist is to tell a better account from a worse one. 'It is not against a body of uninterpreted data, radically thinned descriptions, that we must measure the cogency of our explications,' writes Geertz (1973: 16), 'but against the power of the scientific imagination to bring us into touch with the lives of strangers.' And, for Berger, to be '*a listener to the many stories of human meanings – and then to retell the stories as faithfully as one is able* – this description of what a sociologist does is a restatement of certain methodological principles. It is *also* a statement with a certain moral status' (1981d: 75; emphasis in original).

In this light, sociological and anthropological propositions about people's lives are 'scientific' and 'verifiable' to the extent that they faithfully present and respect the cognitive categories of the people being studied. For the anthropologist this would mean constructing an 'emic' description of the first-order interpretations by the actual participants in a social situation. For the sociologist this would mean exercising the 'cognitive respect' Berger often writes about. The truth of these descriptions, therefore, is empirical without being positivistic. Sociological statements about meanings in people's lives are not falsifiable.

There is available in the American pragmatic tradition an understanding of truth and scientific method that, I believe, can satisfy Berger's wish to sustain a distinction between the scientific and ethical 'moments' in a dialectic between knowing and acting, between detachment and engagement. In fact, Berger has been employing a pragmatic approach in his substantive work without needing to label it as such, and this pragmatic approach has served Berger well in pursuing the calling of sociology as he laid it out in the beginning of his career. In a sense, then, I am calling Berger 'back' to a methodological position to match his practice.

Pragmatism as a way of seeing

American pragmatic philosophy is enjoying a revival in some corners of the interpretive social sciences in the United States. The matter is not quite this simple, of course. The revival involves major interpretations (some say reinterpretations) of what Charles Sanders Peirce, William James, John Dewey, and George Herbert Mead said about truth and scientific method, and the revival features the typical arguments about *whose* version of pragmatism is to become exemplary for the interpretive social sciences of the 1980s (for example, Webb, 1976; Johnson and Shifflett, 1981). Without surveying here the entire revival, I shall follow the pragmatic strain in Berger's work and see where it leads to.

The pragmatic pedigree of Berger's thinking is not difficult to trace. Schutz and Husserl both acknowledge great debts to William James. Berger begins his 'Society as Stage' chapter in *The Precarious Vision* (1961c: 48–50) with a discussion of the social psychology of James, Mead, and Cooley, and references to James and Mead occur across the ensuing two decades of Berger's books. Mead is attracting so much attention now in sociology because it was he among the pragmatists who established most clearly the social nature of knowing and doing (Lewis and Smith, 1980; see also the Fall, 1981, issue of *Symbolic Interaction*, 4: 129–95, a commemorative issue of essays on Mead).

But it is the 'tough-minded' pragmatism of William James, in contrast with the 'tender-minded' pragmatism of Mead, that strikes me as the most important epistemological foundation for Berger's work. While other sociologists are working out the sociology (sociologies, is more like it) implied by Mead, Berger is working out the sociology implied in James's work. Berger might not agree with this assessment, but I believe James's views on the relationship between knowing and doing, between understanding and engagement, provide for Berger and for those of us who would take up Berger's program for humanistic sociology a far more satisfactory example than do Weber's, without violating Weber's valuable interpretive approach to the life-world. In fact, as I hinted earlier, Berger actually practises a substantive sociology closer to James than to Weber.

William James was, in the words of two historians of American philosophy, 'more Kantian than Kant' (Flower and Murphey, 1977: 674; for a sample of recent scholarship on James, see Suckiel, 1982, Barzun, 1963, and Feinstein, 1984). James's *Principles of Psychology* (1890), twenty years in the thinking and twelve in the writing, provided the scientific basis for his extension of psychology into metaphysics. James steered a course different from either the nineteenth-century Rationalists or Empiricists, constructing a psychology and a philosophical method (radical empiricism) that insisted that *all* knowledge, including introspection, has its roots in experience. For James, therefore, human knowing and doing are a teleological system, forever changing, learning, self-correcting.

The world of sensations never presents itself to us raw; it is always experienced selectively by our sense organs and interpreted by our belief systems, primarily by common sense. Moreover, our knowledge is always *about* something; knowledge is always personal. Things are real to us, explain Flower and Murphey (1977: 657), if they are 'interesting and important. Thus the real world, reality, means simply a relation to our own emotional and active life.' This Jamesian point is the origin of Berger's interest in 'relevance structures,' including the scientific relevance structure that carries the body of sociological knowledge against which new phenomena are compared.

Most importantly, James's pragmatism provides a theory of truth and verification completely compatible with Berger's practice, James was quite familiar with nineteenth-century developments in science, mathematics, and logic (Kline, 1980), all of which were moving away from certainty that their formal systems were referring to an 'objective, absolute' reality. The holdouts against whom James railed were the rationalist neo-Hegelians. James wrote:

> *True ideas are those that we can assimilate, validate, corroborate and verify. False ideas are those that we cannot*. . . . Truth *happens* to an idea. It *becomes* true, is *made* true by events. Its verity *is* in fact an event, a process: the process namely of its verifying itself, its veri-*fication*. Its validity is the process of its valid-*ation* (1978: 97; emphasis in original).

Always the emphasis is upon experience. The process of 'verification,' for example, consists of the 'agreeable leading' of our thoughts from one experience to another, and 'assimilability' refers to the constant dialectic between our previously 'funded knowledge and new beliefs' (James, 1978: 103, 107–8). This view is very close to the one propounded by Berger (1981d: 49) in his claim that 'objectivity means that the sociologist's conceptual scheme is in a dialectical relationship with the empirical data.'

This view of truth as always changing, always provisional, leads James to political and ethical stances that foreshadow Berger's. James develops these stances in his later books, notably in *Pluralistic Universe* (1909) and in the posthumously published *Some Problems in Philosophy* (1911). 'James's pluralism,' explains Flower and Murphey, 'is a mediating philosophy . . . His view is neither optimistic on the one hand nor pessimistic on the other, but melioristic – steps can be taken which will make things better' (1977: 684). This describes pretty well Berger's stance *qua* concerned citizen. In his advice regarding public policy, for instance, Berger suggests in detail 'two essential steps in . . . a moral accounting of the probable costs of policy – a calculus of pain and a calculus of meaning' (1974f: 144, 149–82). Related is his 'postulate of ignorance,' to wit: 'Most political decisions must be made on the basis of inadequate knowledge . . . To understand this is to become very gingerly toward policy options that exact high human costs' (1974f: xiii).

James's point that 'truth' is a conditional state of the knowledge/action system in constant feedback and change helps account, I think, for Berger's *ironic* attitude toward action (1961c: 9; 1963: 39). Flower and Murphey (1977: 686) argue that James was developing in his last writings some important thoughts on decision theory, especially the problem of 'decision under risk and uncertainty.' James believed that among those situations calling for decisions when we have inconclusive knowledge are what he called 'forced options,' when not to decide is in effect to choose a side. James recommends action in these cases: 'where two alternatives are equally probable, believe in the one that would yield a richer quality of life' (Flower and Murphey, 1977: 686). Berger, too, understands that in the case of 'forced options' we must choose, ever mindful of the 'postulate of ignorance.' Berger's calculi of pain and meaning are criteria quite consistent with James's. But Berger adds an element, the element of irony. We must act; but *act*, says Berger, with a full understanding of the irony of unintended consequences. 'When it comes to revolutionaries,' he writes in his treatise on 'the movement' and his own 'conservative humanism' (1970a: 19), 'only trust the sad ones. The enthusiastic ones are the oppressors of tomorrow – or else they are only kidding.'

James's concern in his later work with the 'will to believe' and a voluntaristic view of the individual's actions serve quite well Berger's (and Weber's) view of the voluntary self, the 'individualist' who may *choose* social roles and degrees of involvement. Berger is comfortable postulating human freedom because rooted in the 'world-openness' of human biology is the ability to say 'no.' The image of the autonomous individual and the condition of *freedom* weave through both *Invitation to Sociology* and *Reinterpreting Sociology*, providing some of those books' most appealing reading. Like James, Berger postulates the reality of freedom (1963c: 125) and explores the ways in which an individual may live an autonomous, 'authentic' existence. Moving successively from the image of society as a prison to society as a puppet theatre to society as a stage with living actors, Berger finally offers in his concept of 'sociological Machiavellianism' his own version of the free agent in society (1963c: 163). Years later Berger reiterates his earlier argument about freedom, this time advocating Weber's 'ethics of responsibility': 'I am responsible for the consequences of my liberating choices' (1981d: 113). All told, the sociologist ought to act only with caution and doubt. This amounts to a 'pedantic utopianism' (1973b: 235) that seeks the middle ground between the equally unacceptable 'pedantic scientism' and 'messianic utopianism.'

This last point about sociology and utopianism raises some fascinating questions regarding the relationship between the 'sociological imagination' of C. Wright Mills, arising from the same sources (that is, American pragmatism, Mannheim, and Weber) as Berger's 'sociological consciousness' but arriving at what conventional wisdom sees as very different politics and ethics. Although I do not have the space here to pursue these connections, the recent biography of Mills by Irving Louis Horowitz (1983), subtitled 'An American Utopian,' may be an important lead in a revisionist history of the influence of pragmatism upon American sociology of the 1950s and 1960s and of the relation between the sociologies of Mills and Berger.

I understand, of course, the dangers of pushing Berger so far in the direction of William James that I shall have violated the differences between and subtlety of the thought of both men. But I am convinced that Berger's actual practice of sociology (as opposed to his writing 'about' sociological theory and method) is Jamesian, just as I am convinced that Berger's constant litany of the Weberian distinction between science and politics has led too many interpretive social scientists (for example, those in Haan, *et al.*, 1983) to dismiss Berger as a reactionary sociologist with nothing to offer their concerns. James offers a rationale for Berger's past work and a program for the future. So how has Berger's past work been Pragmatic?

Crucial to Berger's location in the pragmatic tradition is an understanding of his *inductive* approach to truth. Berger devotes an entire chapter of the 1981 book to 'the problem of relativity' in interpretive sociology. Once the sociology of knowledge debunks the truth claims of all plausibility structures and definitions of reality, including sociology's, how is the sociologist to escape the 'logical flaw of circularity'? Berger (1981d: 64–5) notes that several theorists have proposed 'escape hatches' from this logical dilemma of radical relativism, but he concurs with Mannheim that these attempts to 'contain' relativity by finding 'a particular social location that renders one immune or minimally less susceptible to, the ravages of relativity' are bound to fail. The search for a privileged social location for seeing the truth really carries a sort of 'hidden positivism,' a faith that we really can know the truth from a privileged standpoint. But, says Berger, 'there is no magical trick by which one can bypass the act of interpretation.'

So, within the scientific attitude toward the life-world, Berger sees only two strategies for transcending the relativity dilemma or trap. The first is the aforementioned strategy of depending upon the 'multiplicity of relevance structures' within the consciousness of Peirce's 'community of investigators,' and the second is the comparative method: '*all* human societies and meaning systems have some things in common. This implication constitutes a transcendence of radical relativism. . . .' But the comparative method at this level of generalization is in Berger's view very abstract and borders on the 'philosophical anthropology' outside the domain of a scientific sociology (1981d: 72–3).

What is missing in this discussion is Berger's other major strategy for escaping the relativity dilemma – namely, 'relativizing the relativizers,' described at length in *A Rumor of Angels* (1969b). Berger omits this strategy because it is one he adopts writing as Berger *qua* moralist and not *qua* sociologist. I reject his distinction in the case of this strategy and want to argue instead that his scientific sociology is loaded with examples of his adopting the inductive approach to truth described in *A Rumor of Angels* and in other works he would call non-scientific.

A Rumor Angels (1969b) is the believer's sequel to *The Sacred Canopy: Elements of a Sociological Theory of Religion* (1967c) in that the goal of *Rumor* is to ask whether theological thinking is possible, *given* (in a sense) the sociological analysis of the social constructedness of religion. Berger's strategy is to pursue 'the relativizing dragon' to its logical conclusion. Once every plausibility structure, including scientific sociology's, has been relativized, 'the question of truth reasserts itself in almost pristine simplicity,' writes Berger. 'Once we know that all human affirmations are subject to scientifically graspable socio-historical processes, *which affirmations are true and which are false*?' (1969b: 40, emphasis original). Berger calls this act 'relativizing the relativizers,' and clearly it is a form of *ecstasy*, a 'stepping away from' the natural attitude toward the life world:

> One (perhaps literally) redeeming feature of sociological perspective is that relativizing analysis, in being pushed to its final consequence, bends back upon itself. The relativizers are relativized, the debunkers are debunked – indeed, relativization itself is somehow liquidated. What follows is *not*, as some of the early sociologists of knowledge feared, a total paralysis of thought. Rather, it is a new freedom and flexibility in asking questions of truth (1969b: 42).

Berger turns to philosophical anthropology to propose an empirical starting point for theology's asking questions of truth. 'I would suggest,' offers Berger, 'that theological thought seek out what might be called *signals of transcendence* within the empirically given human situation. And I would further suggest that there are *prototypical human gestures* that may constitute such signals.' Signals of transcendence are empirical phenomena we encounter in our natural attitude toward the world 'but appear to point beyond that reality.' Prototypical human gestures are 'certain reiterated acts and experiences that appear to express essential aspects of man's being, of the human animal as such' (1969b: 52–3, emphasis original).

Berger then proceeds to offer his tentative list of five prototypical human gestures that signal a transcendent reality: ordering, play, hope, damnation, and humor (1969: 54–72). Rather than repeat his entire argument here, I shall make a few points relevant to our purposes. First, this method of inquiry takes the phenomena of everyday life as its data. Berger holds up as a model German protestant theologian Wolfhart Pannenberg's use of empirical history and empirical anthropology to examine historical instances of what Berger is calling prototypical human gestures. Second, this is an *inductive* method, an 'inductive faith' in the case where it is used to discover signals of a transcendent reality. Third, Berger makes no claim that this method presupposes a static human nature or yields eternal, unchanging truth. 'Truths can be discovered or rediscovered. Truths can also be lost and forgotten again. . . . Each claim to truth must be looked at on its own merit' (1969b: 73). Fourth, this method requires an interdisciplinary conversation, especially between theology, sociology, history, and philosophical anthropology.

A fifth and final point is one that Berger makes not in *Rumor* but elsewhere – namely, that this method can be pushed past matters theological to the pursuit of 'truthful' propositions about the secular life-world. Berger well might resist my asserting this last point, but I see in his novels (Mechling, 1984) and in a few shorter pieces his extending the method outlined in *Rumor* to deal with questions he otherwise claims are properly sociological and, hence, scientific. In his essay, 'In Praise of New York: A Semi-Secular Homily' (1977c), for example, Berger adds New York City to his tentative list of signals of transcendence. As the prototypical city, New York embodies for Berger universalism and freedom, a signal of the 'final liberation' that is to come with the Kingdom of God. New York City is also a place of hope and of play. But, above all, New York City is 'a place of strangers and of strangeness,' and herein lies its specialness as a signal of transcendence: 'Reality is not what it seems; there are realities behind the everyday reality of everyday life; the routine fabric of our ordinary lives is not self-contained, it has holes in it, and there is no telling what wondrous things may at any moment rush in through these holes' (1977c: 62). This 'magic' of New York City is not religious, but it is a related realm of experience. Berger's fascination with Robert Musil's novel, *The Man Without Qualities*, (1970c), and his own fictional exploration of the 'cracks in everyday reality' revealed by certain sorts of mundane experiences (Mechling, 1984) inform us that the supernatural reality is not the only alternative reality 'signalled' by our everyday lives.

Similarly, Berger's 'Reflections on Patriotism' (1974g) makes a distinction between two basic kinds of patriotism – communal patriotism and abstract patriotism – and considers the more 'real' or more 'true' that sort rooted in the 'concrete everyday experiences in ordinary life.' In other words, some descriptions of American identity and of American patriotism (which Berger defines as 'loving one's own') are more 'true' than others to the extent that they are inductive, rooted in concrete experiences. Moreover, this concretization 'serves as a *limit* to the arbitrariness of abstract definitions of identity' (1974g: 22). From this inductive approach Berger draws two conclusions. One is a value, or at least political, proposition – namely, that 'American democracy will be vital to the degree its basic propositions are linked to the patriotism inspired by the concrete experiences of American life.' The other is less clearly a value proposition, for Berger uses his ruminations on patriotism to propose a universal human right: '*Every human being has the right to his own tradition*. Put differently: *No one may be deprived of his own childhood*' (1974g: 23; emphasis in original).

In fact, the whole matter of human rights is an important test case for Berger's inductive approach to truth (or, better, truths). In an essay, 'Are Human Rights Universal?' that appeared in *Commentary* in 1977, Berger begins with a familiar theme, i.e., how is it that modernization's pluralization of meanings has meant, as well, the pluralization of moral judgments? Moralities are not unlike other ideological systems, and Berger notes that 'contemporary notions of human rights,' as in the United Nations Universal Declaration of Human Rights, are derived from the Enlightenment, a quite specific historical and Western phenomenon. The sociological consciousness, it seems, must relativize some cherished American notions of human rights.

But Berger pushes ahead, determined to sort the narrower, Western catalogue of 'human rights' from those that 'derive their warrant from a wider consensus,' from the 'human condition, as such.' The latter, I conclude, must therefore be 'truer' in contemporary life. Separate, says Berger, the specifically Western 'rights' based on the Western Enlightenment values of liberty and equality; this category includes most American civil rights and civil liberties, such as freedom of speech, due process, economic justice, and especially the recent expansion of these 'rights' to women, children, homosexuals, and others (1977a: 62). What is left is a broad category of government acts that violate the 'human rights' on which (says Berger) there is a more universal consensus, acts such as genocide, enslavement, forced separation of families, religious persecution, and the destruction of the institutional and symbolic carriers of ethnic identity. This strategy is the comparative one Berger proposes as a possible 'escape hatch' from the relativity dilemma, and it is a strategy Berger has adopted elsewhere in his focus on the common 'no's' humans say to certain oppressions. What Berger recommends is an attitude toward human rights that eschews ethnocentrism and shows respect for 'the remarkably consensual moral scope' of human civilizations (1977a: 63).

This brief view of Berger's grappling with the issue of universal human rights is instructive; here as elsewhere, I believe, Berger's methodological distinction between questions properly answered by scientific sociology and those properly answered by 'philosophical anthropology' (or theology or ethics) fades and there emerges in his thinking something very close to the Pragmatists' views on truth, knowing and acting (Berger, 1981d: 95). My point is that all of these examples, from signals of a supernatural transcendent reality to taking New York City as a signal of a surreal world beneath the surface of everyday life to ruminations about patriotism and human rights, all privilege *experiences* in the everyday reality as signals of and tests of the truth of propositions. This is the case in most of Berger's substantive work on the sorts of issues on which, he believes, the sociological consciousness can 'humanize' our views, issues such as race, homosexuality, capital punishment (1963c: 156–62), the war in Vietnam, student radicalism in the university (1970a), the separation of church and state (Mechling, 1978), and the family (Berger, 1983e). So the best test of my claim that we ought to think of Berger as belonging to the American pragmatic tradition is to turn to one of these particular studies in order to see how Berger actually constructs the relation between sociological knowledge and value judgments. Does the Weberian separation between knowledge and engagement work, or does Berger collapse the analysis, as he seems to do in his essay on human rights? In short, does Peter L. Berger satisfy his own agenda for the sociological consciousness? To answer these questions, I shall offer a brief analysis of Berger and Berger's recent, controversial book, *The War Over the Family* (1983e).

The bourgeois family as fact and value

Brigitte Berger and Peter L. Berger plunge headlong into a debate that has a long history in both social science and ideology. The substantive interest in the family is Brigitte Berger's (Berger and Callahan, 1979), and to this Peter Berger (1977e) brings his theoretical perspectives regarding modernization, mediating structures, and public policy. There is no faint-heartedness here, as Berger applies sociological consciousness and partisan judgments to all three major camps on the issue of the family in America

– the critical, the neo-traditional, and the professional. Berger wishes, not surprisingly, to hold and elaborate the 'middle-ground' position in the family, believing that most Americans 'gravitate' toward the middle in their beliefs about the family, that the middle ground is the 'most plausible intellectually,' and that 'it is also the position that has the best political prospects.'

Berger adopts the familiar Weberian strategy and distinguishes from the outset those matters that are sociological and those that are 'judgments of value.' Part I of the book describes the history, language, and issues in the current ideological battle over the bourgeois family. Part II offers a 'social-scientific' understanding of the contemporary family, with great attention to the dialectic between the modernization of thought and changes in the institutional carriers of modernity. Both Parts I and II attempt what the sociological consciousness ought to do in any case; that is to say, Berger seeks to debunk and radically relativize the three contemporary alignments, primarily by showing the class interests displayed by and fought for by each camp. Finally, Part III develops a 'reasonable defense of the bourgeois family,' recommending the middle ground on policy. For the sake of clarity and focus, I shall address here only one issue raised by the book, one treated deftly by Peter Berger in an 'excursus,' and then explicitly abandoned for the remainder of the volume. This is the tough issue of abortion.

Abortion is a particularly rich issue for making both Berger's point and mine. The public rhetoric about abortion is the most heated we have, and we are faced with James's classic dilemma of the 'forced option.' Berger's social-scientific observations on the matter are brief. There is an 'enormous cognitive gulf' between the antagonists on the fundamental question, 'Is the fetus a person – yes or no?' Science, of course, cannot answer this question, it is so fundamentally a cognitive, definitional question. In fact, the question uncovers precisely the nineteenth-century epistemological revolution that was the context for Peirce's and James's writing, for biological science recognizes in the case of a fetus that the answer is purely *interpretive*, depending upon where one wants to draw the boundary between something that is merely 'living' and something that is organized enough to be called a human being (or, more properly for legal purposes, 'a person'). The 'truth' of an answer to this question has nothing to do with the 'objective reality' and everything to do with the intimate relation between knowing and doing. This Berger knows and, in effect, says.

Scientific sociology essentially has two observations to make about this conflict. First, Berger draws our attention to the use of language (for example, the 'pro-life' and 'pro-choice' labels) and other symbolic systems (for example, posters of bloody, aborted fetuses) in the ideological conflict. Second, this rhetoric is the symptom of the class conflict Berger sees over the issue, as elsewhere in the debate over the fanily. The new 'knowledge class' appears to be strongly pro-abortion, 'pro-choice,' a connection wholly explicable as in their interests, while the anti-abortion, 'pro-life' camp appears to Berger to include the classes, ethnic groups, and races that feel most 'victimized' by the bureaucratic New Class (Bruce-Briggs, 1979) that controls even the most private aspects of their lives.

It is in his 'Excursus – Abortion and the Postulate of Ignorance' that Berger deliberately steps 'across the line that separates sociological analysis from political affairs,' denying to himself any 'more ethical competence than any other thoughtful citizen in a democracy.' The matter is rather straightforward, given Berger's twenty-years' attention to the effects of modern society. The cognitive and religious pluralism in our everyday lives, a feature well explicated by James, leads inevitably to a *moral pluralism*. Our Jamesian 'forced option' arises from the fact that, unlike cognitive pluralism, moral pluralism cannot endure the peaceful coexistence wherein people 'agree to disagree.' Some moral differences affect 'actual conduct in social life' and, therefore, demand legal regulation. Hence, argues Berger, the two camps in the abortion debate are unlikely to become mere 'denominations' and the moral pluralism on this matter may be unresponsive to the mechanisms by which Americans customarily negotiate their cognitive pluralisms.

The lessons of two similar moral conduct issues, slavery and prohibition, are not reassuring, and Berger admits to being not 'overly optimistic' about the chance for a 'new consensus' of the 'vital center.' Still, Berger acts, choosing in the face of uncertainty, though hovering over his 'exercise in hope' are the postulate of ignorance and the calculi of meaning and pain. To the 'pro-choice' camp Berger recommends a 'revival of awe' in human reproduction, and to the 'pro-life' camp he recommends 'a recognition of ignorance,' that is, that 'any new consensus on this issue will emerge from common reflection about uncertainties, rather than from shared certitude' (1983e: 81). Accordingly, Berger advocates a 'middle-ground' policy decision on abortion, in lieu of (or while waiting for) the hoped-for new consensus: 'While it would not proscribe all abortions, it would tend to set a fairly narrow time frame (certainly not beyond the first trimester and probably below it) as the period when abortion is to be permitted' (1983e: 82). This position is conservative (the calculus of pain) in presuming when the fetus is a person, but it is liberal (the calculus of meaning) in leaving the choice entirely in the hands of the woman within the time frame (postulate of ignorance). This middle-ground policy recommendation on abortion is typical of the later recommendations of the book as a whole. Finally, Berger calls for humility on both sides, reminding us that, in the Judeo-Christian tradition at the base of the American civil religion, 'redemption comes from forgiveness, rather than self-righteousness.'

Berger's handling of the abortion issue seems to me much closer to James's approach than to Weber's. There is, in fact, no 'value-neutral,' scientific statement that helps the matter at all. The proposition that the 'pro-choice' people tend to be members of the New Class is empirically verifiable and, hence, falsifiable in a narrow sense; but there are problems galore. Not only is there not much agreement on how one should operationalize the concept of the 'New Class' (see, for example, the essays in Bruce-Briggs, 1979), but at best one would have to make an arbitrary decision at what level to reject the null hypothesis that there is no patterned relationship between membership in the New Class and a 'pro-choice' stand on abortion. In other words, there are precious few uninterpreted 'facts' in this scientific inquiry. All the more difficult is it to see how one could falsify an *interpretive* proposition – an explanation – of the putative correlation between the two variables.

The point is that Berger has something interesting, something 'true,' to say about the abortion issue *not* because he has mustered a value-free scientific sociological method but because he is an intelligent person whose insights are 'verifiable' to the extent that the working hypotheses they offer lead us to other 'agreeable' hypotheses, as James said. What's more, Berger invokes the 'inductive method' in searching American historical experience (for example, mechanisms for dealing with cognitive pluralism) for 'signals' of the 'truths' that should guide public policy regarding abortion. And he demonstrates the characteristic Jamesian courage to choose in the face of risk and uncertainty.

My argument that Berger might better be thought of (and better cast himself as) primarily a Jamesian and less a Weberian may seem to some readers nit-picking, an elaborate exercise in drawing lines and making distinctions without differences. In closing I want to insist otherwise. I am quite comfortable with Berger's eclectic mix of Weber, Durkheim, Mannheim, Habermas, Gehlen, Peirce, James, Mead, and perhaps a dozen other major thinkers, just so long as the eclecticism leads him to offer interesting insights into modern society. This is, after all, the final test of explanations in hermeneutic, interpretive sociology: are the 'truths' offered by this interpretation 'relevant' to our interests, do they persuade us, and do they lead to other interesting 'truths'? So on that score, Berger satisfies me.

What troubles me is that some of Berger's Weberian and Popperian rhetoric seems to land him in a place increasingly isolated from current trends in interpretive sociology and anthropology. Many of these social scientists are puzzled that Berger (and Mary Douglas in anthropology) offer such radically debunking forms of analysis, only to arrive at some politically conservative conclusions. The result has been for many of these people to dismiss or ignore Berger's work, even though they are inspired by the liberating sociological consciousness they thought Berger was describing in *Invitation to Sociology* (1963c). And Berger seems only to have negative words for many of these social scientists. This is unfortunate for both sides, all the more so because it is unnecessary.

What I am advocating, in short, is a return of interpretive sociology not only to Mead but to James. While the symbolic interactionists argue about what Mead 'really meant,' they are overlooking a philosopher who not only offers a solution to the epistemological questions but who, more importantly, offers a thoughtful opinion on how the individual might lead a meaningful, moral life. A 'return' to James would put Berger's work back into the center of interpretive sociology, where it belongs. At the same time, this convergence would put Berger into conversation with James, C. Wright Mills, and others in the American pragmatic tradition. That is a conversation I would like to hear.

Epilogue

Peter L. Berger

The editors of this volume, I understand, have sternly advised the contributors not to indulge in personal reminiscences, recriminations or ruminations. Presumably this admonition applies to me as well. For obvious reasons impersonality is more difficult for me than for the other contributors; it would mean my looking at my own work as if it were someone else's – a rather improbable feat of intellectual detachment even for one committed to Weberian 'value-freeness.' I must ask the indulgence of both editors and readers if the following remarks take on a more personal tone.

Indeed, I must begin right off with two personal observations. First, I must express my appreciation to the editors for undertaking what must have been a demanding task and to all the contributors for a set of commentaries that, without exception, are eminently fair-minded even (and especially) when they are critical. I'm very grateful for this, especially in a period where invective has often taken over from analysis in the writings of social scientists.

Second, I must confess that I respond with a good deal of reluctance. I'm embarrassed by this volume, not because of 'false modesty' (is not all modesty false?), but because my sense of the comic kept intruding as I was reading essay after essay, all about me and my scribblings. The very adjective 'Bergerian,' so liberally sprinkled over these preceding pages, makes it hard for me to keep a straight face. It leads me to anticipate its successors 'neo-Bergerian' and (intimation of mortality) 'post-Bergerian.' I remember once asking Werner Stark, that very eminent sociologist, about a book of his published some time ago. He replied: 'About books of mine that have been published I feel as Calvin felt about the dead: There is nothing more we can do for them; they have gone on to their doom.' I suspect that all autobiographical (or, to coin an adjective, 'autobibliographical') reflection typically presupposes a deficient sense of humor. And, in any case, I'm deeply immersed in ongoing work and have little time or inclination to reflect at length about my work in the past. Still, I owe a response, and I will do my best to do it responsibly. Since I have no quarrel with the very logical sequence of essays, I will do so *seriatim*.

Nicholas Abercrombie gives a very good account of the theoretical intentions and the major thrust of the redefinition of the sociology of knowledge undertaken by Thomas Luckmann and myself in the early 1960s. It should be emphasized that this undertaking was very much a joint one, especially in *The Social Construction of Reality*, to the point where both Luckmann and I, in re-reading that book, have had difficulty recalling which of us suggested this or that argument in it. Of all the books I wrote or coauthored during the earlier part of my career, this is the one that I would change least if I were to revise it today (and I know that Luckmann feels the same way). Abercrombie is also correct in his view that this theoretical undertaking went far beyond the sociology of knowledge proper in its implications, a point that Luckmann and I realized early on and to our own surprise. It seemed to us then that we were putting together a conceptual tool that would have wide applicability, and I have certainly found it so when I moved into substantive areas that were far from my mind then (such as the areas of Third World development or of domestic social policy).

Abercrombie, I think, is also correct when he detects in the undertaking a tension between structure and action, and thus between pessimism and affirming the possibilities of human autonomy. At the core of this theoretical perspective is the determination to take full cognizance of the objective and the subjective side of human social experience. 'Structure,' from Emile Durkheim on, has been the *idée-clef* for the coercive objectivations of society; 'action,' both in its Marxian ('labor'/praxis) and its Weberian versions, has been the term expressing a recognition of the constructedness of society. Any sociological theory that denies the one or the other side of this tension cannot do justice to the empirical reality of human social life. Abercrombie is quite right that the existential correlate of this theoretical tension is the ambivalence of pessimism and autonomous efforts. The political implications of this double tension (theoretical and 'practical') are taken up in James O'Leary's essay, but Abercrombie understands them very well indeed. A theoretically sound sociology will show both the limits and the possibilities of what individuals experience as their freedom; if praxis in the social world is informed by this kind of sociology, it will be pessimistic in the sense of being anti-utopian, but this need not mean an attitude of cynicism or passivity: even in extreme situations of constraining structures, there are openings for autonomously inspired actions by individuals and groups of individuals.

When *The Social Construction of Reality* and other early writings of mine were taken as a warrant for the various utopian eruptions of the late 1960s and early 1970s, this was due to a profound misunderstanding. When I reacted sharply and negatively to these utopianisms, some erstwhile readers of mine were disappointed by my having 'moved to the right' and thus, from their point of view, having moved away from the radicalism of my youth. I may have 'moved to the right' on specific political issues, but it is they who misread radicalism into these early writings. It was never there, either objectively or in intention. This original misunderstanding and the ensuing disappointment, however, has greatly influenced my own relation to sociology as an organized discipline. (I might add that Luckmann's experience has been very similar, only in a personally more aggravating fashion, at least for a while, since he returned to teach in West Germany where sociological utopianism came to be institutionalized in much more thorough-going fashion than in the United States.)

I also find nothing to disagree with in Stephen Ainlay's analysis of my relation to the phenomenological tradition. Unlike others with whom I worked in the early stages of my career (notably Thomas Luckmann and Maurice Natanson), I never entered in great depth into the Husserlian universe of discourse; Alfred Schutz was my major connection with the latter, and, as Ainlay correctly understands, this always left me in the antechamber rather than the inner sanctuary of the phenomenological edifice. This in no way diminishes my debt to Schutz, but it is to Schutz the sociological theorist much more than to Schutz the philosopher. My meta-scientific presuppositions, taken up later in the volume by S.D. Gaede, have religious rather than philosophical roots. From time to time I have had a bad conscience about this and with it the feeling that I ought, as it were, to clean up my act philosophically. I have not found it possible to do so. There are only so many things one can do and this, it seems, is not going to be one of them. One aspect of this, though, which I have always taken seriously is the obligation to make clear my methodology to others and to myself (and here, I think, I must disagree with Ainlay's assertion that I have failed to indicate a methodology for sociology). I have tried to be clear about my *modus operandi* from the beginning and, in collaboration with Hansfried Kellner, restated my methodological presuppositions in *Sociology Reinterpreted*. These presuppositions have remained Weberian throughout and (Jay Mechling notwithstanding) they are likely to remain so. If I have not written more extensively on these matters, it is because I always felt that I had nothing very original to contribute here.

There is one observation of Ainlay's, though, that I must take exception to more emphatically, namely, the observation that I have failed to confront Marxism. On the level of Marx's basic theoretical approach, *The Social Construction of Reality* (like all the sociology of knowledge since Max Scheler and Karl Mannheim) could not have been written without the 'struggle with the ghost of Marx,' and it seems to me that this was made very clear in that book and in other writings of mine during the 1960s. While I was editor of *Social Research* (the journal of the Graduate Faculty of the New School) during the same period, I edited a special issue on contemporary Marxist sociology (this was published as a book, under my editorship, 1969a). While the *Social Research* issue dealt only with Marxist sociologists writing in the socialist countries of Europe, this was the time when Marxism in various forms began to be very influential in Western academia. I never had any political sympathies with this Marxist renascence, but I felt that its intellectual claims should be taken seriously. Later on, when my attention turned to the substantive problems of modernization and development, Marxism was an ever-present intellectual challenge. My book *Pyramids of Sacrifice* dealt with this challenge very explicitly. All of this has led directly to the work I'm currently engaged in, which is precisely to draw the outline of a non-Marxist sociological theory of capitalism, Ainlay may not agree with the *manner* in which I have confronted Marxism (with some sympathy for its anthropological assumptions and in sharp disagreement with virtually all its empirical assertions), but the charge that I have not confronted it will not stand up.

Anton Zijderveld's essay spans my early work on religion and the concern with modernization that has preoccupied me since the early 1970s. I suppose that my entire published opus revolves monomaniacally around two questions: What is modernity? And, how can one come to terms with it personally and politically? I agree with Zijderveld that the collapse, or at least the weakening, of the canopy of meaning is at the core of these questions. I also agree that, *au fond*, this has been the central problem of sociology as a discipline from its beginnings, although many sociologists in recent decades have found less interesting questions to preoccupy them. Like Zijderveld, I admire Max Weber's stoicism in the face of the modern dilemma. But Zijderveld is quite right when he ascribes to me a less melancholy view than Weber's. In part this is due to some differences in my understanding of how modernity works empirically. I accept Zijderveld's charge (if it can be called that) to the effect that, in the final analysis, my greater optimism is grounded in Christian faith: under the aspect of this faith, modernity, like any other era of human history, is simultaneously relativized and transcended. To say this in no way detracts from my admiration for the sort of stoicism with which Zijderveld identifies.

Zijderveld observes that there is a good deal of inconclusive ambivalence in the final chapters of *Pyramids of Sacrifice*. He is right. This is exactly where I was in 1972 and 1973, when I was working on this book. In the meantime I have become less ambivalent. I would today take back nothing I wrote then about the moral criteria for the assessment of any development model, notably the criteria of the 'calculus of pain' and the 'calculus of meaning.' Nor, heaven knows, would I retract what I wrote about the 'postulate of ignorance' hanging over the arena of political action. But I'm no longer so even-handed as between capitalist and socialist development models. Rather, with all due regard to the empirical uncertainties, I would recommend betting on a model of democratic capitalism. The reason for this change of mind is quite simple: when I wrote *Pyramids*, my only significant acquaintance with the Third World was in Latin America; in the second half of the 1970s I 'discovered' East Asia, the region of the world where the big capitalist 'success stories' are located. Rio de Janeiro looks very different once one has seen Singapore.

I do not agree with Zijderveld that, even then, I transferred the problem from social-scientific analysis to theology and ethics. I felt then, as I do now, that social-scientific problems must be solved within the empirical frame of reference of the social sciences; one cannot produce a theological or ethical *deus ex machina* to resolve empirical ambiguities. The very ambivalence Zijderveld detects in my work of that period has led directly to my present work, which is emphatically a social-scientific, and *not* a theological or ethical, enterprise. As to the welfare state of North-Western Europe, whose praises Zijderveld sings here (a little surprisingly, in view of various criticisms he has made of it elsewhere), it seems to me that it has enough problems of its own without being held up as a shining example for the rest of the world to follow. But, in any case, it certainly cannot serve as a model for Third World development: no Third World country could afford this type of welfare state. Where the attempts were made to establish such 'tropical Scandinavias' (the phrase was coined by a Jamaican critic of Caribbean socialism), the results have invariably been detrimental to the very people who were intended to be the major beneficiaries – namely, the poor. The reason for this is simple too: One must produce wealth before one can redistribute it. Whether the redistributionist experiments of North-western Europe should be a model at least for the advanced industrial societies is another question. I tend to think that there are better models, especially in the United States, but this question cannot be pursued here.

James Hunter concentrates on the question of the *costs* of modernity. Once again, I have no quarrel with his basic exposition of my ideas on that subject. I accept his observation that my early criticism of the American churches was in line with the general trend of social commentary of that period and that my major step beyond that commentary was in terms of a social psychology of modernity. As with Ainlay's assertion that I fail to confront Marxism, I cannot accept Hunter's that I fail to deal with different versions of modernity, notably the capitalist and socialist versions. If anything, since the early 1970s I have been obsessed with these differences: *vide supra*.

A more telling criticism of Hunter's is to the effect that empirical data, especially in the United States, suggest that certain costs of modernity may be smaller than I and other social critics have assumed. This, he argues, is particularly the case with the alleged loss of community. I believe that this point of Hunter's will stand up. Modern American society is certainly *not* the cesspool of alienations that I, along with many others (in sociology actually going back to the so-called Chicago School), believed to be there. In my own work, I would contend, I have corrected this misperception in my more recent emphasis on 'mediating structures.' The phrase was coined in my collaboration with Richard Neuhaus and the concept provided the major thrust of the Mediating Structures Project of the American Enterprise Institute, which Neuhaus and I directed from 1976 to 1979. This resulted in four books (none of them written by Neuhaus or myself) on various areas of domestic social policy. We have derived some satisfaction from the currency gained by these ideas in the American policy community, but that is another question. In terms of the 'costs of modernity,' the 'mediating structures' perspective makes clear that most individuals in a modern society are *not* plunged into devastating anomie and that these institutions provide the major defense against such a condition. Similar institutions provide a cushion against the much more cataclysmic alienations of the modernizing process in Third World societies – and, for that matter, even in the societies of totalitarian socialism. The continuing collaboration with Neuhaus and others who were engaged in the Mediating Structures Project (especially Robert Woodson and his National Center for Neighborhood Enterprise) has provided me with another satisfaction – that of seeing very vividly how insights derived from my brand of 'interpretive sociology' can have practical implications for very concrete policy areas.

I appreciate Donald Redfoot's exposition of my interest in the empirical question of how freedom in the contemporary world can be protected from various threats brought about by modernity. I think he sees correctly the linkage here between personal existential concerns ('How can I be an autonomous individual?') and the dilemmas of political praxis ('What are the *institutions* by which individual autonomy can be maintained?'). And I'm grateful to him for his fair-minded treatment of some of my views with which he evidently disagrees. His essay, however, contains some basic (and somewhat surprising) misunderstandings of my position on a number of questions.

He is quite right in his assertion that I have moved from a celebration of liberating debunking in my early work (as in *Invitation to Sociology*) to a much more cautious sense of the built-in limits and dangers of liberation. And, of course, he is right that this move has put me in the company of politically more conservative groups on the American scene. But that is where he stops being right. He is emphatically wrong in ascribing to me the view that the countervailing forces to the threat of technocratic domination (Max Weber's 'iron cage') should be sought outside the political sphere. Even the concern for 'mediating structures' is a predominantly political one: what Neuhaus and I, and the others involved in the Mediating Structures Project, were trying to explore was a framework of *policies* that would protect and utilize these institutions. What is at issue here in the broadest sense is the search for an alternative model of the modern welfare state, one that would be more appropriate to American society than the prevailing (essentially European) model. But, beyond the question of 'mediating structures,' my work on development issues since the early 1970s has revolved consistently around the question of what *political* strategies can meet the moral criteria of reducing human deprivation and safeguarding human meanings. I have done some writing on the problems of democracy and of human rights in this context. My current work on capitalism has as one of its major foci the relation between this 'mode of production' and the empirical possibility of democratic governance. Whatever I may be reproached with, it can hardly be an apolitical attitude.

Redfoot states that there is 'no example of a modernized society in which the libertarian critics have established a totalitarian system.' Does he believe that Communist totalitarianism was started by critics advocating more repression? The reverse of his statement is empirically correct: the major totalitarian systems of the modern world *all* have their roots in doctrines of liberation, propagated by critics of Western bourgeois society. But leave that aside. It is difficult to disprove Redfoot's view that I have 'come down solidly on the rightist side' in current social disputes in this country: what is 'rightist'? I have no idea from what he derives his assertion that I believe that 'gay rights and day care centers are the first steps toward the Gulag.' (For the record, long before the Gay Liberation movement, I wrote in *Invitation to Sociology* that one of the tests of a sociologically informed humanism was revulsion against the traditional persecution of homosexuals in Western societies. As to day care, I believe with every other sensible analyst that day care is a necessity in contemporary society; the question that I have raised, mainly in my collaboration with Brigitte Berger, is *what kind* of day care we should institutionalize.) Finally, Redfoot's suggestion that, in my recent writings, I view the role of the sociologist along the lines of Dostoevsky's Grand Inquisitor is preposterous. I have written, again and again, that the role of the intellectual in society is to make a carefully circumscribed contribution to democratic discourse and *not* to represent any kind of cultural or political elite.

Robert Wuthnow treats as a virtue what Jay Mechling, later on, looks upon as a methodological failing – namely, that most of my theoretical work deliberately lays itself open to falsification. Wuthnow, of course, concentrates on my work in the sociology of religion, but I have always believed that all theorizing that occurs within the frame of reference of the social sciences must be open to empirical testing. (Admittedly, there are elements of my sociology of knowledge that may be meta-theoretical in this sense; I have usually been careful to mark them off as such.) Since in recent years I have not followed the sociology of religion closely, some of the studies cited by Wuthnow are not known to me. I take his word for it that they tend to support some of my theoretical contentions; needless to say, I'm happy to hear it.

Wuthnow makes one interesting criticism, that the manner in which I originally defined my concept of 'plausibility structure' suggests that social context *precedes* religious belief, so that the latter appears as a sort of dependent variable of the former. Such sociological determinism, of course, was never intended by me. I think that the cause of this difficulty (Wuthnow is right in seeing it as such) is the way in which Thomas Luckmann and I originally defined the Weberian-derived category of 'legitimation.' This perhaps is one of the few terms in *The Social Construction of Reality* (and, consequently, in *The Sacred Canopy*) that I would prefer to reword today, even though the *mot juste* does not immediately occur to me. 'Legitimation' suggests that the social structure legitimated is indeed prior, logically as well as chronologically, to whatever the legitimating ideas are. This is generally distortive, and particularly so in the case of religion. Wuthnow recognizes that such a view of the relation between social structure and religion is not mine, but I agree with him that my language has invited misinterpretation.

I'm less persuaded by his criticism that my view of religion is overly subjective and overly rational. My approach to sociology dictates that subjective meanings be given great attention, but I have always paid due attention as well to the institutions in which human meanings are objectivated. Nor have I ever believed that *homo religiosus* is a sort of do-it-yourself philosopher. Thus the great question of theodicy is primarily not a 'philosophical' problem: to make sense of suffering, injustice, and death is a need of the human being as a whole; it has profoundly existential and emotional sides, as well as the theoretical side that preoccupies those few individuals who do theology or philosophy.

Phillip Hammond gives a very clear account of my attempt to delineate, by way of definition, the religious phenomenon; I think that he misunderstands my definition somewhat when he discusses its implications. I have been concerned for a long time to define religion *substantively* rather than *functionally*; both my Weberian and my phenomenological prejudices have compelled me in this direction: Only after the meaningful substance of religion is apprehended by way of *Verstehen* should one, logically, turn to the question of how religion functions in society; the reverse starting point, typical of structural functional theories, puts the cart before the horse. So far, so good. But I don't agree with Hammond that this procedure precludes the sociological study of new religious meanings that may appear under the garb of secularity. If these meanings really are religious, then one will not be misled by the secular garb; if, by the aforesaid definition, one will call these meanings quasi- or even pseudo-religious, this appellation by no means precludes their being studied sociologically. Hammond is correct in stating that, in my recent work, I have not paid much attention to new religious movements, at least not those in the United States (a cost, perhaps, of living on the East Coast). My early work in the sociology of religion, including my doctoral dissertation on the Baha'i movement, was very much concerned with such movements – but, admittedly, not in the frame of reference of the sociology of knowledge.

It has occurred to me recently that perhaps the best way to conceptualize the phenomena at issue is to think of the 'supernatural' and the 'sacred' as two intersecting circles. Only the common area of the two circles contains what traditionally has been known as religious experiences. There has always been a relation to the supernatural without a sense of the sacred – magic, and such of its latterday embodiments as parapsychological research. The effects of secularization might then be described as an increase in the area denoting the sacred without supernatural aspects – as in the sanctification of such secular entities as science, or the nation, or the revolutionary movement. The phenomena that Hammond has in mind would then also fall under this category. In any case, as Hammond clearly understands, choices of definition should facilitate, not hamper, empirical research.

I have been very intrigued by S.D. Gaede's discussion of the relation of sociology and theology in my thinking. I'm somewhat puzzled by the 'investigative journalism' tone of this essay: I have always tried to be very up-front on this issue and my intercourse with Christian theology has taken place (often enough literally) in the lobbies and conference facilities of hotels rather than sneakily in locked bedrooms. This fact, of course, doesn't preclude the possibility that there are aspects of this of which I myself have not been aware and which, therefore, await hermeneutical disclosure. I'm not sure that I'm quite prepared to accept Gaede's hermeneutics.

He argues that my sociology limits my theology by ruling out certain types of 'fundamentalism.' I think that I must agree with this, though I doubt if it is just sociology that rules out this kind of theology: much more so than sociology it is an acceptance of philosophical reason and of modern historical method that rules out 'fundamentalism.' Still, if sociology keeps me from this sort of theological position, so be it. But Gaede also argues that my theology influences my sociology by imputing transcendent meanings to certain empirical human 'gestures.' In this, I believe, he is mistaken: in *The Rumor of Angels*, where I make this argument, I never suggested that the transcendent meanings can be discovered by sociology or any other scientific discipline in these empirical phenomena. Imputing transcendence to these 'gestures' is in itself an act of faith. The theological procedure advocated in that book is 'inductive,' *not* in the sense of modern scientific method, but in the sense of taking ordinary human experience as its starting point. The same meaning of 'induction' is applied to religious experience proper in *The Heretical Imperative*. Perhaps I invited this misunderstanding by the use of the term. Using more conventional Christian language, I might say that my approach is 'sacramental' – an apprehension of God's presence 'in, with and under' the elements of common human experience – though this usage might invite yet other misunderstandings.

I had been more impressed by an earlier expression of Gaede's interest in detecting illicit theological intrusions into my sociology, when, in a criticism of *The Heretical Imperatives* (Gaede, 1981), he suggested that my typology of modern theologies was distorted by a theological bias. He criticized my three-fold typology of 'deduction,' 'reduction' and 'induction' as mixing up two heterogeneous themes – the deductive/inductive and the orthodox/heterodox dichotomies. Thus my category of 'reduction' should properly be called 'deductive heterodox,' my 'deduction' becomes 'deductive orthodox' and my 'induction' re-emerges as 'inductive heterodox.' He then noted, very astutely, that one box in his four-fold table remains blank in my analysis – that of 'inductive orthodox.' He suggested that this blind-spot was due, not to my sociological analysis, but to a theological prejudice: I find it hard to believe that anyone would move from personal experience to an orthodox theological position. Maybe so, Gaede argued, but as a sociologist of religion I should take note of the fact that many people make precisely this claim – such as millions of Evangelical Protestants. I was persuaded by the validity of this argument and, ever since, have made frequent reference to Gaede's modification of my typology.

There is another point to be made: *The Heretical Imperative*, at least in those sections discussed here by Gaede, deals with theological options – that is, with choices made within a theoretical enterprise. It is important to distinguish religious faith from all exercises in theorizing. A good portion of my 'Protestant liberalism' is a matter of theological method rather than religious content. This is why a number of Evangelicals, for example, have felt themselves to be close to me in faith while not much liking my theology. This is not the place to pursue this matter further.

James O'Leary brings out the relation between my sociology of knowledge and my politics more clearly than I have thus far seen it myself. I believe that he is correct in seeing the notion of 'cognitive respect' as a crucial link between the two spheres. Within the frame of reference of the sociology of knowledge, and indeed of sociology in general, 'cognitive respect' means that one takes with utmost seriousness the meanings held by living human beings in any given situation. This, again, is what *Verstehen* is all about; of course, this is a methodological, not a moral, principle. It links up, though, with a particular stance in politics. It is conservative, at least in the (Burkean) sense of respecting the common values and traditions of people, and of rejecting all notions of 'raising the consciousness' of people or of otherwise pretending to know better than they what is good for them. This conservatism, of course, also predisposes one toward democracy as a form of government and toward the market economy. This notion of 'cognitive respect' is a unifying thread in my work on development strategies, on 'mediating structures' and on human rights. It is also at the root of my criticisms of socialism and of the pretensions of intellectuals, the 'New Class' and other putative 'vanguards of the people.' I'm very grateful to O'Leary for bringing out this theme very lucidly.

Jay Mechling's essay, finally, is intriguing, stimulating, and not altogether persuasive. I, for one, am not persuaded that the methodology proposed by Hansfried Kellner and myself in *Sociology Reinterpreted* is an untenable mix of phenomenological and 'Popperite' elements. As to phenomenology, I might just refer once more to Ainlay's essay. But I don't see why an insistence on the falsifiability of sociological propositions makes one a 'Popperite.' I rather think that, while the *term* is Popper's, the *methodological principle* is one accepted by the vast majority of social scientists. It is certainly consonant with Max Weber's methodology. I'm quite willing to entertain the notion that I might find William James congenial. I must confess that I haven't read James (with the exception of *The Varieties of Religious Experience*) for many years; Mechling is also correct in surmising that I originally read James while under Alfred Schutz's instruction. If this makes me a Pragmatist without knowing it, I find myself in the position of Molière's character who one day discovered that he had been writing prose all his life. Maybe so. I must also confess, however, that the possibility of such a discovery somehow fails to thrill.

I have been much more stimulated by Mechling's recent discussion of my two excursions into fiction (Mechling, 1984), especially as Mechling is one of the infinitesimally small number of people who have ever read these novels. Mechling was able to show the interconnections between the latter and both my sociological and theological work, including some interconnections that had previously escaped me. 'Relevance structures' can be kept apart in the act of theorizing; they inevitably intersect in the inner biography of any living and thinking individual.

The editors have asked me to include in this response some observations on the present stage and the future prospects of 'interpretive sociology.' I could reply by simply saying that the present state is dismal and the future prospects are dim. A number of contributors to this volume evidently share this opinion. Contemporary sociology, both in this country and everywhere else, is dominated by two equally depressing factions, the narrow positivists grinding out masses of mostly trivial data and the ideologues propagating various more or less odious political agendas. In some places the two factions actually appear to have merged. Individuals with more traditional understandings of the discipline are typically marginalized or have left the field altogether. In my own case, I have become very much alienated from the ongoing life of sociology as an organized discipline, my work mostly brings me together with people and with contributions from other fields, and I have paid little attention to what most sociologists are actually doing. I'm told by some that there has been a change, that younger sociologists are tired both of technocratic expertise and of ideological dogma, that the time has come for a revival of the classical spirit of sociology. I'm enough of a conservative to be skeptical.

A case could be made that sociology has always been more of a perspective than a specific field. If so, it has enormously influenced every one of the human sciences, indeed has become an important ingredient of modern thought as such. If so, it is possible that the development of sociology as a distinct social science may have been unnecessary in the first place and that, in any case, its present degeneration and its possible future demise may not do irreparable harm to the scholarly enterprise. The empirical test of these notions may not be far off. Be that as it may, I see no reason, because of this, to take back what I wrote more than twenty years ago on the distinctively liberating qualities of sociological consciousness as originally understood. It retains these qualities wherever sociology is practised in the classical tradition. If, as the authors in this volume claim, I have been able to make a contribution to this tradition, I'm not ashamed of it. There are still a few of us Mohicans around and, when we get together, we have a very good time.

The bibliography of Peter L. Berger

Books

1961a *The Noise of Solemn Assemblies*, Garden City, NY: Doubleday.

1961c *The Precarious Vision*, Garden City, NY: Doubleday.

1963c *Invitiation to Sociology*, Garden City, NY: Doubleday.

1964a *The Human Shape of Work* (ed. and contributor), New York, Macmillan.

1965b *The Enclaves* (novel published under the pen-name Felix Bastian), Garden City, NY: Doubleday.

1966e *The Social Construction of Reality* (with Thomas Luckmann), Garden City, NY: Doubleday.

1967c *The Sacred Canopy*, Garden City, NY: Doubleday.

1969a *Marxism and Sociology* (ed.), New York: Appleton Century.

1969b *A Rumor of Angels*, New York: Doubleday.

1970a *Movement and Revolution* (with Richard Neuhaus), New York: Doubleday.

1972e *Sociology: A Biographical Approach* (with Brigitte Berger), New York: Basic Books.

1973b *The Homeless Mind* (with Brigitte Berger and Hansfried Kellner), New York: Random House.

1974f *Pyramids of Sacrifice*, New York: Doubleday.

1975d *Protocol of a Damnation*, New York: Seabury.

1976a *Against the World for the World* (co-ed. with Richard Neuhaus and contributor), New York: Seabury.

1977b *Facing Up to Modernity*, New York: Basic.

1977e *To Empower People* (with Richard Neuhaus), Washington, American Enterprise Institute.

1979a *The Heretical Imperative*, Garden City, NY: Doubleday.

1981c *The Other Side of God* (ed. by Berger), Garden City, NY: Doubleday.

1981d *Sociology Reinterpreted* (with Hansfried Kellner), Garden City, NY: Doubleday.

1983e *The War Over the Family: Capturing the Middle Ground* (with Brigitte Berger), Garden City, NY: Doubleday.

1986 *The Capitalist Revolution*, New York: Basic Books.

Articles

1954 'The Sociological Study of Sectarianism,' *Social Research*, 21, p. 467.

1955 'Demythologization – Crisis in Continental Theology,' *Review of Religion*, 20, p. 5.

1956a 'Symbol Reutlingen – Der Goldene Engel dreht sich in Wind,' *Christ und Welt*, April.

1956b 'Von den Langweile zum Mobilismus,' *Christ und Welt*, July.

1957 'Motif Messianique et Processus Social dans le Bahaisme,' *Archives of the Sociology of Religion*, Part 4, p. 93.

1958a 'Evangelical Academies in America?', *Christianity and Crisis*, 18, p. 40.

1958b 'Sectarianism and Religious Sociation,' *American Journal of Sociology*, 64, p. 41.

1959a 'Camus, Bonhoeffer and The World Come of Age,' *Christian Century*, April, p. 451.

1959b 'Die Gesellschaftliche Bedeutung der Amerikanischer Kirchen,' *Die Mitarbeit*, February.

1959c 'Relationship of Self-esteem and Gossiping Behaviour,' *Journal of Social Psychology*, 50 (August), p. 153.

1959d 'The Second Children's Crusade,' *Christian Century*, December, p. 1399.

1960a 'The Best Jokes are Jewish: A Christian Footnote,' *Village Voice*, June.

1960b 'Christliche Gemeinschaft und Moderne Gesellschaft,' *Lutheran Runschau*, May.

1960c 'The Problems of Christian Community in Modern Society,' *Lutheran World*, 7, p. 14.

1960d 'Religious Liberalism and the Totalitarian Situation,' *Hartford Seminary Bulletin*, 28 (March), p. 28.

1960e 'Die Sociologische Struktur einer Kirchengemeinde,' *Zeitwende*, May.

1960f 'Sociology in the Theological Curriculum,' *Hartford Quarterly*, 1 (No. 1, Winter), p. 41.

1960g 'Thorstein Veblen y la Sociologia de la Religion,' *Revista de Ciencas Sociales*, 4, p. 447.

1961b 'Note on Sociology and Homiletics,' *Hartford Quarterly*, 1 (No. 3, Spring), p. 113.

1962a 'Church Commitment in An American Suburb: An Analysis of the Decision to Join' (With Dennison Nash), *Archives of the Sociology of Religion*, 13, p. 105.

1962b 'The Family, The Child and the Religious Revival in Suburbia' (with Dennison Nash), *Journal for the Scientific Study of Religion*, 1, p. 85.

1962c 'The Religious Establishment and Theological Education,' *Theology Today*, 19, p. 178.

1962d 'Sociology and Ecclesiology,' in Martin Marty (ed.), *The Place of Bonhoeffer*, New York: Association Press, p. 224.

1962e 'Sociology and the Technicians,' *Hartford Quarterly*, 2 (No. 4, Summer), p. 73.

1962f 'Zur Sociologie Kognitive Minderheiten,' *Internationale Dialog Zeitschrift*, part 2.

1963a 'Charisma and Religious Innovation: The Social Location of Israelite Prophecy,' *American Sociological Review*, 28, p. 940.

1963b 'The Human Shape of Personnel Work,' in Hall (ed.), *On-the-Job Ethics*, New York: National Council of Churches.

1963d 'A Market Model for the Analysis of Ecumenicity,' *Social Research*, 30, p. 77.

1963e 'Prophetic Mantle Disclaimed,' *Christian Century*, 80 (May), p. 649.

1963f 'Sociology of Religion and the Sociology of Knowledge' (with Thomas Luckmann), *Sociology and Social Research*, 47, p. 417.

1964b 'Letter on the Parish Ministry,' *Christian Century*, 81 (April), p. 547.

1964c 'Marriage and the Construction of Reality' (with Hansfried Kellner), *Diogenes*, 46, p. 1.

1964d 'Some General Observations on the Problem of Work,' in Peter L. Berger (ed.), *The Human Shape of Work*, New York: Macmillan Co., p. 241.

1964e 'Social Mobility and Personal Identity' (with Thomas Luckmann), *European Journal of Sociology*, 15, p. 331.

1964f 'Value Aspects of American Funeral Practices,' *New Wine*, March.

1965a 'Arnold Gehlen and the Theory of Institutions' (with Hansfried Kellner), *Social Research*, 32, p. 110.

1965c 'Reification and the Sociological Critique of Consciousness' (with Stanley Pullberg), *History and Theory*, 4, p. 196.

1965d 'Towards a Sociological Understanding of Psychoanalysis,' *Social Research*, 32, p. 26.

1966a 'Identity as a Problem in the Sociology of Knowledge,' *European Journal of Sociology*, 7 (Spring), p. 105.

1966b 'On Existential Phenomenology and Sociology II,' *American Sociological Review*, 31, p. 259.

1966c 'Response to Brewster,' *New Left Review*, 35.

1966d 'Secularization and Pluralism' (with Thomas Luckmann), *Internationales Jahrbuch fur Religionssociologie*, 2, p. 73.

1967a 'Conservative Reflection About Vietnam,' *Christianity and Crisis*, 27, p. 33.

1967b 'Religious Institutions,' in N. Smelser (ed.), *Sociology: An Introduction*, New York: Wiley.

1967d 'A Sociological View of the Secularization of Theology,' *Journal for the Scientific Study of Religion*, 6, p. 3.

1967e 'Sociology and Theology,' *Theology Today*, 24, p. 329.

1968a 'Between Tyranny and Chaos,' *Christian Century*, 85 (October), p. 1365.

1968b 'In Memoriam: Frederick Neumann, 1899–1967,' *Hartford Quarterly* 8 (Winter), p. 59.

1968c 'In Richardson's Cybernetic Chapel,' *Una Sancta*, 25, p. 100.

1968d 'Reflections on Law and Order,' *Christianity and Crisis*, 28, p. 296.

1968e 'Some Sociological Comments on Theological Education,' *Perspective*, 9, p. 217.

1969c 'Sociological Theory as an Area of International Collaboration,' *Acta Universitatis Carolinae . . . Philosophica et Historica*, part 2.

1970b 'On the Obsolescence of the Concept of Honor,' *European Journal of Sociology*, 11, p. 339.

1970c 'The Problems of Multiple Realities (Alfred Schutz and Robert Musil),' p. 213 in Maurice Natanson (ed.), *Phenomenology and Social Reality*, The Hague, Nijhoff.

1971a 'The Blueing of America' (with Brigitte Berger), *Theology Today*, 28, p. 216.

1971b 'Call for Authority in the Christian Community,' *Princeton Seminary Bulletin*, 64.

1971c 'Preface' to Caporale and Grumelli (ed.), *The Culture of Unbelief*, Berkeley: University of California Press.

1971d 'Sociology and Freedom,' *American Sociologist*, 6, p. 1.

1971e 'Zukunft der Religion,' *Evangelische Kommentare*, 4, p. 317.

1972a 'The Arithmetic of Happiness Doesn't Add Up,' *Fortune*, 86 (October), p. 151.

1972b 'The Assault of Class' (with Brigitte Berger), *Worldview*, 15 (No. 7), p. 20.

1972c 'Languages of Murder,' *Worldview*, 15 (No. 1), p. 9.

1972d 'The Liberal as Fall Guy,' *Center Magazine*, 5 (July/August), p. 38.

1972f 'Two Paradoxes,' *National Review*, 24 (May, 12), p. 507.

1973a 'Demodernizing Consciousness' (with Brigitte Berger and Hansfried Kellner), *Social Policy*, 3 (No. 6), p. 3.

1973c 'On Not Exactly Reaping the Whirlwind,' *Christian Century*, 90, p. 19.

1973d ' "Sincerity" and "Authenticity" in Modern Society,' *Public Interest*, 31, p. 81.

1974a 'Berrigan – Nixon Connection,' *Worldview*, 17 (No. 3), p. 4.

1974b 'Cakes for the Queen of Heaven,' *Christian Century*, 91, p. 1217.

1974c 'Consciousness Raising – To Whom? By Whom?' *Social Policy*, 5 (No. 3), p. 38.

1974d 'The Devil and the Pornography of Modern Consciousness,' *Worldview*, 17 (No. 12), p. 36.

1974e 'Modern Identity: Crisis and Continuity' in Wilton Dillon (ed.), *The Cultural Drama*, Washington: Smithsonian.

1974g 'Reflections on Patriotism,' *Worldview*, 17 (No. 7), p. 19.

1974h 'Religion in a Revolutionary Society,' published in pamphlet form, Washington: American Enterprise Institute.

1974i 'Some Second Thoughts on the Substantive versus Functionalist Definitions of Religion,' *Journal for the Scientific Study of Religion*, 13, p. 125.

1975a 'Bestrangement in Stockholm,' *Christian Century*, 92, p. 1022.

1975b 'False Consciousness of Consciousness Raising,' *Worldview*, 18, p. 33.

1975c 'Hartford Declaration' (with eighteen others), *Theology Today*, 32, p. 94.

1975e 'Rejoinder to Critiques of the Hartford Declaration,' *Theology Today*, 32, p. 189.

1975f 'Response to Richard Relevant on the Hartford Appeal,' *Christian Century*, 92, p. 271.

1976b 'The Greening of American Foreign Policy,' *Commentary*, 61, p. 23.

1976c 'In Praise of Particularity: The Concept of Mediating Structures,' *Review of Politics*, 38, p. 399.

1976d 'The Socialist Myth,' *Public Interest*, 44, p. 3.

1977a 'Are Human Rights Universal?' *Commentary*, 63, p. 60.

1977c 'In Praise of New York,' *Commentary*, 63, p. 59.

1977d 'Secular Theology and the Rejection of the Supernatural,' *Theological Studies*, 38, p. 39.

1978a 'Comment Under the General Heading Capitalism, Socialism and Democracy,' *Commentary*, (April), p. 33.

1978b 'Ethics and the Present Class Struggle,' *Worldview*, 21 (No. 4), p. 6.

1978c 'On the Conceptualization of the Supernatural and the Sacred' (with Hansfried Kellner), *Dialog*, 17, p. 36.

1979b 'Religion and the American Future,' in Seymour Lipset (ed.), *The Third Century*, Chicago: University of Chicago Press, p. 65.

1979c 'The Worldview of the New Class: Secularity and its Discontents,' in Bruce Briggs (ed.), *The New Class*, New Brunswick, NJ: Transaction Books.

1980 'From Secularity to World Religion,' *Christian Century*, 97 (January), p. 41.

1981a 'The Class Struggle in American Religion,' *Christian Century*, 25 (February), p. 194.

1981b 'New Attack on the Legitimacy of Business,' *Harvard Business Review*, 59 (October), p. 82.

1981c 'Symposium: The Heretical Imperative,' *Journal for the Scientific Study of Religion*, 20, p. 193.

1982 'Secular Branches, Religious Roots,' *Society*, 20 (No. 1), p. 64.

1983a 'Democracy for Everyone?' *Commentary*, 76 (No. 3, September), p. 31.

1983b 'Secularity, West and East,' *This World*, Winter, p. 49.

1983c 'The Third World as a Religious Idea,' *Partisan Review*, 50 (No. 2), p. 183.

1983d 'Toward an Alternative Vision of the Welfare State,' *Catholicism in Crisis*, November, p. 19.

1984a 'Can the Caribbean Learn from East Asia?,' *Caribbean Review*, 13 (No. 2), p. 7.

1984b 'Robert Musil and the Salvage of the Self,' *Partisan Review*, 51, p. 4.

1984c 'The Asian Experience and Caribbean Development,' *Worldview*, (No. 10).

1984d 'Underdevelopment Revisited,' *Commentary*, 78 (No. 1), p. 41.

General bibliography

Abercrombie, N. (1980), *Class, Structure and Knowledge*, New York: New York University Press.

Adorno, T., W. E. Frenkel-Brunswick, D. J. Levinson, and R. N. Sanford (1950), *The Authoritarian Personality*, New York: Harper.

Adorno, Theodor and Max Horkheimer (1972), *Dialectic of Enlightenment* (English edition), New York: Herder & Herder.

Aidala, Angela, A. (1984), 'The Consciousness Reformation Revisited,' *Journal for the Scientific Study of Religion*, 23: 44–59.

Ainlay, Stephen C. (1983), 'Intentionality and the Investigation of the Social World,' in Scott McNall (ed.), *Current Perspectives in Social Theory, Volume IV*, Greenwich, Conn.: JAI Press.

Anderson, Nels. (1923), *The Hobo*, Chicago: University of Chicago Press.

Apostle, Richard A., Charles Y. Glock, Thomas Piazza, and Marijean Suelzle (1983), *The Anatomy of Racial Attitudes*, Berkeley: University of California Press.

Bainbridge, William Simms and Rodney Stark (1981), 'The "Consciousness Reformation" Reconsidered,' *Journal for the Scientific Study of Religion*, 20: 1–15.

Barth, Karl (1964), *Evangelical Theology: An Introduction*, New York: Doubleday.

Barzun, Jacques (1963), *A Stroll with William James*, Chicago: University of Chicago Press.

Baum, Gregory (1980) 'Peter L. Berger's Unfinished Symphony,' *Commonweal* (May), pp. 263–70.

Becker, H. and H. Dahlke (1973) 'Max Scheler's Sociology of Knowledge,' *Towards the Sociology of Knowledge* (ed. Remmling), New York: Humanities Press.

Beckett, Samuel (1965) *Waiting for Godot*, London: Faber & Faber.

BELL, DANIEL (1970), 'Modernity and Mass Society: On the Varieties of Cultural Experience' in *Paths of American Thought*, Arthur M. Schlesinger, Jr. and Morton White (eds), Boston: Houghton Mifflin.

(1976), *The Cultural Contradictions of Capitalism*, New York: Basic Books.

BELLAH, ROBERT N. (1970), *Beyond Belief*, New York: Harper & Row.

BENNIS, WARREN C. and PHILIP E. SLATER (1968), *The Temporary Society*, New York: Harper and Row.

BERGER, BRIGITTE, and CALLAHAN, SIDNEY (eds) (1979), *Child Care and Mediating Structures*, Washington, DC: American Enterprise Institute for Public Policy Research.

BREYSPEAK, WILLIAM A. (1974), 'Toward a Post-Critical Sociology of Knowledge: A Study of Durkheim, Mannheim, Berger and Polanyi,' Duke University, Unpublished Doctoral Dissertation.

BOWLES, SAMUEL and HERBERT GINTIS (1976), *Schooling in Capitalist America*, New York: Basic Books.

BRINTON, CRANE (1938), *The Anatomy of Revolution*, New York: Norton.

BRUCE-BRIGGS, B. (ed.) (1979), *The New Class*? New Brunswick, NJ: Transaction Books.

BRUMMER, VINCENT (1982), *Theology and Philosophical Inquiry*, Philadelphia: Westminster Press.

BRUNER, JEROME S., ROSE R. OLIVER, and PATRICIA M. GREENFIELD (1966), *Studies in Cognitive Growth*, New York: John Wiley and Sons.

Bureau of the Census (1975), *Historical Statistics of the United States: Colonial Times to 1970*, Washington, DC: U.S. Department of Commerce.

(1984), *Statistical Abstracts of the United States*. Washington, DC: U.S. Department of Commerce.

BURNHAM, JAMES (1972), 'Selective, Yes. Humanism, Maybe. Reply to Berger: Two Paradoxes,' *National Review*, p. 513ff.

CAIRNS DAVID (1974), 'The Thought of Peter Berger,' *Scottish Journal of Theology*, 27, pp. 181–97.

CLANTON, GORDON (1973), 'Peter Berger and the Reconstruction of the Sociology of Religion,' Union Theological Seminary

Unpublished Doctoral Dissertation.

CHRISTIE, RICHARD and MARIE JAHODA (eds), (1954), *Studies in the Scope and Method of 'The Authoritarian Personality'*, Glencoe: Free Press.

DAHRENDORF, RALF (1964), *Homo Sociologicus*, Koln-Opladen: Eestdeutscher Verlag.

DILTHEY, WILHELM (1961), *Pattern and Meaning in History*, (ed.) H.P. Rickman, New York: Harper.

DIXON, K. (1980), *The Sociology of Belief: Fallacy and Foundation*, London: Routledge & Kegan Paul.

DOLGIN, JANET L., DAVID KEMNITZER, DAVID SCHNEIDER (eds) (1977), *Symbolic Anthropology: A Reader in the Study of Symbols and Meaning*, New York: Columbia University Press.

DOUGLAS, MARY (1982), 'The Effects of Modernization and Religious Change,' in Mary Douglas and Steven M. Tipton (eds), *Religion and America*, Boston: Beacon Press.

DRUCKER, PETER F. (1968), *The Age of Discontinuity: Guidelines to Our Changing Society*, New York: Harper and Row.

EDWARDS, LYFORD (1927), *The Natural History of the Revolution*, Chicago: University of Chicago Press.

ELLUL, JACQUES (1957), *The Technological Society*, New York: Vintage.

(1965), *Propaganda*, New York: Vintage Books.

(1967), *The Political Illusion*, New York: Vintage Books.

FARB, PETER (1973), *Word Play*, New York: Knopf.

FEINSTEIN, HOWARD M. (1984), *Becoming William James*. Ithaca, NY: Cornell University Press.

FEYERABEND, PAUL (1975), *Against Method: Outline of an Anarchistic Theory of Knowledge*, London: Verso.

FILMER, PAUL with MICHAEL PHILLIPSON, DAVID SILVERMAN, and DAVID WALSH (1972), *New Directions in Sociological Theory*, Cambridge, Mass: MIT Press.

FLOWER, ELIZABETH and MURRAY C. MURPHEY (1977), *A History of Philosophy in America*, New York: G. P. Putnam's Sons.

FRAZIER, E. FRANKLIN (1932), *The Negro Family in Chicago*, Chicago: University of Chicago Press.

FROMM, ERICH (1932), 'The Method and Function of an Analytic Social Psychology: Notes on Psychoanalysis and Historical Materialism,' *Zeitschrift fur Sozialforschung*, I, 1/2.

(1941), *Escape from Freedom*. New York: Holt, Rinehart and Winston.
(1955), *The Sane Society*. New York: Holt, Rinehart and Winston.

GAEDE, STAN D. (1981), 'Review Symposium of "The Heretical Imperative",' *Journal for the Scientific Study of Religion*, 20, 2, pp. 181–5.

GALBRAITH, JOHN KENNETH (1958), *The Affluent Society*, Boston: Houghton Mifflin.

Gallup Organization (1982a), *Self Esteem Study*, Princeton, NJ.
(1982b), *Faith Development Study*, Princeton, NJ.

GARFINKEL, H. (1967), *Studies in Ethnomethodology*, Englewood Cliffs, NJ: Prentice-Hall.

GEERTZ, CLIFFORD (1973), *The Interpretation of Cultures*, New York: Basic Books.

GEHLEN, ARNOLD (1956), *Urmensch and Spatkultur*, Bonn: Athenaum.
(1957), *Die Seele in Technischen Zeitalter*, Hamburg: Rowholt.
(1963), 'Uber die Geburt der Freiheit aus der Entfremdung,' in *Studien zur Anthropologie und Soziologie*, Neuwied am Rheim: Luchetrhand.
(1980), *Man in the Age of Technology*, trans. P. Lipscomb, New York: Columbia University Press.

GEIGER, THEODOR, (1963), *Demokratie ohne Dogma*. Munich: Szczesny Verlag.
(1969), 'The Mass Society of the Present' in *On Social Order and Mass Society*, Chicago: University of Chicago Press.

GIDDENS, ANTHONY (1976), *New Rules of Sociological Method*, New York: Basic Books.
(1977), *Studies in Social and Political Theory*, New York: Basic Books.

GILL, ROBIN (1974), 'Reply to Cairns: The Thought of Peter Berger,' *Scottish Journal of Theology*, 27, pp. 198–207.

GOODMAN, PAUL (1956), *Growing Up Absurd*, New York: Vintage.

GREEN, MARTIN (1974), *The Von Richthofen Sisters*, New York: Basic Books.

HAAN, NORMA, ROBERT N. BELLAH, PAUL RAINBOW, and WILLIAM M. SULLIVAN (eds), (1983), *Social Science as Moral Inquiry*, New York: Columbia University Press.

HABERMAS, JURGEN (1968), *Toward a Rational Society: Student Protest, Science, and Politics*, Boston: Beacon Press.

(1973), *Legitimation Crisis*, Boston: Beacon Press.

HAMMOND, PHILLIP E. (1969), 'Peter Berger's Sociology of Religion: An Appraisal,' *Soundings*, 52, 4, pp. 415–33.

(1985) (ed.), *The Sacred in a Secular Age: Toward Revision in the Scientific Study of Religion*, Berkeley and Los Angeles: University of California Press.

HAMMOND, PHILLIP E. and JAMES DAVISON HUNTER (1984), 'On Maintaining Plausibility: The Worldview of Evangelical College Students,' *Journal for the Scientific Study of Religion* 23: 221–38.

HART, JEFFREY (1972), 'Peter Berger's "Paradox": Reply to Berger: Two Paradoxes,' *National Review*, pp. 511–13.

HARVEY, VAN. A. (1973), 'Some Problematic Aspects of Peter Berger's Theory of Religion,' *Journal of the American Academy of Religion*, 41, pp. 75–93.

HEGEL, GEORG W.F. (1967), *The Phenomenology of Mind* (1807), J. B. Braillie (trans.), New York: Harper.

HENRY, JULES (1963), *Culture Against Man*, New York: Vintage Books.

HERNDON, JAMES (1971), *How to Survive in Your Native Land*, New York: Simon and Schuster.

HODGES, B. (1983), 'Perception is Relative and Veridical,' Unpublished manuscript, Gordon College.

HOLT, JOHN (1964), *How Children Fail*, New York: Delta.

HOOK, SIDNEY (1961), 'Panel Discussion,' in Norman Jacobs (ed.), *Culture for the Millions?*, Boston: Beacon Press.

HORKHEIMER, MAX (1974), *Eclipse of Reason* (1947), New York: Seabury.

HOROWITZ, IRVING LOUIS (1983), *C. Wright Mills: An American Utopian*, New York: Free Press.

HUGHES, H. STUART (1961), 'Mass Culture and Social Criticism,' in Norman Jacobs (ed.), *Culture for the Millions?* Boston: Beacon Press.

HUNTER, JAMES DAVISON (1983), *American Evangelicalism: Conservative Religion and the Quandary of Modernity*, New Brunswick, NJ: Rutgers University Press.

ILLICH, IVAN (1971), *Deschooling Society*, New York: Harper and Row.

ISRAEL, JOACHIM (1971), *Alienation from Marx to Modern Sociology*. New Jersey: Humanities Press. Sussex: Harvester Press.

JACOBS, NORMAN (ed.), (1959), *Culture for the Millions: Mass Media in Modern Society*, Boston: Beacon Press.

JAMES, WILLIAM (1958), *The Varieties of Religious Experience*, New York: Mentor (first published in 1902).

(1978), *Pragmatism and the Meaning of Truth*, Cambridge, Mass.: Harvard University Press.

JANOWITZ, MORRIS (1977), *Military Institutions and Coercion in the Developing Nations*, Chicago: University of Chicago Press.

JASPERS, KARL (1963), *Leonardo, Descartes and Max Weber*, London: Routledge & Kegan Paul.

JOHNSON, G. DAVID and PEGGY A. SCHIFFLETT (1981), 'George Herbert Who? A Critique of the Objectivist Reading of Mead,' *Symbolic Interaction* 4: 143–55.

JONES, HUGH (1978), 'Spirit of Inquiry and the Reflected Self,' *Scottish Journal of Theology*, 31, pp. 201–16.

JOSEPHSON, ERIC and MARY JOSEPHSON (eds) (1962), *Man Alone: Alienation in Modern Society*, New York: Dell.

KACHEL, THEODORE A. (1984), 'Theodicy: Tragedy or Masochism? A Critique of Peter Berger's Rhetoric,' *The New England Sociologist*.

KALBERT, STEPHEN (1980), 'Max Weber's Types of Rationality,' *American Journal of Sociology*, 84, pp. 1145–79.

KANT, IMMANUEL (1949), *Fundamental Principles of the Metaphysic of Morals* (1785) trans. T. K. Abbott, Indianapolis: Bobbs-Merrill Co.

(1963), *On History*, ed. L. W. Beck, Indianapolis: Bobbs-Merrill Co.

(1965), *The Metaphysical Elements of Justice* (1797) trans. J. Ladd, Indianapolis: Bobbs-Merrill Co.

KATONA, GEORGE (1964), *The Mass Consumption Society*, Chicago: McGraw-Hill Book Company.

KELLY, R. GORDON (1983), 'The Social Construction of Reality: Implications for Future Directions in American Studies', in Jack Salzman (ed.), *Prospects 8*, New York: Cambridge University Press, pp. 49–58.

KLAPP, ORRIN E. (1969), *Collective Search for Identity*, New York: Holt, Rinehart and Winston.

KLINE, MORRIS (1980), *Mathematics: The Loss of Certainty*, New York: Oxford University Press.

KOHL, HERBERT (1967), *36 Children*. New York: Signet Books.

KUHN, Thomas S. (1962), *The Scientific Structure of Scientific Revolutions*, Chicago: The University of Chicago Press.

(1970), *The Structure of Scientific Revolutions*, 2nd ed., Chicago: University of Chicago Press.

KUYKENDALL, GEORGE (1976), 'God and Peter Berger: A Critique of the Sociology of Religion, *Thought*, 51, pp. 428–37.

LAFFERTY, WILLIAM M. (1977), 'Externalization and Dialectics: Taking the Brackets Off Berger and Luckmann's Sociology of Knowledge,' *Cultural Hermeneutics*, 4, pp. 139–61.

LANDESCO, JOHN (1929), *Organized Crime in Chicago*, Chicago: Illinois Association for Criminal Justice.

LARKIN, P. (1964), *Whitsun Weddings*, London: Faber and Faber.

LASCH, CHRISTOPHER (1978), *The Culture of Narcissism*, New York: Norton.

(1984), *The Minimal Self: Psychic Survival in Troubled Times*, New York: Norton.

LEFEBVRE, HENRI (1968), *Everyday Life in the Modern World*, New York: Harper and Row.

LEVINE, DONALD N. (1981), 'Rationality and Freedom: Weber and Beyond,' *Sociological Inquiry*, 51 (1), pp. 5–25.

LEWIS, J. DAVID and RICHARD L. SMITH (1980), *American Sociology and Pragmatism: Mead, Sociology and Symbolic Interaction*, Chicago: University of Chicago Press.

LICHTMAN, R. (1970), 'Symbolic Interactionism and Social Reality,' *Berkeley Journal of Sociology*, 15.

LINDBECK, GEORGE A. (1984), *The Nature of Doctrine: Religion and Theology in a Postliberal Age*, Philadelphia: Westminster Press.

LOEWITH, KARL (1970), 'Weber's Interpretation of the Bourgeois-Capitalistic World in Terms of the Guiding Principle of "Rationalization",' in D. Wrong (ed.), *Max Weber* (1932), Englewood Cliffs, NJ: Prentice-Hall.

LUCKMANN, BENITA (1978), 'The Small Life-Worlds of Modern Man,' in T. Luckmann (ed.), *Phenomenology and Sociology* (1980), Harmondsworth, England: Penguin.

MACDONALD, DWIGHT (1953), 'A Theory of Mass Cultures,'

Diogenes, 3 (Summer), pp. 1–17.

McClelland, David (1961), *The Achieving Society*, Princeton, NJ: Van Nostrand.

Macquet, J. (1951), *The Sociology of Knowledge*, Westport, Conn: Greenwood Press.

Mannheim, K. (1960), *Ideology and Utopia*, London: Routledge & Kegan Paul.

(1971), 'The Problem of a Sociology of Knowledge,' in K. Wolff (ed.), *Karl Mannheim*, New York: Oxford University Press, p. 59.

Marcuse, Herbert (1955), *Eros and Civilization*, New York: Vintage.

(1960), *Reason and Revolution*, Boston: Beacon Press.

(1964), *One-Dimensional Man*, Boston: Beacon Press.

(1968), *Negations*, trans. J. Shapiro, (1965) Boston: Beacon Press.

Marx, K. (1867), *Capital: A Critique of Political Economy* (ed. Engels), New York: New World.

(1959), 'Preface to a Contribution to the Critique of Political Economy,' in L. Fewer (ed.), *Marx and Engels: Basic Writings on Politics and Philosophy*, New York: Doubleday.

Mechling, Jay (ed.) (1978), *Church, State, and Public Policy: The New Shape of the Church–State Debate*, Washington, DC: American Enterprise Institute for Public Policy Research.

(1979), 'Myth and Mediation: Peter Berger's and John Neuhaus' Theodicy for Modern America,' *Soundings*, 62, pp. 338–68.

(1984), 'Peter L. Berger's Novels of Precarious Vision,' *Sociological Inquiry*, 54, 4, pp. 359–81.

Merleau-Ponty, Maurice (1962), *The Phenomenology of Perception*, London: Routledge & Kegan Paul.

(1973), 'The Crisis of Understanding,' in *Adventures of the Dialectic*, Evanston, Ill.: Northwestern University Press.

Merton, R. (1968), *Social Theory and Social Structure*, New York: Free Press.

Mowrer, Ernest (1927), *Family Disorganization*, Chicago: University of Chicago Press.

Mowrer, Ernest and Harriet Mowrer (1928), *Domestic Discord*, Chicago: University of Chicago Press.

Mumford, Lewis (1934), *Technics and Civilization*, New York: Harcourt, Brace.

(1938), *The Culture of Cities*, New York: Harcourt, Brace and World.

(1967), *The Myth of the Machine: Technics and Human Development*, New York: Harcourt, Brace, Jovanovich.

MURDOCK, G. P. (1949), *Social Structure*, New York: Macmillan.

NATANSON, MAURICE (1973a), *Edmund Husserl: Philosopher of Infinite Tasks*, Evanston, Ill., Northwestern University Press.

(1973b), *Phenomenology and the Social Sciences* (2 vols.), Evanston, Ill., Northwestern University Press.

NIETZSCHE, FRIEDRICH (1955), *Die frohliche Wissenschaft*, in *Werke in Drei Bander*, Band III, Munchen: Hauser Verlag.

O'NEILL, JOHN (1972), *Sociology As Skin Trade*, New York: Harper and Row.

ORTEGA Y GASSET, JOSE (1932), *The Revolt of the Masses*, New York: Norton.

PACKARD, VANCE (1957), *The Hidden Persuaders*, New York: David McKay.

(1960), *The Waste Makers*. New York: David McKay.

PARETO, VILFREDO (1935), *The Mind and Society. The Treatise on General Sociology*, trans. A. Bongiorno, A. Livingston, New York: Dover Press.

PARSONS, TALCOTT (1977), *The Evolution of Societies*, ed. J. Toby, Englewood Cliffs, NJ: Prentice-Hall.

PHILLIPSON, MICHAEL (1972), in Filmer *et al.* (1972).

PICCONE, PAUL (1971), 'Phenomenological Marxism,' *Telos*, 9: 3–31.

PSATHAS, GEORGE (1973), *Phenomenological Sociology: Issues and Applications*, New York: John Wiley.

QUEBEDEAUX, RICHARD (1982), *By What Authority*, New York: Harper and Row.

RABINOW, PAUL and WILLIAM M. SULLIVAN (eds) (1979), *Interpretive Social Science: A Reader*, Berkeley: University of California Press.

REMMLING, G. (1967), *Road to Suspicion: A Study of Modern Mentality and the Sociology of Knowledge*, Englewood Cliffs, NJ: Prentice-Hall.

RIEFF, PHILLIP (1961), *Freud: The Mind of the Moralist*, New York: Harper and Row.

(1966), *The Triumph of the Therapeutic: Uses of Faith After Freud*. New York: Harper and Row.

RIESMAN, DAVID (1950), *The Lonely Crowd*, New Haven and London: Yale University Press.

ROOF, WADE CLARK (1978), *Community and Commitment*, New York: Elsevier.

ROSENBERG, BERNARD (1957), 'Mass Culture in America,' in Bernard Rosenberg and David Manning White (eds), *Mass Culture*, Glencoe, Ill.: Free Press.

ROSENBERG, BERNARD and DAVID MANNING WHITE (eds), (1957), *Mass Culture: The Popular Arts in America*. Glencoe, Ill.: Free Press and The Falcon's Wing Press.

(1971), *Mass Culture Revisited*, New York: Van Nostrand Reinhold.

ROSENBERG, BERNARD, ISRAEL GERVER and F. WILLIAM HOWTON (eds), (1964), *Mass Society in Crisis: Social Problems and Social Pathology*, New York: Macmillan.

ROTH, GUENTHER and WOLFGANG SCHLUCHTER (1979), *Max Weber's Vision of History*, Berkeley: University of California Press.

SCHELER, MAX (1980), *Problems of a Sociology of Knowledge*, London: Routledge & Kegan Paul.

SCHELSKY, HELMUTH (1965), 'Ist die Dauerreflexior institutionalisierbar?' in H. Schelsky, *Auf der Suche nach Wirklichkeit*, Dusseldorf-Koln: Eugen Diederichs Verlag.

SCHILLER, HERBERT, I. (1973), *The Mind Managers*, Boston: Beacon Press.

SCHLUCHTER, WOLFGANG (1981), *The Rise of Western Rationalism*, trans. G. Roth, Berkeley: University of California Press.

SCHUTZ, ALFRED (1962), 'On Multiple Realities,' *Collected Papers*, vol. I, The Hague: Nijhoff.

(1970), *Reflections on the Problem of Relevance*, New Haven, Conn: Yale University Press.

(1971), *Collected Papers, I: The Problem of Social Reality*, ed. Maurice Natanson, The Hague: Martinus Nijhoff.

SCHUTZ, ALFRED and THOMAS LUCKMANN (1973), *Structures of the Life-World*. Evanston, Ill: Northwestern University Press.

SCHLEIERMACHER, FRIEDRICH (1958), *On Religion. Speeches to Its Cultured Despisers*. trans. J. Oman, New York: Harper Torchbooks.

SEELEY, JOHN, R.A. SIMM and E. LOOSELY (1956), *Crestwood Heights*, New York: Basic Books.

SENNETT, RICHARD (1974), *The Fall of Public Man*, New York: Vintage Books.

SHILS, EDWARD (1959), Mass Society and its Culture,' in *Daedalus*, 89, 2: 228–314.

(1962), 'The Theory of Mass Society,' in *Diogenes* (39).

SHINER, LARRY (1967), 'The Concept of Secularization in Empirical Research,' *Journal for the Scientific Study of Religion*, 6: 207–22.

SIMMEL, GEORG (1950), *The Sociology of Georg Simmel*, trans. K. Wolff, New York: Free Press.

SIMONDS, A. (1980), *Karl Mannheim's Sociology of Knowledge*, New York: Oxford University Press.

SLATER, PHILIP (1970), *The Pursuit of Loneliness: American Culture at the Breaking Point*, Boston: Beacon Press.

SLAWSON, JOHN (1926), *The Delinquent Boy*, Boston, R.C. Badger.

SMITH, WILFRED CANTWELL (1979), *Faith and Belief*, Princeton, NJ: Princeton University Press.

SPEIER, M. (1967), 'Phenomenology and Social Theory: Discovering actors and social acts,' *Berkeley Journal of Sociology*, 12.

SPENGLER, OSWALD (1932), *Man and Technics*, London: Allen and Unwin.

SPIEGELBERG, HERBERT (1971), *The Phenomenological Movement* (two vols), The Hague: Martinus Nijhoff.

SPURLING, LAURIE (1977), *Phenomenology and the Social World*. London: Routledge & Kegan Paul.

STARK, WERNER (1958a), *The Sociology of Knowledge*, London: Routledge & Kegan Paul.

(1958b), *Social Theory and Christian Thought*, London: Routledge & Kegan Paul.

SUCKIEL, ELLEN KAPPY (1982), *The Pragmatic Philosophy of William James*, Notre Dame, Ind.: University of Notre Dame Press.

SUTHERLAND, EDWIN (1937), *The Professional Thief*, Chicago: University of Chicago Press.

SUTHERLAND, EDWIN and HARVEY LOCKE (1936), *10,000 Homeless Men*. Chicago: University of Chicago Press.

TAYLOR, GRAHAM and the CHICAGO COMMISSION on RACE RELATIONS (1922), *The Negro in Chicago*, Chicago: University of Chicago Press.

TAYLOR, MARK C. (1984), *Erring: A Postmodern Antheology*. Chicago: University of Chicago Press.

TIRYAKIAN, EDWARD (1965), 'On Existential Phenomenology and the Sociological Tradition,' *American Sociological Review*, 30: 674–88.

(1966), 'Reply to Kolaja and Berger,' *American Sociological Review*, 31: 260–4.

TONNIES, FERDINAND (1957), *Community and Society* (1887), trans. Charles Loomis, New York: Harper and Row.

TURNER, B.S. (1981), *For Weber*, London: Routledge & Kegan Paul.

TURNER, STEPHEN and REGIS FACTOR (1984), *Max Weber and the Dispute Over Reason and Value: A Study of Philosophy, Ethics and Politics*, London, Routledge & Kegan Paul.

VAN DEN HAAG, ERNEST (1959), 'Dissent from the Consensual Society,' *Daedalus*, 89, 2: 315–22.

VARACALLI, JOSEPH (1984), 'Peter L. Berger and the Problem of Modern Religious Commitment,' *The New England Sociologist*, 143–51.

VIDICH, ARTHUR and JOSEPH BENSMAN (1958), *Small Town in Mass Society*, Garden City, NY: Anchor Books.

WEBB, RODMAN B. (1976), *The Presence of the Past: John Dewey and Alfred Schutz on the Genesis and Organization of Experience*, Gainesville: University Presses of Florida.

WEBER, MAX (1946), *From Max Weber*, trans. H. H. Gerth and C. W. Mills, New York: Oxford University Press.

(1949), *The Methodology of the Social Sciences*, trans E. Shils and H. Finch, Glencoe, Ill.: Free Press.

(1959), *The Protestant Ethnic and the Spirit of Capitalism* (1904), trans. T. Parsons, New York: Scribner.

(1963), *The Sociology of Religion* (1922), trans. E. Fischoff, Boston: Beacon Press.

(1968), *Economy and Society* (1922), trans. G. Roth and C. Wittich, Berkeley: University of California Press.

WELLER, ROBERT and LEON BOUVIER (1981), *Population: Demography and Policy*, New York: St Martin's Press.

WHITE, DAVID MANNING (1971), 'Mass Culture Revisited,' in Bernard Rosenberg and David Manning White (eds), *Mass Culture Revisited*, New York: Van Nostrand Reinhold.

WHYTE, WILLIAM H. (1957), *The Organizational Man*, Garden City, NY: Doubleday.

WILENSKY, HAROLD L. (1975), *The Welfare State and Equality*, Berkeley: University of California Press.

WILSON, Bryan (1966), *Religion in Secular Society*, London: C. A. Watts and Co.

WILSON, JOHN (1969), 'The De-alienation of Peter Berger,' *Soundings*, 52, 425.

WISDOM, J. O. (1973), 'The Phenomenological Approach to the Sociology of Knowledge,' *Philosophy of Social Science*, 3, pp. 257–66.

WOLFE, D. (1982), *Epistemology: The Justification of Belief*, Grove, NY: Intervarsity Press.

WOLTERSTORFF, N. (1976), *Reason Within the Bounds of Religion*, Grand Rapids: William B. Eerdmans.

WUTHNOW, ROBERT (1976), *The Consciousness Reformation*, Berkeley: University of California Press.

(1981), 'Two Traditions in the Study of Religion,' *Journal for the Scientific Study of Religion*, 20, 16–32.

WUTHNOW, ROBERT, JAMES DAVISON HUNTER, ALBERT BERGESEN and EDITH KURZWEIL (1984), *Cultural Analysis: The Work of Peter L. Berger, Mary Douglas, Michel Foucault, and Jurgen Habermas*, London: Routledge & Kegan Paul.

YANKELOVICH, DANIEL (1981), *New Rules: Searching for Self-Fulfillment in a World Turned Upside Down*, New York: Bantam Books.

ZIJDERVELD, ANTON (1963), 'The Sociology of Humor and Laughter,' *Current Sociology*, 31, 3 (Winter).

(1970), *The Abstract Society*, New York: Doubleday.

(1979), *On Clichés: The Supersedure of Meaning by Function in Modernity*, London: Routledge & Kegan Paul.

Index